HOW
TO
FIND
FLOW

Dr Cameron Norsworthy
aka The Flow Coach

HOW TO FIND FLOW

3 steps for high performance and deep resilience

First published in the UK in 2025 by Blink Publishing
An imprint of Bonnier Books UK
5th Floor, HYLO, 105 Bunhill Row,
London, EC1Y 8LZ

Copyright © Dr Cameron Norsworthy, 2026
Page 88 Illustrations by Envy Design Ltd

All rights reserved.

No part of this publication may be reproduced, stored or transmitted in any form or by any means, electronic, mechanical, photocopying or otherwise, without the prior written permission of the publisher.

The right of Dr Cameron Norsworthy to be identified as Author of this work has been asserted by him in accordance with the Copyright, Designs and Patents Act, 1988.

A CIP catalogue record for this book is available from the British Library.

Trade Paperback ISBN: 9781785307867

Also available as an ebook and an audiobook

1 3 5 7 9 10 8 6 4 2

Design and Typeset by Envy Design Ltd
Printed and bound by CPI (UK) Ltd, Croydon CR0 4YY

Every reasonable effort has been made to trace copyright holders of material reproduced in this book, but if any have been inadvertently overlooked the publishers would be glad to hear from them.

Some names have been changed to respect the privacy of those mentioned.

The authorised representative in the EEA is
Bonnier Books UK (Ireland) Limited.
Registered office address: Block B, The Crescent Building
Northwood, Santry
Dublin 9, D09 C6X8, Ireland
compliance@bonnierbooks.ie

www.bonnierbooks.co.uk

CONTENTS

Introduction	1
Part 1 READY	33
Chapter 1 Recognise Flow	37
Chapter 2 Reset for Flow	57
Chapter 3 Demystify Flow	114
Chapter 4 Prioritise Flow	130
Part 2 STEADY	181
Chapter 5 Build a Blueprint	184
Chapter 6 Invite the Intensity	203
Chapter 7 Shape Your State	236
Part 3 FLOW	255
Chapter 8 Be Absorbed	261
Chapter 9 Be Effortless	285
Chapter 10 Being Flow	315
Conclusion Over to You	344
References	362
Acknowledgements	376

INTRODUCTION

THERE ARE MOMENTS IN LIFE THAT MAKE IT ALL worthwhile, when everything clicks into place, as if our best self takes the lead and spontaneously knows precisely what to do as each moment unfolds. It just flows. We feel unusually alive, confident and creative. But these moments – so rich with meaning and satisfaction – are all too fleeting. And I've always wondered: why can't it be like that all the time?

Humans all share a common desire to feel and be our best. Whether it is being a better professional, sports player, parent, artist or human being, there is an inbuilt desire to improve, be more effective and embody the best version of ourselves – it is linked to our survival. Yet, facing life head-on can be difficult. Competing for our career, striving for satisfaction, craving connection and being our best is complex and challenging. Too often, we can find ourselves stretched and stressed. As we try to live a life that

How to Find Flow

makes us proud, we usually meet these challenges with varying degrees of success and fall short of the ideal, left feeling dissatisfied with the experience, frustrated by our actions and stressed for our future – excusing ourselves because it all seemed too hard or took too much energy to embody our best. The majority of us continue to turn up each day and strive through life's challenges, 'pushing on' through the difficulty or mediocrity of life, hoping that our finest is just around the corner. For the most part, we tolerate these underwhelming and suboptimal experiences, as we expect that other deeply satisfying and fulfilling moments will eventually come our way. But will they? In a world where we are increasingly challenged and our attention interrupted, making it all too easy to lurch from one stressor and distraction to another, are we really applying ourselves in the right way to be rewarded with the deep satisfaction that we all crave?

Do you get frustrated by life's challenges, only to feel flat, stressed or disappointed by the result, wishing you could do better, be better?

Well, if you do, you're not alone. In fact, the majority of people often feel that things are just not clicking into place. Whether it's struggling to fulfil our potential, falling short of our ability in moments that matter or feeling like there must be more to life, my research suggests that a trail of dissatisfaction lingers in the back of most of our minds. But what if I said that stepping into your best self is entirely within your control, a mindset and habit that

Introduction

you can curate, and one that takes less energy than the effort of 'pushing on through', 'surviving another day' or 'just doing enough not to fail'? And what if this wasn't just a hyperbolic comment or a charlatan promise, but a real possibility that could change how you tackle challenges and complexity? How would life be different for you?

The stark reality is that over 79 per cent of people are not fully engaged with what they do, and feel a sense of dissatisfaction with work and life.[1] Furthermore, my research suggests that over 90 per cent of people feel that they could do better, or be better, when it matters; and fewer than 20 per cent of people feel they already have the tools to do so – and these results were from a high-achieving sample. Whether it's talking to our boss, serving for match point or flirting with a potential romance, when the moment comes, it is common for most of us to tighten up, get nervous and fluster. We may know what we want to say or do, but we are not all equipped with the mental tools to actualise our ability.

There are other moments in life, however, in which everything seems to come together. We say what we want to say, hit an ace in the corner and charm the person standing before us with such ease and fluency that we surprise ourselves by our own ability. Fleeting, mislabelled and overlooked, these effortless moments are special and stand out from the mundane. They resonate deeply, reverberating in our memories, leaving a trace of fulfilment and confidence behind. So subtle, yet at the

How to Find Flow

same time profoundly rewarding, they act as catalysts for our future action. These moments, in which life seems easier than normal, effortless and enjoyable, are the scientific phenomenon known as 'flow'.

When in this zone, we become so absorbed in the task that nothing else seems to matter – self-consciousness disappears and self-confidence reigns. Beyond the fleeting moments of flow, we can become so engaged that time can feel different – hours go by unnoticed or the moment seems to occur in slow motion. We paint, work or train deep into the night forgoing food or rest, regardless of the rewards. Why? Because it just feels so good.

This joyous state is thought to account for humankind's richest experience, and yet we spend more time out of it than in it. In truth, we don't treasure it and give it the attention it deserves, because, for the most part, we don't understand it or know how to reproduce it. Yet it doesn't need to be this way. This optimal state of functioning – this flow – is very tangible. In fact, I'm going to show you how we have come to understand this state better now than ever before, and how we can all invite more of it into our lives.

I've spent the past twenty years working with some of the world's elite professionals to help them understand and apply the science behind these transformative moments and release untapped potential inside the world of sport, education, the arts and business. Now, in this book, I will teach you everything I know about flow and how

Introduction

it can not only be a focus for the moments that matter, but also a new way to approach the daily challenges of everyday life, in whichever sphere you currently operate. I will show you how to bypass those gritted performances and strained experiences that more often than not simply result in a relief that the grind is over. I will lay out the proven methodology used by many world champions and professionals to help you fulfil your ultimate potential and reap the rewards of all your hard work.

Let's begin.

MY MOMENT OF MAGIC

Playing tennis as a junior professional, I lived for those sublime moments on the court in which everything clicked into place – moments of crystallised ability as the heat of competition brought out the best in me, so focused on the ball, the world around me seemed to melt into insignificance. I still can recall in detail those shots that seemed destined to find their target. Shots that seemed to play themselves. Moments in which time itself would seem to slow down, and my mind and body moved effortlessly with miraculous synchronicity.

Why this one memory stands out more than most, I do not know, but I remember playing a tennis point that was no less ordinary than any of the other points played that day. Equally, the game was far from being a special match. But, while preparing to make a return, I was suddenly

How to Find Flow

filled with an unusual awe for my surroundings. I could see the detail of distant blades of grass being lit up by rays of sunlight gracing the British countryside, while also noticing my opponent brace for the point to come. I didn't reflect on this awareness at the time – I just felt plugged in. Most noticeably, I felt unusually light and confident. Not the conscious confidence that I tried so hard to install, but rather a deep sense of clarity and lack of concern laced with a knowingness of what was to come.

Dialled in on the tennis ball hurtling towards me, without thought, my body intuitively reacted, hitting the return effortlessly at the server's feet. I hadn't planned the shot, nor purposefully aimed it there, yet in that millisecond it felt like the right shot. My opponent, who was rushing towards the net, surprisingly adjusted his footwork with such speed and poise that he hit an amazing half-volley that sent the ball into the corner way out of my reach. Without debate, as if my body was on autopilot anticipating such a shot, I felt my body float through the air towards the corner. As if time itself slowed down, I could see, with impeccable clarity, the yellow fluff that carpeted the surface of the ball. My body stretched out an arm, shifted its weight and, in perfect harmony, my muscles made all the minute adjustments necessary to whip my racquet over the top of the ball. I could feel the ball sink into the racquet bed as if my nerves were hardwired to the strings. Still in motion, I watched as the ball sailed down the line and over the net towards a

Introduction

seemingly predestined spot in the corner of the court. In one instance, I could see the spectators looking on with surprise and my opponent dipping his head in defeat, all as I felt my feet sliding to a halt.

Again, I didn't consciously think about placing the shot there; it just seemed to play itself. I did not purposefully take on all this peripheral awareness – I just seemed to deeply absorb what was relevant. I take no personal credit for hitting, let alone reaching, the shot because I seemed to be a passenger in the process. It was as if my mind had surrendered control and instead was implicitly trusting my innate ability as the moment unfolded, and it couldn't have felt easier or more 'right'. For some reason, my body had taken over control of my brain, dismissing my authority in the process, and was doing a much better job of it – exceeding my normal ability. It was a shot that most racquet-wielding athletes will be familiar with, but, on considered reflection, in its own subtle manner, it felt somewhat magical and pure – a moment I will never forget.

Although this moment felt surprising, I had felt this feeling before, regularly, in fact, throughout my tennis career, to varying levels of intensity. It felt unexpectedly familiar; I knew I had also felt and seen it elsewhere in everyday life, but couldn't easily place it. The feeling wasn't like the highs of raptured applause or momentary elations that many of us may seek in our achievement pursuits or during our weekend kicks; rather it was a deep

How to Find Flow

satisfaction of everything coming together in a state of union. Ordinarily, I may have put such moments of high performance down to luck or potentially even basked in self-praise, but this felt different; it felt more inherently satisfying, like the sweeping love for a child.

Seconds later, I lined up to play the next point, but this time wasn't the same. I was now concerned with how well I was playing and whether I could replicate such a point. I was still focused and determined, but my reactions were slower and my actions forced. The fluency and accuracy had gone. Focused on winning the next point, I quickly moved on and forgot about the experience.

It wasn't until I reflected upon this moment, hours later, that it truly stood out. 'What had happened?' I thought. 'How could I excel in one second only to fluster the next? Why and how were these two experiences so different, yet only seconds apart?' I thought this state must have been an act of muscle memory or the culmination of all the years of intense training camps. Then the realisation dawned on me that I had rarely played this nuanced shot. Further, I hadn't been playing competitively for nearly two years. I was mentally, physically and nutritionally far from match-ready or peak performance, and yet the shot I had just played was possibly one of my best.

Perhaps you can recall a similar moment of magic in which a joke successfully slipped off your tongue, an email wrote itself, a spontaneous riff played itself, or you hit a sublime shot or made a precision pass during

Introduction

a match without time to think. However big or small, these moments that are undeniably recognisable against the mundane frequently go by undetected and almost always misunderstood. Not because they hold no value, but because we know so very little about them.

A renewed purpose

Insofar as I dwelled on it back then, I referred to these moments as being 'in the zone' – moments that were so rich and intrinsically rewarding that they motivated me to play three hours of tennis every day, and six on the weekends, in the hope of feeling that internal union once again. I wasn't always consciously aware of it, but every time I stepped onto the court was an exploration towards this state, its attraction even stronger than the desire to win. As the physician Dr Larry Doser wrote, 'In experiencing and realizing what flow is, we are no longer satisfied with the ordinary and mundane. Having passed through the eye of this needle, for many there is no going back. We have seen.'[2]

A propensity to find myself in this state on the tennis court surely helped me reach the English National Championships finals, represent my country and play three World Championships in my junior years, but my connection to this under-celebrated state ended up reaching far beyond the court. When a persistent elbow injury forced me to retire from tennis prematurely, aged seventeen, I found myself crippled with frustration and

How to Find Flow

fear, hiding in a fog of depression. Staying competition-ready for months and years, while hoping my forearms would recover, was exhausting. Spending endless hours in the gym, watching what I ate and sacrificing social engagements, only to feel my arms scream in pain every time I stepped back onto the tennis court was taking its toll. The problem was not merely this frustrated persistence nor the fact that I had dedicated my life to the game – leaving my family and a conventional education at home in England some four years earlier to attend America's superior training academies. Tennis had also provided me with an outlet to help distract me from my biggest fear in life: speaking.

Up until this point, I had lived with a stammer and crippling fear of public speaking, and became adept at hiding it from those around me. Being abroad with the unusual freedom of living like a university student many years older, I revelled in the liberty of my schedule. I soon found myself hanging out with older kids who liked to party, ducking and diving from conversational situations and getting stoned whenever I could to evade my inner turmoil. Preoccupied with running around a tennis court in the day and partying till I hit oblivion at night, I made sure there was very little time for engaging interactions. I became a master of ensuring I was always on the fringes of social conversations, replete with one-liners that could redirect attention and avoid any conversational uncertainties. I tried to avoid intellectual or emotionally

Introduction

complex conversations that would otherwise trigger my stutter, and evaded spaces that encouraged even the slightest chance of public speaking. Instead of working on my social skills and projecting my persona, I built my character and self-worth around impressing people through physical acts and impressive achievements. Never wanting to say no to a challenge, however, paired with my desperate need to be with others as I was estranged from my family, I would continually find myself among friends only to be repeatedly 'triggered', frozen in thought and unable to control the feelings in my chest or the deliberations racing through my mind. I felt restricted by my own voice. The only one true comfort I felt in life was the buzz of being high or the rewarding feeling of finding flow on the tennis court.

So, when my injury forced me to return to my family and homeland, I felt naked from both the psychological crutches of training several hours a day to find my flow and the escapism of partying till I passed out. With my identity as a tennis player stripped, and no arena to find those special moments of being in the zone, I felt void of purpose and exuberance, numb to the joys of life. My insecurities became exposed, my anxiety spiked and my speaking inadequacy grew ever more obvious. It was insufferable. I felt imprisoned by the potential stress and embarrassment of spiralling anxieties and unexpected stammers.

Continually feeling in flux, unable to articulate exactly

How to Find Flow

how I felt or what I wanted to say, it quickly seemed like life was spiralling out of control. Disconnected and discontent, an inner void was increasingly consuming my experience. Not wanting to be reliant on the need for drugs and alcohol to wipe away my emotional turmoil, and with no tennis on the horizon to give me purpose or evade these insecurities, my family and I thought the best solution was to check into a rehab centre, and face the biggest challenge of all – myself.

While I learnt more street smarts in rehab than I did in the real world, the months of psychodynamic counselling and supportive therapies were tectonic – possibly one of the most profound experiences of my life. I learnt to love myself, respect my emotions and appreciate the fragile value of each day. As I became better equipped to overcome my own dysfunctions, above all, this period of introspection lit a fire in my soul to continually grow. Emerging somewhat raw and still a child, while I felt stronger and more competent, at the same time I felt even more disconnected from society and my past. Peers my age struggled to identify with my experiences, and my world had taken a psychological lens few teenagers were happy to encourage. So, for the most part, I kept this psychological submersion to myself. The only place I could get identification and support was in adult self-help groups, but those had the problematic requirement to participate orally. As others were fascinated by my youth, I was frequently asked to speak at these events.

Introduction

Not wanting to cower under a challenge, I would painfully persist through these talks, stammering continuously, often causing more unease to those listening and cringing in silence. While, on reflection, I could perceive this as brave, this drive to push on only led to gritted and unpleasant experiences, entrenching seemingly helpful coping strategies. The way I approached these challenges chipped away at my confidence, drawing more dissatisfaction and relief than enjoyment and growth. Years later, still living with a daily fear of being exposed and feeling somewhat victimised, as if my injuries had robbed me of a life of tennis stardom, when a friend offered me a free around-the-world plane ticket she had won in an online student lottery, I leapt at the opportunity.

Nine months and nine countries later, I found myself wandering up a street in an ancient Inca village in Peru, where a busker's music and demeanour stopped me in my tracks. The tune was mesmerising, and I was instantly lifted to a new vantage point. The spellbinding view was of a man who seemed to be in that 'zone' which I had only associated with my tennis until that point. Here was a weathered young man, covered in colourful blankets, playing a harmonica with all his heart. He was busking in the back streets for pennies, yet he would not have been out of place in the Royal Albert Hall. I was transfixed by every note, as if gravity itself was pulling me into the song. I was in awe of his commitment to each bar, not least because he was playing the instrument with not one but

How to Find Flow

two amputated arm stubs. Seeing this man's application, despite his disadvantage, seemed to instantly lift my veil of self-pity; if he could do what he was doing with the cards he was dealt, I told myself, surely I still had the world at my feet.

Then it suddenly dawned on me, the moment the busker was experiencing was this same deep engagement and effortless action that I missed from playing tennis. Like a flicker of lightbulbs going off in my head, I quickly realised that it was not the hitting of hundreds of balls a day, the living out of a suitcase or the prestige that came with international competition that I missed, it was this state that the humble man in front of me was finding in his music. I wasn't depressed because I didn't have a purpose or couldn't continue to be a successful tennis player, I was deeply dissatisfied because nothing brought the same meaning as finding those magical moments on the tennis court.

If this state of being was as versatile a phenomenon as I might be witnessing, then surely I could find it elsewhere and perhaps even use it to speak confidently in public. Elevated by both the music and this train of thought, I started to see these absorbing moments in a new light – not restricted by context or my past, but open to whoever, wherever.

From that moment on, an overwhelming sense of purpose took over. This state of flow and its pursuit had offered me so much up until now. It had given me my

Introduction

greatest moments on a tennis court and helped stave off my existential pain from feeling disconnected and rudderless in life. I knew I had to get to the bottom of what this state actually was. I wanted to know why it brought such joy and meaning to those who experienced it, and how it enabled so many to act with such freedom.

FINDING FLOW

This thirst to understand flow and the music that inspired it stayed with me, all the way back to England and university. Where I swiftly discovered the 'godfather of flow', Mihaly Csikszentmihalyi, and began devouring his books, one after another, in quick succession. Csikszentmihalyi (don't worry, it took me two years to pronounce his name correctly: chick-sent-me-hi), a Hungarian psychologist and a prisoner during World War II, developed a curiosity about the nature of happiness. In the 1970s, Csikszentmihalyi studied how and why people do what they do, and what creates a life worth living. Interestingly, he found that people valued the process of participation as more important than the end product or outcome. For example, the sense of meaning gained during the act of painting far exceeded the satisfaction of seeing the finished painting; a painter might spend months finishing a painting only for it to sit in the cupboard on completion. Specifically, he discovered that people felt their best and performed their best,

How to Find Flow

thus drawing a huge sense of meaning to the act, when their actions or performance 'flowed'. The experience of what is now labelled as 'flow' was found to foster greater performance, creativity, talent development, productivity and self-esteem, and, perhaps most noticeably, acted as a natural and attainable buffer to life's stresses. Regardless of any subsequent internal or external reward, the experience itself was repeatedly described as one of humankind's richest and most enjoyable experiences.

This research was instrumental to a post-war shift in the field of psychology. Up to this point, traditional psychology had focused on fixing 'damaged people' and finding labelled solutions to 'mental illness', largely because funding was directed to finding a psychological cure for affected war veterans. However, when Martin Seligman became President of the American Psychological Association, a cohort of minds changed the orientation of psychological treatment to focus on the most positive qualities of an individual in what many called 'positive psychology' (a change from dysfunction to function, problems to purpose). Essentially, Seligman and many others believed that, to live a rich and fulfilling life, we cannot simply remove what is wrong or problematic, only to hope the void turns into fulfilment. Instead, we need to identify patterns that can lead us to where we want to head. In his words, 'Curing the negatives does not produce the positives.'[3] Csikszentmihalyi and Seligman

Introduction

asserted that happiness could be learnt and nurtured by cultivating our signature strengths as opposed to shoring up our weaknesses. While some researchers thought that more pressing issues, such as poverty, obesity or mental illness, were a better use of researchers' time, the 'positive psychology movement' felt this perspective was short-sighted, in the belief that it is often one's ability to recognise and employ one's strengths that can help to resolve such pressing problems. If we could understand the elements that made people happy, for example, and then focus our attention on creating these elements in our lives, happiness would prosper and the depression and poor mental health that we are otherwise trying hard to fix would diminish. This approach shifted the paradigm away from pathology, victimology and mental illness to positive emotions, virtues and positive applications. And so, the trail that led to the emergence and phenomena that we now know as 'flow' was set, and the world of flow was born.

Csikszentmihalyi claimed that this intrinsically rewarding state of deep engagement was an optimal experience, an experience that helped to explain both fleeting moments of optimal functioning and deep satisfaction, as well as continued motivation and engagement in people's pursuits in which extrinsic gains were low or absent. 'Flow is important both because it makes the present instant more enjoyable, and because it builds the self-confidence that allows us to develop skills and

How to Find Flow

make significant contributions to humankind,' explains Csikszentmihalyi.[4] Flow was positioned as a somewhat deeper state underpinning creativity, connection, optimal performance and many of the desirable states that we readily seek – a notion echoed by many philosophies and authors, such as Thomas Edward Lawrence (better known as Lawrence of Arabia), who said that happiness is not an end in itself, but rather 'a by-product of absorption'.[5]

Flow research flourished across psychological literature. It was noticeable across education and work-related research due to its association with self-determined engagement. It became central to happiness literature because of the intrinsically motivating nature of flow. It also became of interest to developmental research due to the inherent 'growth principle' of flow; the skill acquisition and confidence evident in flow creates self-efficacy, psychological growth and an emergent motivation to re-engage, fostering continual participation and progression. Due to flow's linkage with optimal human functioning, flow research was frequently cited in sports and performance psychology, which is where I first came across it. While elite performers would whisper its name in closed circles, not wanting to jinx future attainment, and coaches would indirectly strive for it, despite the academic uptake, flow mainly stayed an intellectual concept reserved for the academic archives or those examining optimal experience scientifically.

To date, the flow state has attracted over sixty years

Introduction

of research, spanning disciplines such as sociology, psychology, neuroscience, physiology and philosophy. It has attracted bestselling books, become a common term for commentators and been readily embraced by performers and those striving for an optimum. Practically, questing flow offers a framework or philosophy for engagement and achievement that focuses on the quality of subjective experience rather than the outcome – a differentiated approach that doesn't see experiential satisfaction and performance as mutually exclusive.

Csikszentmihalyi's research and writing is profound, and it continues to inspire me to this day. His work is a major strand of decades worth of excellent research by the scientific community, that my work is indebted to. Seminal as Csikszentmihalyi's research was, it was largely preoccupied with identifying and observing the flow state from his perspective as a researcher, and most noticeably a philosopher; while his research helped to describe the experience of flow, it didn't venture into explicit techniques for attaining the state or explain how someone could be as bad at finding flow in their speech as they were good at it in a sport.

Despite flow's prominence in our everyday life, like the microdoses of flow that occur far more frequently than many of us may realise (such as playing with a yo-yo or favouring rhythmic household chores), I couldn't understand why a clear pathway to flow didn't exist already – surely something so satisfying and actualising

How to Find Flow

of our abilities was worth intentionalising and charting, I thought. The need for such a map seemed to be blindingly obvious – it would be priceless for myself and others taking on any of life's challenges.

Unable to run with the practical wisdom of others, I began to ponder on whether flow really could be found intentionally. I intuitively knew that the knowledge I had managed to accumulate through finding flow in tennis had won me many a match, helped me overcome my nerves, buffered stress and engineered bucketloads of enthusiasm in order to thrive through exhausting training regimes. It didn't feel so intangible to me. But were my skills of finding flow in tennis transferable, to both other domains and other people? If so, could I articulate them in a way that others could follow? Could I make these teachings into a profession, even though the practice of intentional flow didn't exist?

A vision was born

Having noted that flow had been found by others in almost any task that involves a high degree of challenge, I thought it pertinent to start testing and charting whether I could find flow in other activities that my injured elbows allowed. To this end, I jumped into scuba diving, running, coding, skiing, snowboarding and surfing, to name but a few. To support these passions, I set up, with my brother, an adventure sports tour company, called Active Adventures, that also gave others the chance of

Introduction

adventure outside their comfort zone and to dabble with finding flow.

These years were, in many ways, a perfect playground to experiment with finding flow and continue my academic learning on the side. Other than the entrepreneurial learnings and having a great time with so many clients, these years gave me a safe space to practise re-engaging in sports in a whole new way. Building a business provided me with an endless list of challenging tasks that gave me ample daily opportunities for finding flow, something that I never thought was possible when walking up those back streets in Peru years earlier. But perhaps most impactful of all was the improvement of my speech. Since flow had become a conscious focus, I felt more relaxed and less concerned about the outcome of events or how I may or may not come across to others. Instead, when I spoke, I focused on finding my own rhythm, slowing down my brain to be in sync with my mouth. Having flow as a guiding star seemed to take some of the pressure away. The need to force the words out of my mouth when my stammer was triggered lifted. As the focus was on my inner experience, I naturally became more compassionate with myself in order to improve the quality of my experience. I would recognise when I was out of flow and readjust to find more synchronicity. The confidence of finding flow across other activities I enjoyed also seeped into my daily experience. The more I found flow in my life, the

How to Find Flow

less stress I felt, and the more satisfied I became. I felt more empowered, less consumed and reactive to my thoughts, and more confident socially. I became better able to pick my moments, talking more frequently when I felt safe and competent. These conversational wins were massive, something I had not felt for as long as I could remember.

Despite this success, I still stammered in emotional situations, avoided intimate conversations and refrained from public-facing positions that might require such daunting prospects as making a speech. But while my progress was incremental, I had turned the tide and was heading in the right direction. And perhaps most unexpected, questing to be in flow taught me two vital lessons that have been instrumental in my life ever since: how to collaborate with my stress constructively and how to deal with an overactive mind.

As the travel business grew, I felt torn. On the one hand, I drew confidence from setting up a business and being featured in the UK's *Director* magazine with my brother, Adam, as a young and bold entrepreneur. On the other hand, deep down, I knew I wanted to pursue my fascination with flow more directly. The business was all-consuming. It involved endless marketing, operational management and dealing with ridiculous client demands – and since my default to dealing with stress at that stage was to 'power on', it was finally taking its toll. I felt demotivated and exhausted, and was close to burnout. As difficult as it

Introduction

was to leave this business – my baby that I had nurtured and spilt blood to help build – I knew I needed to make the space to focus on what grabbed me most: flow. So I not only left the business to pursue flow more directly, but I also moved to live in Australia and commit to the woman I loved.

Having trained in sport psychology, been a tennis and mindset coach, helping athletes, financial traders and my own staff become better equipped to find their flow over the years, I seemed to naturally fall into the role of a high-performance coach – specifically, a Flow Coach. I was certainly more comfortable asking questions than giving lengthy answers, and coaching people towards flow combined my passions for personal development, performance psychology, Eastern philosophies and peak performance. Feeling like I was pioneering a new profession, this work continued to fuel my sense of adventure and fascination with finding flow.

As the years rolled on, I founded the Flow Centre to bring together scientists and expert practitioners to help bridge the science and practice of flow. And the results were rewarding. I loved every minute of working to build an organisation of meaning. Never had I worked with such a variety of people from different backgrounds. The common love for flow brought us all together, and we all felt that the world needed more flow. Initially, Dr Susan Jackson, co-author with Csikszentmihalyi of the book *Flow in Sports*, and I created an applied pathway

How to Find Flow

to flow. Soon, our list of practical tips for finding flow stacked up, and the practice of Flow Coaching evolved. To help professionalise this approach, the Flow Coaching Federation was established to standardise the practices and ethics of Flow Coaches, and continues to serve as a beacon for all those seeking to pursue this career.

Which brings me back to this book and a question I have for you. While you may not want to become a Flow Coach, if you are reading this book, it is a safe bet to say that you may want to experience more flow in your life. But before you can do this, a fundamental lesson that I have learnt from my experience is that, in every moment, throughout every day, our mindset, mental processing and inner game are already dictating how we think, feel and act. This happens whether we like it or not, often to our detriment if not purposefully optimised. To rewire these inner workings for flow, we first must take responsibility for this inner game. So the question I want to ask you is: Are you committed to taking charge of these inner workings, or not? If you are, this book is designed to help you understand this inner game and tweak it towards flow. It is designed to provide you with the tools to enhance your daily performance, increase your satisfaction and cultivate the mental skills that foster a state of flow. But first and foremost, you must be willing to change and ready to work on your mindset.

Introduction

THE BOOK

I am far from being the first to have linked flow with performance, life satisfaction, meaning and well-being – we are several decades beyond that juncture. In this book, I do, however, help to bridge the science and practice of flow which has been missing to date, and explain how you can manage your inner game towards intentional flow. I will share the learnings from my PhD on flow science and present a simple model for you to understand the core concepts of flow and give you the same educational flow training programme that has helped participants engaging in scientific studies to improve their performance, reduce anxiety, utilise their stress and find more flow.

Managing their inner game towards flow has helped my clients not just cope with, but perform better and feel better when facing life's challenges. Whether it is an over-brimming mailbox, cleaning the house, delivering a presentation at work or creating a work of art, to having a testing moment in a relationship, getting a toddler somewhere in a timely fashion despite their untimely tantrum, facing irrational fears or winning sporting contests, putting on a Flow Mindset will help. I have seen people recover from trauma, transition out of addictive behaviour, discover new meaning in life, enhance their relationships, amplify productivity, sustain focus and even become a world champion. How? Because this book deals

How to Find Flow

with the most fundamental part of your life – you; your approach to life and how you fundamentally deal with difficulty. I make no promises to you. There are no silver bullets or magic milkshakes to finding flow on demand. Like getting fit, it will take *your* continued effort to change your habits and redirect your focus towards flow – which I will help you to do.

I will guide you through how to become more aware of your inner experience, approach challenges in a flow-orientated manner, attune your attention to bypass rising distractions and then step into flow. Put simply, you will walk away from this book with an overarching theme to approach both personal excellence and self-development – one that connects and enjoys both high-performance and well-being.

At the core of this book it's suggested that you adopt and integrate a Flow Mindset into your life. It is my way to hopefully enact what the psychologist Abraham Maslow called the 'actualised self'. In other words, it is a way of satisfying the needs and motivations shared by all humans to realise our full potential. Adopting a Flow Mindset has helped countless professionals and can also offer you a new way to perform. Lorraine Huber, freeride skier, who became World Champion after we had worked together, remarks: 'The lessons have affected my entire life for the better. Learning about flow has been life-changing for me in all areas of life. It has helped me strengthen my mindset and mental approach to elite skiing, and it will give you a

Introduction

tried-and-tested system to use in any challenge. I wish I had started much earlier with this, because you really can learn how to find flow.'

At a time in life when stress is abundant, focus is fractured and mental health issues are on the rise, this book aims to address these three significant problems. As it has done for me, this book will help you understand why we are wired to overthink, stress and be more anxious than we think we should be. It aims to liberate your experiential freedom, allowing you to tune out distracting noise and focus your attention on what matters. And it will give you a roadmap and a toolbox of mental skills to optimise the overall quality of your life and find your flow when it matters most. On this journey, you will learn:

- How your biology and psychology unintentionally get in your own way.
- How overthinking can cannibalise your success.
- The latest science and practice of flow.
- How flow is already a noticeable and valuable part of your life.

I will then guide you to:

- Approach your challenges in a way that is conducive to flow.
- Use your natural stressors as a stepping stone to flow.
- Direct your thoughts and emotions towards flow.
- Synchronise your brain's faculties to step into flow.

How to Find Flow

- Entrust your intuitive intelligence to guide your actions.

By the end of the book, you will:
- Understand the satisfaction that comes with intentionally finding flow – as a goal in its own right.
- Learn how to be *experientially intelligent* and collaborate with your day-to-day experiences, including uncomfortable moments such as fear.
- Appreciate how adopting a Flow Mindset can improve both your performance and your life satisfaction.
- Own your own personalised three-step ritual to prepare for flow for any given situation.

The book is split into three main parts, each representing an important pillar of the Flow Mindset. Together, they aim to give you the tools and rituals to aid your preparation skills for specific events. The name of each part represents a mantra – 'READY, STEADY, FLOW' – that you can use to synthesise and trigger your learnings from each stage to instantly prepare yourself for moments that matter.

Part 1 (READY) is concerned with your *self-leadership* and your approach. Your psyche, when untrained, will naturally get in your way, and this is where the Flow Model comes in to help you instantly self-assess where your experience is in relation to flow. By taking charge

Introduction

of your mindset and orientating your approach to flow, you can create helpful neurochemicals, open your mind to the moment and reduce the friction that readily derails your ability for flow. If you are stuck in an unhelpful state, you may need to 'reset' and 'release' – to wipe your psychophysiological slate clean, before putting on your Flow Mindset to 'rewire'.

Part 2 (STEADY) of a Flow Mindset is all about *self-regulation*. If you are not managing the contents of your consciousness, then your thoughts, emotions and sensations will manage you. To find flow, you need to take charge of your momentary experience prior to events and proactively build the experience you want. If left unattended, the mind will naturally project to future events, most often self-determining suboptimal experiences. To help shape your state, in this part, you will create clear short-term achievable visions of flow that will train your brain to experience flow when the moment comes.

Part 3 (FLOW) allows you to *self-actualise* your ability. To become absorbed in the act and be effortless in your actions, you need to intentionally allow yourself to become absorbed and be effortless. This section will show you how the Flow Mindset aims to develop trust in your intuition and remove the unnecessary effort that typically laces your experience. You'll also learn several lifestyle skills to help naturally attract flow experiences.

In each chapter, I will conclude with a quick recap and a simple challenge for you to integrate what we have

How to Find Flow

covered – allowing you to establish the nuances of a Flow Mindset as you go through the book.

You can apply this book to your most important activity or as a lifestyle approach, or both. Initially, my suggestion is to pick one activity to experiment with the lessons and challenges in this book – preferably an activity removed from your usual setting, something that you enjoy and can do at a moment's notice when reading this book. Some ideas include a yoga move you are trying to master, a handstand, writing a poem, juggling, playing a song, drawing, singing or origami. It doesn't matter what it is, as long as it is easy to pick up and put down and doesn't disrupt your reading of the book too much. Use the same task the whole way through the book, so you can see the evolution of your training as you add layers to what a Flow Mindset means. By practising the challenges I give you as you read the book, you will gain a better understanding of the practice of flow.

While this book offers an entire toolkit of useful flow skills, I suggest working on only a few skills at a time. Overload the psyche and these skills will be difficult to implement. Take the time to practise each skill, then move on to new ingredients. The ultimate aim is to make these flow skills become unconscious habits, but first, we need to build a toolkit of flow skills that you can dip into when needed and intuitively pick the relevant skill.

Before we begin, I would like to clarify a few terms that I will use frequently. I may use the word 'performers'

Introduction

or 'performances', which relates to us all. Performers are often associated with artists or athletes, but our brains and muscles perform within any given task. We could view an executive as a white-collar athlete or a scientist as a cognitive athlete, for example. Whether it is powering through our emails or doing the gardening, we all 'perform' our actions. It often helps people to take authority and responsibility for their actions if they see themselves as always performing their tasks. Secondly, while I may refer to the mind and body as separate entities, they are more accurately inextricably integrated. I may do this on occasion to either isolate concepts or adhere to a common language, but I will regularly refer to this integration as the human 'psyche', derived from the Greek '*psykhe*', which reflects an integrated mind and spirit that is inseparable from the physical body.

If you're ready, then let's get into it.

Part 1
READY

CASTING BACK TO BEFORE I EVEN KNEW WHAT FLOW was, the idea of my thoughts getting in my way was ever-present as a youngster playing tennis. I often knew what shots I wanted to play, but, as many athletes would attest to, despite the hours of training drills hitting the very same shot, sometimes the mind games were all too much and the ball just wouldn't go where I wanted it to go. Likewise, I often knew what I wanted to say when talking to others, but, just as I would be about to speak, my mind would race ahead, leaving me jumbled. Caught up in my thoughts, unable to articulate the multitude of threads that were occurring, often in some mild state of paranoia, I became my own bottleneck. It was confusing and often crippling. The more I sank into my thoughts, the more aloof I would become, the more I stammered and the worse I felt about myself.

To overcome these frustrations, the only tool I had at the time was to push on and grind it out. Belittling any inner conflict and hiding any unhelpful inner chatter seemed to be a revered strength surrounding elite athletes at the time. The old-fashioned lessons to 'Ignore

Ready

it like it doesn't exist'; 'Just stay positive'; 'Tell yourself you're better than that'; 'Just keep going'; 'Pull your socks up'; 'Power on'; 'Force it if you have to' were ever-present. And so, not knowing another way, I did just that. I kept stumbling through conversations, pushing away the embarrassment and forcing the stammer out when I had to talk. It was painful, but what other choice did I have? I kept approaching my tennis in the same way, hoping that the more I criticised myself into playing better, training harder and forcing a result, the more my mind would stop being distracted and the ball would land exactly where I wanted it to. While this dogmatic and dogged approach awakened my attention, it also marred my experience, adding more deliberation and doubt. Further, the internal conflict that I had otherwise been suppressing would eventually catch up with me. Like a live volcano, the bottled thoughts and feelings would erupt, often at the most inopportune moment; I would shout and swear on court, punch the fence or find myself slating my own lack of competence. When I did win, rather than celebrating in joy, it was more of a relief that the mind games and dissatisfying journey was over.

On reflection, this approach that afflicted my youth was clearly outdated and never led me to perform at my peak or feel at my best. Flow would come and go but often when I was playing about or had nothing to lose. Ignoring the chance to change my inner game for the

How to Find Flow

better only led to more distracted thinking and discorded experiences.

Many of us still approach our careers and daily challenges by pushing through difficulty, ignoring our momentary inner experience in favour of other agendas. Often forcing our performance in an authoritarian manner, and being discompassionate to ourselves in the process. However, learning about flow has shown me another way to meet my challenges – it has given me a new way to perform, one in which I can still strive for excellence but without the need to diminish my inner experience or motivate myself through fear or dogged demands. It's an approach in which I don't have to apply the stick to get me over the line or beat myself up when making a mistake. Instead, learning about flow has shown me how to work with my brain rather than despite it – and I want to share that with you now.

Part 1 will begin by outlining a comprehensive education on flow. After understanding the nuances of flow which will help you refine what you are aiming for, we will cover how to recognise flow, how to use the Flow Model in your challenges and how to change your approach to challenge and complexity. By unpacking the foundations of a Flow Mindset and the type of self-leadership that is required to find flow frequently, you will be READY to enter your journey to flow.

Ready to get READY?

Chapter 1

RECOGNISE FLOW

FLOW IS OFTEN OVERLOOKED BECAUSE WE DON'T fully understand it, placing it in the illusory or 'too hard' basket. My experience and research suggest that flow becomes more attainable when we receive an education on it. Understanding the nuances surrounding flow will provide your brain with the details it needs to trust the process, as well as the levers your mind requires to home in on flow. After all, how can you expect your brain to attain a vague and ambiguous target, unless by chance?

In this chapter, we will therefore cover the idea and benefits of flow so that you can start to recognise how flow is appearing in your life already.

THE IDEA OF FLOW

Centuries ago, in a sunlit grove of olive trees that was dedicated to the goddess Athena, the young orphan

How to Find Flow

Aristotle questioned the teachings of Socrates and debated the meaning of life with Plato. Looking for an answer to the meaning of his own name – 'the best purpose'[6] – Aristotle, revered as one of the most influential thinkers ever to walk this planet, identified *eudaimonia* (nowadays loosely translated as 'human flourishing') as the optimum activity of the soul and the aim of all human deliberate action. Among Aristotle's teachings, one prominent message is his distinction between action and production. He proposed that our greatest rewards came from actions that were driven not by productivity but by a search for our greatest self. Aristotle's moral call for us to discover and live with our 'daimon' or 'true self'[7] suggested that our greatest path was to follow our interests and realise our full abilities. Ever since, we have searched for the right term for the deeply satisfying experience drawn from finding the best version of ourself in the real challenges of everyday life. While the Greeks quested to find one's 'daimon', the Romans remarked on one's 'genius' and early Western psychologists wrote about the embodiment of 'self-actualisation', modern scientists have called our most optimal state of functioning 'flow'. Now, thanks to the work of so many distinguished researchers, the actualisation of our greatest self – flow – is now better understood than ever before.

When in flow, athletes get into the zone, scientists find breakthroughs, writers' pens flow and students walk away from exams exhilarated. 'Flow sits at the heart of

Recognise Flow

most, if not all, great athletic performances – and those achieved without flow would have been made even more memorable via the experience of this optimal psychological state,' explains flow scientist Susan Jackson. Kobe Bryant, considered to be one of the greatest basketball players the NBA has ever seen, describes flow in the following way:

> 'When you get in that zone, it's just a supreme confidence that you know it's going in. It's not a matter of if – it's going in ... Everything slows down. You just have supreme confidence. When that happens, you really do not try to focus on what's going on, because you could lose it in a second ... You have to really try to stay in the present, not let anything break that rhythm ... You get in the zone and just try to stay here. You don't think about your surroundings, or what's going on with the crowd or the team. You're kind of locked in.'[8]

Innate in all of us is a desire to survive and/or prolong our genes. Humans naturally, therefore, turn their attention to developing their own unique potential, knowingly or not, as it sharpens our chances of survival and progression. In doing so, we inevitably become attracted to flow-inducing activities because these activities allow us to express our potential and actualise our ability. A fundamental premise of flow's link to positive progression is the growth principle inherent within flow. Since flow

How to Find Flow

is most frequently found when our skills are challenged and we play with our limits, we become more skilful, confident, brave and adept at dealing with complex situations. Within the activity, for those brief moments of flow, we witness our true unreserved self in action. Unshackled from the limitations of our mind, we glimpse upon our strengths, our potential and our actualised self, feeling more satisfied and whole because of it. These benefits of flow are so rewarding that we will seek flow regardless of extrinsic pressures or the sacrifice of other personal needs. It is why rock climbers risk their lives or some work into the night without recognition. To re-enact this feeling of flow and the subsequent development, we seek increasingly challenging or complex tasks to match our increasingly sophisticated skills, initiating a growth principle that engineers continual learning and layering complexity that helps us to become more capable and complex human beings. We become better equipped to survive and progress among the herd, passing down a more evolved gene to our progeny.

Deeply enriching, flow experiences garner a greater meaning than other daily experiences and help to shape our future thoughts, choices and actions. Even though our genetics, the environment and our cultural inheritance help to shape our life's trajectories, our mind also plays a moment-to-moment active role in selecting information and making decisions; this is known as our 'psychological selection'. Since the internal harmony experienced during

Recognise Flow

flow is so intrinsically rewarding, there is a continuous bias towards flow that governs much of our decision-making, spurring us to return to flow-inducing activities. In this manner, flow shapes what narratives and activities we deem to be valuable. The activities in which we find flow become meaningful and important to us, in and of themselves; so much so that we are happy to identify with these activities as if they represent who we are – 'I *am* a golfer', 'I *am* an engineer', 'I *am* an artist' ... and so on. I wonder what activities form part of your identity. No doubt, flow is a major reason why. This ongoing process of self-definition not only facilitates our personal growth as we become more 'defined', but also helps to consolidate our personal identity. It helps us to understand why we participate in certain activities over others, and how we position ourselves in the world. In doing so, these chosen activities become important self-defining activities and help us to reveal our true interests and strengths.

Flow is often talked about as being the missing link between performance and well-being or the glue that binds so many varying benefits. I like to term flow as a meta-state, an underlying state that spurs other attractive outcomes. It is a catalyst within consciousness that allows us to embody the person we otherwise try so hard to engineer. Flow is undeniable in the world around us, whether seeing a comedian own the room or watching a child skip along the top of some jagged rocks – when in flow, our psyche produces an almost identical experience;

How to Find Flow

but it never fails to surprise me how this incredible and developmentally integral meta-state is rarely prioritised in our thinking.

One of our failings is the low light it gets in popular culture. But whether it is a fleeting *mild* moment of flow, such as when embroiled in a fascinating conversation, or an unforgettable *intense* state of flow from an important event, flow is already part of our human experience that we readily acknowledge, albeit by many different names. Musicians talk about being in the 'groove', jazz musicians find the 'pocket', fighter pilots enter the 'bubble', athletes go 'into the zone', executives 'nail it', coders become 'wired in', traders are 'in the pipe', bowlers talk about being 'on a roll' and basketballers go 'on fire' – to name just a few cultural references. Regardless of the label we use, we readily appreciate this optimal state of control indirectly, but seldom directly. While flow irrefutably stands out in stark contrast to the inner experiences that otherwise consume much of everyday life, it is my experience in talking to others that many of us have become accustomed to glancing over the state, not because we don't appreciate it, but because we don't fully understand it. When we try to capture the essence of these treasured moments, we often end up confused. We are left pondering how we paradoxically felt both highly in control and out of control at the same time, how we were seemingly more present than usual yet can't recall immediately after the act how we did what we just did.

Recognise Flow

A surgeon, Enita, describes her experience after leaving her consultancy exams:

> 'I can't remember too much, to be honest. I know it went well, because I seemed to enjoy answering the questions, but I can't recall much of what I said. The answers just seemed to come to me; they popped out of my mouth. It is only now, as I deeply reflect, that I can recall being aware of the examiner's facial expressions, structuring the answer in my mind, and speaking, all at the same time. I was able to take in so much more information and speak with more authority than my mock exams; it was as if someone else was speaking through me.'

Often, the more we think about these moments of magic, the more perplexed we seem to become, as Olympic archer Denise Parker explains:

> 'I don't know what happened. I wasn't concentrating on anything. It didn't feel like I was shooting my shots, but like they were shooting themselves. I try to remember what happened so I can get back to that place, but when I try to understand it, I only get confused. It's like thinking how the world began.'[9]

Since most of us are left bewildered as to what just happened, when we pop out of flow, we label the experience as luck and quickly move on, rave about our talents like an egomaniac or marvel at the mystery, but try not to talk about it in case we jinx ourselves from rediscovering it. In the difficulty to fully comprehend these experiences of flow, they become blind spots in our memory, and, for most of us, this extra potential that flow seems to unbottle remains untapped.

THE BENEFITS OF FLOW

Across domains and cultures, the experience of flow achieves outcomes that are not only highly sought after in the short term, but fundamental to human evolution in the long term. Across hundreds of scientific journals, I have found that flow:[10]

1. furthers our *positive development* by enhancing our confidence, self-concept, well-being, positive emotions, ability to handle stress and sense of meaning derived from these actions
2. *improves human functioning* by facilitating increased performances, skill acquisition, creativity and cognitive efficiency
3. *furthers our engagement* with activities through increased commitment, motivation and ability to sustain attention with the task at hand, not least the increased desire to re-engage for the sake of finding flow once again

Recognise Flow

POSITIVE DEVELOPMENT	HIGH FUNCTION
Positive Emotions • Joy • Meaning • Happiness **Well-being** • Enhanced Well-being • Improved Mental Health • Reduced Stress • Physiological Health **Developmental** • Personal Development • Growth Complexity • Enhanced Self-concept • Enhanced Self-efficacy • Increased Self-identity	• High Performance • Optimal Functioning • Increased Creativity • Academic Achievement • Cognitive Efficiency • Skill Acquisition **FURTHER ENGAGEMENT** • Continued Engagement Sustained Attention • Commitment • Increased Motivation • Increased Flow

Researched outcomes to flow[11]

In business

World leaders and entrepreneurs such as Virgin's founder Richard Branson have sung the praises of flow. The McKinsey Global Institute spent ten years studying the workplace to conclude that executives are five times more productive in flow.[12] As such, Google, Red Bull and many other leading companies are integrating the principles of flow into their workplace. Andy Mckinley, a biomedical engineer from the United States Air Force Research Laboratory, states that, in flow, results show 'a twofold improvement in how long a person can maintain performance'.[13]

How to Find Flow

In education

Flow is one of the key principles of creating optimal learning environments. David Shernoff, Director of the Center for Math, Science and Computer Education at Rutgers University in New Jersey, carried out one of the largest reviews of research on flow in educational settings and then decided to test the effect of flow on learning firsthand.[14] He assessed whether a variety of instructional activities intentionally designed to facilitate flow would affect the learning experience. And it did. Flow has been found to facilitate optimal learning environments and prolong student engagement, increasing enjoyment, gratification, academic confidence, academic adherence and a sense of mastery from learning tasks.[15] John Hendry, awarded the Order of Australia Medal (OAM) for his work in education, suggests:

> 'Flow captures the intention of all life experiences and is certainly the intention or stated purpose of every human endeavour, be it individual or group, team or institution. All the "iatry" (care) aspects of the helping sciences, e.g. psychiatry and psychology, medicine and all the human sciences and social sciences, are embroiled in the task of pursuing flow. This is ultimately the purpose of human existence for we wish always to have a better world laced with care and of course a living performance level

Recognise Flow

that enables all to contribute to the best of their capacity moment to moment.'

Flow is so integral to student development and optimal learning that many researchers believe that the Montessori schooling method, while using different language during its genesis, systemically designed the classroom environment and culture to empower student flow.[16]

In creativity

In music, artists live for these special moments of deep flow and pick up the instrument daily to immerse themselves in the music. Peter Buck, the lead guitarist of R.E.M., describes:

> 'When I think about "Losing My Religion" [the band's most famous song], I think about the process of writing and recording it, and how dream-like and effortless it was. The music was written in five minutes; the first time the band played it, it fell into place perfectly. Michael [Stipe] had lyrics within the hour, and while playing the song for the third or fourth time, I found myself incredibly moved to hear the vocals in conjunction with the music. To me, "Losing My Religion" feels like some kind of archetype that was floating around in space that we managed to lasso. If only all song writing was this easy.'[17]

How to Find Flow

In innovation, flow has been positively associated with employee creativity and reported to be an essential component of creativity in group decision-making.[18] So much so that one's ability to find flow is seen as a valid predictor to employees finding creativity in their work.[19] Not only are individuals who experience flow thought to be more creative, 'they are more inclined to *implement* creative ideas,' states Dr Nicola Baumann – Professor of Differential and Personality Psychology at the University of Trier in Germany.[20] Flow experiences seem to promote a faster transition from the idea phase to the subsequent initiation and implementation stages of innovation. 'The higher the flow experience, the greater the chance of successful implementation of the idea,' explains Dr Miha Škerlavaj – Professor of Leadership and Organisational Behaviour at BI Norwegian Business School.[21]

In health

Flow is often linked to positive well-being and mental health. In recent decades, the practice of flow therapy has emerged, successfully helping people to learn about the flow experience, identify it in their life and, more importantly, become more proactive in managing or producing future flow occurrence. Studies show that finding flow has played a crucial role in treatment adherence, treatment outcomes and improved functioning in daily life among individuals undergoing programmes in physical rehabilitation, eating disorders and obesity.[22] A main

Recognise Flow

reason for this is that flow not only improves engagement and adherence of interventional programmes, but is seen as an effective and rewarding coping mechanism for anxiety and stress reduction when facing daily life challenges. As flow is often reported to be the antithesis of task anxiety, these intrinsically rewarding experiences of effort-less control result in improved confidence, personal satisfaction and motivation. Consequently, over time, flow facilitates a more consolidated construction of an individual's self-efficacy and self-worth.

For example, Clemens Ley, a researcher at the Institute of Sport Science in Vienna, studied how flow could help soldiers with post-traumatic stress disorder (PTSD). Experiences of flow are ever-present in battle as soldiers facing life-threatening scenarios are literally forced into 'flow or die' situations. Soldiers report that, within the heat of battle, they feel more alive in flow than in any other moments of their life. The desire to re-experience this sensation often drives soldiers to return to the blood-soaked battlefields, even in the knowledge that they themselves may end up lying among the dead. War has its price, and survivors often suffer from PTSD. As a result, these affected war veterans become depressed, and can hardly focus on the here and now in their post-war life; they deeply miss the state of presence they found in flow when at war. To help alleviate these distressing conditions, Ley conducted a three-year flow-inducing intervention study with patients of HEMAYAT –

How to Find Flow

a non-profit organisation for medical, psychological and psychotherapeutic care of torture and war survivors.[23] The subjects had come from conflict-torn countries, mostly Chechnya, Afghanistan, Iran and Iraq, and varied by social-cultural background, asylum status, age, language skills, past experiences, family and living situation, mental health, physical condition and previous sport and exercise skills. Twice a week for three months, the participants engaged in a sport and exercise therapy programme which included flow-inducing games and activities such as basketball, dance tasks and art therapy. What Ley found was astonishing. In only a short space of time, the survivors, who were depressed and had poor mental health, were able to experience flow once again, and not only did they find relief from their everyday trauma, they also relished in participating in the flow-inducing activities. The participants reported that the intervention facilitated an experience of pleasure, a distraction from illness-related thoughts and an ability to be in the 'here and now'. It helped them to experience a sense of mastery and achievement, adding joy and meaning to their actions. These sample results are no doubt why other flow-inducing programmes such as 'Operation Surf', an organisation that teaches wounded soldiers how to surf, have had such success, reporting that participants have decreased their PTSD symptoms by 36 per cent, depression by 47 per cent and increased confidence by 68 per cent.[24]

Recognise Flow

Considering that nearly 20 per cent of sample populations are receiving registered mental health treatment;[25] that 17 per cent of the American population,[26] 18 per cent in Australia[27] and 15 per cent in England[28] are on psychiatric drugs; and that a longitudinal study over ten years examining psychotropic medicine consumption in 65 countries and regions highlighted a 4.08 per cent relative average increase annually,[29] it is clear that there are few gold-standard solutions for mental health, if any. Even though statistics for mental health vary in differing reports, these numbers are alarming. Whilst individual anecdotal benefits are common, meta reviews show little improvement in mental illness from most psychological interventions,[30] so it is worth questioning how flow can aid, facilitate or replace existing interventions for treating stress-related health disorders.

While the pharmaceutical solution to anxiety, stress and depression is certainly beneficial for big pharma, it also does a lot to create a dependent population, bottlenecked health services and many unwanted side effects. Perhaps most devastating of all is the associated rhetoric that individuals who cannot effectively deal with stress are 'broken' and require fixing through external means; it does little to empower an individual's capability to direct oneself through life's stressors, let alone lead oneself towards optimal functioning. On the contrary, flow interventions aim to do just that; they empower individuals to embrace the challenges in their lives.

How to Find Flow

Even outside of clinical settings and diagnosed mental health labels, the human population is struggling. Often, we don't find ourselves flourishing or in flow, but rather settle for suboptimal results or just saying 'enough', because we don't have the energy or the impetus to strive for a better experience. This appetite is starved not because we are incapable or do not logically know that these heights are worth aiming for, but because, over time, life has seemed to get the better of us. Let me be more specific: the pressure we all face in life is so potent that it can be exhausting. We are so compelled to do more, keep up with the Joneses or achieve a certain status that we can easily forget how we genuinely feel or, at extremes, who we even are. Many of us readily suppress how we might think, feel and act in order to get through the day, week, and year.

We all face a host of environmental and cultural pressures that subtly and sometimes explicitly shape our minds. Whether that is from corporate influence, values from our parents, religious ideals, cultural norms, political messaging or commercial messages suggesting how we should dress and behave, we are bombarded with scripts to adhere to. While some of these messages are well-meaning, they often conflict with what our authentic self feels. When we add to this the internal pressures we face from our upbringing, past traumas, expectations and emotional and mental stuff that we haven't fully processed, we find that much of our

Recognise Flow

psychic energy is secretly being drained. These external and internal pressures consume a tremendous amount of energy just to keep at bay, let alone overcome. So much so that the pressure just to get through the day can be intense. While we may be better at side-stepping these pressures at certain times, for the most part, they are overwhelming and, in our exhaustion, we surrender, conform and take to living in a straitjacket of suppression and conformity. Overwhelmed but operating, struggling but surviving, comfortable but not content, many of us who are not mentally ill may not feel depressed, but we don't feel exuberant either. Braced and belted in our own jacket of suppression, a growing sense of disconnection, meaninglessness and 'meh' is kept at bay. If continued, we inevitably become numb to what we are doing and seeing, and suffer in silence, as there is no urgency to our dismay. In short, we languish and wonder why life feels dissatisfying, even if we achieve great things.

Dr Corey Keyes, a pioneering sociologist and psychologist, whose groundbreaking research delves into the importance of recognising and addressing languishing, highlights that over 35 per cent of people are languishing, and this is on top of those who are already depressed or anxious.[31] When we combine this tendency to languish and conform to life's pressures with the trend to alleviate such stress and numbness with immediate gratification, the internal discord only grows. As we become preoccupied with anticipating the next dopamine hit from our mobile

How to Find Flow

notifications or consuming an endless range of media available at our fingertips, our inner expressions and intuitive voice get lost among the noise. As this avoidance and suppression compound, we disengage, disconnect and stop being present. We become uninspired, unexpressed and unactualised. Our vitality for life diminishes, our vibrancy in each moment lessens and our internal flame reduces to a flicker. In effect, in trying to 'get by', we restrict our own actualisation. Mental health symptoms come and go and, perhaps most importantly, the opportunity for flow diminishes.

I say 'most importantly', because flow potentially offers the most excellent antidote to this problem. To combat languishing, people need to find meaning and deep engagement again – something flow offers on tap. People feel innately alive after experiencing flow. The deep engagement, actualisation of our strengths, inspired behaviour and intuitive action inherent within flow are precisely the opposite feelings and self-narratives to languishing in suppression and suffering. It is no surprise that, during the early days of the Covid-19 pandemic, the best predictor of well-being wasn't optimism or mindfulness – it was flow.[32] People who became more immersed in their projects were able to avoid languishing and maintain their pre-pandemic happiness.

While increasing the frequency of flow may not be the panacea for all mental health challenges, it certainly provides a pathway to significantly improve engagement

Recognise Flow

and satisfaction, and diminish the crippling effects of anxiety, stress, suffering, languishing and depression.

Hopefully, I have adequately outlined why flow is essential to every performance endeavour and to those wishing to live a satisfied and actualised life. Yet, despite these benefits, flow is constantly and continuously restricted. Why? Because, for the most part, aspects of our biology and psychology that once served us have evolved to restrain us. The next chapter explores these evolutionary errors and why it is so difficult to tap into flow in the modern world.

> **LET'S RECAP**
>
> In this chapter, we have looked at how the state of flow:
> - is one of, if not the richest human experience
> - can be an everyday experience
> - fosters positive development, higher functioning and further engagement
> - is relatable to any domain
> - bridges the often-neglected gap between well-being and performance

YOUR CHALLENGE

To help flow become more real for you, let's take a moment to look back over your past experiences of flow.

How to Find Flow

Flow is as egalitarian as a French baguette. There are thousands of examples every day, in work and in play, in which flow occurs, and I'm sure if you reflect closely enough, you too may notice how flow has already appeared in your life.

It is important that you start to recognise flow, identify it and label it, in order to give your brain signposts to follow. It is in reminiscing over these deeply satisfying moments of flow that we best remind ourselves of their importance and, at the same time, subconsciously give ourselves the permission to experience them again.

Reflect on your childhood, younger years or yesterday, and try to identify a moment in which you were able to act spontaneously, surprising yourself by your actions – perhaps flying down the stairs or playing in the back garden. No matter how mild or intense the experience, start to recognise these moments as potential flow experiences. It can be helpful to externalise these ideas by talking them through with others or writing them down on a timeline.

If you are unsure as to whether the flow experience was a flow experience or something else, do not be too concerned or overthink it. Later in the book, when we give details on the Flow Model and the latest science on flow, you will become more familiar with recognising and labelling a flow experience.

Chapter 2
RESET FOR FLOW

IF, AS ELEANOR ROOSEVELT SUGGESTED, 'THE PURPOSE of life, after all, is to live it, to taste experience to the utmost, to reach out eagerly and without fear for newer and richer experience,'[33] then why do we not seek and find flow more frequently?

Put simply, we get in our own way. For example, when humans face difficulty and mistakes occur, one of our most frequent reactions is to think more. At best, we give a motivating pep talk; at worst, we berate our ability and existence. Do you recall ever saying, 'Argh, I'm such an idiot' after making a mistake, or 'I hope that doesn't happen' after thinking about an uncertain future? While there are certainly times when it is important to cognitively recalibrate or think through our options, when we know what to do but just can't execute it, thinking more about the situation doesn't help – in fact, it often

How to Find Flow

makes it worse. Just when we want to click back into the groove, we become distracted by our thoughts. Instead of executing the next move, we overload our attentional bandwidth with unnecessary concerns, assumptions or worries about what others may (or may not) be thinking, for example. Before we know it, we are consumed by our thoughts. Mind racing, we leave our presence and performance behind. It is not only that our performance suffers from overthinking, but this barrage of mental activity is stressful. To enable flow, we need to learn how to reset and get out of our own way.

In this chapter, I will lift up the hood on our neuro-psychophysiology – by which I simply mean I will explain neuroscientifically (neuro), psychologically (psycho) and physiologically exactly why we have a tendency to overthink, and how we get in our own way. I will explain the three main aspects of our psychobiology (are you with me?) that we need to rewire or overcome in order to allow flow into our lives, and highlight the five big mistakes we all fall into.

As you may have guessed by now, this chapter is a more scientific one. While it forms the foundations of this book, explains the terms I use later on and is imperative for those working in the human performance space, if it gets a bit heavy for you and you feel the need to skip ahead to the more practical Flow Model, by all means do; you can always come back later. However, the information coming up radically changed how I approach human

Reset for Flow

performance and, of course, flow – and, if you can stay tuned, I hope it will do the same for you.

THINK LESS, BE MORE

When I look back over the decades of working with others, the most common nemesis that inhibits both people's success and the quality of their life is themselves. Despite their best intentions, their thinking almost always gets in their way.

When I coached advanced tennis players in my early years, for example, they would often get frustrated by their lack of execution. They knew what they wanted to do, but just couldn't maintain a high level of excellence. I would be amazed at how much time was spent on the details of their technique, equipment, racquets, diet, clothes or trying to control their opponent, and how little time was spent on their inner game. Even once they came to me to raise their inner game, their focus would still be on their outer game, wanting to chat about the latest technical or strategic enhancements. So, like many coaches trying to meet the client where they are, I would continuously give them technical or strategic feedback on almost every ball: 'Follow through more', 'That's right, well done', 'Hit it deeper', 'Now shorten your back swing', and so on. The client would hit the ball back across the court, thinking about my words, tweaking their game with every shot. This continuous obedience to my instruction was pleasing

How to Find Flow

as a coach; it seemed to confirm my value, as their shots would mould to what I was saying. I was helping them to learn and develop, I thought. It also seemed pleasing to the athlete, as they were getting expert support and advice to perform better and feel better, they thought.

However, what I grew to learn was that, with every comment, I was doing two very unhelpful things. Firstly, by drawing their attention towards technical or strategic improvements, I was activating parts of the brain that would only later inhibit their performance when the intensity increased, such as changing from feeding them balls to playing points. Secondly, while intently listening to me waffle on, we were subtly creating a dependence on external input rather than developing their own intuition and self-trust; my continuous direction to focus on the outer game was preventing them from mastering their inner game and, by default, strengthening their bias towards prioritising their outer game. When the client left the coaching session, while somewhat inspired and more knowledgeable of what they needed to do, their game continued to struggle in matches. Match play pressure led them to overthink their shots as they tried to replicate what had been said in the lesson; in the absence of my continual direction and affirmation, they would hesitate in their decision-making and not trust their own feedback. They struggled to find fluidity in match play, as they were not used to self-regulating their inner game during their training sessions. In response to this underperformance,

Reset for Flow

they would feel that they had failed, denting their confidence in the process. They were confused and frustrated as to why their hard work was not paying off. And rightly so.

My coaching, while optimal by most tennis coaching playbooks, was slowly eroding their ability to find their own flow. It was not until I changed my coaching style to talking less and only asking questions as to what they might do to find their own flow that they started to intuitively self-correct and find more fluency, not just in the coaching session but in matches as well. Direct technical feedback and advice are helpful at times, especially for beginners, but I found this only to be truly effective for the player if done infrequently. I also found that this dissemination of advice was far more effective if done before the lesson started, ideally away from the court. The court then became an anchored cathedral for intuitive action, not overthinking.

No matter the profession, the need to overthink when things get difficult is a common trait for all my clients, and I see it today everywhere I look. Whether it is trying too hard in an exam, over-controlling a relationship, overthinking a delicate procedure, stressing about an upcoming presentation or trying to influence what other people are thinking, we all put far too much emphasis on thinking our way through life's hurdles. At extremes, overthinking makes us become self-conscious, distressed and even paralysed in our own analysis. Even intervening

How to Find Flow

with positive self-talk, while intentionally positive, chews up our limited attentional bandwidth from the task at hand, often decreasing our momentary performance.

In examining this more closely, for the most part, overthinking isn't our fault. Even outside of difficult or high-performing moments, we are rarely free from thinking. While we may not be aware of our habit to incessantly think, the Cleveland Clinic Lou Ruvo Center for Brain Health suggests that the brain contains over 100 billion neurons and 500 trillion synapses, allowing us to have between an estimated 15,000 and 70,000 thoughts every day.[34] However, it is not the number of thoughts that is the issue, but rather our inability to utilise them successfully. Most of our thoughts don't even improve our situation. While many philosophers, such as Eckhart Tolle, highlight that much of our thinking is pre-scripted[35] and hundreds of unverified reports online quote that 95 per cent of our thoughts are repetitive and 80 per cent negative (any numerical number would be nearly impossible to determine and vary between each individual and their mood on a given day), what seems to be widely accepted is that our thoughts seem to manage us rather than the other way around; we are not in control of what we think and are relentlessly reacting to them like a soldier to their superior. Whether it is the simmering frustrations that make us shout at the traffic light for being red and 'making us late' or the cyclical projections that make us stress over a future event, the thoughts that drive these situations are, more often than not, combatively tarnishing our inner experiences and accumulatively affecting our overall life satisfaction. Humans are so negatively entangled with their own thoughts that the World Health Organization stated in 2019 that 301 million people – over 4 per cent of the population – were suffering with an anxiety disorder, which is ultimately a disorder of overthinking unhelpful thoughts.[36] Of note, this is not people who are simply frustrated by their anxiety levels, but people with diagnosed disorders. Just as mindboggling is the 2023/4 National Study of Mental Health and Wellbeing from the Australian Bureau of Statistics, which states that 42.9 per cent of people aged 16–85 years experience a mental disorder at some time in their life.[37] Dr Twenge, a psychology professor at San Diego State University, in her study examining the change in anxiety, found that the average teenage girl has the same anxiety that someone in 1950 would be institutionalised for.[38] Even half of retired athletes, a population sample who are used to dealing with stressors, report to have concerns over mental and emotional well-being as they cannot deal with their anxiety and stress.[39] In business, anxiety is ever-present, causing 71 per cent of workers to be disengaged, 53 per cent close to burnout and 48 per cent planning to look for a new role within the next twelve months.[40] In education, reports now suggest that a mind-blowing 75 per cent of students report to be

How to Find Flow

either 'often' or 'always' stressed about achieving good grades, and problems with anxiety and overthinking are commonplace in five-year-olds.[41] All in all, it is now assumed that the average person spends over 70 per cent of their life living in modes of survival and stress, entrenched in excessive unhelpful thinking.[42] Fast forward to the end of the day, and it is no wonder that most of us choose to relieve ourselves from this absurdity through booze, sugar highs, TV, immersing ourselves in our mobile devices or frankly anything that distracts us from listening to our own psyche. What we seem to crave more than anything is to escape our own minds. Our inability to think less and stress less seems to be the most pressing healthcare issue of today and, if unchanged, for future generations too.

Just as the successes of positive psychology have shown us that engineering and embodying our desired states can be more effective than dealing with the dysfunction, to progress from our current disposition of thinking more and becoming less, we first need to 'think less' in order to *be more*. Thinking less to be more may sound like the practice of mindfulness, but there are several differences between being mindful and thinking less to *be* more, as we are in flow. Jon Kabat-Zinn, creator of the mindfulness-based stress-reduction programme at the University of Massachusetts Medical School, and possibly the most famous mindfulness advocate in academia, describes mindfulness as 'the awareness

Reset for Flow

that arises through paying attention, on purpose, in the present moment, non-judgmentally'.[43] While flow and mindfulness both aim towards presence, they each have a different relationship to the present. Mindfulness seeks to raise and maintain a conscious non-judgemental awareness of what is happening in the present, diffusing us from the rising aspects of each moment, such as the distractions of the past and future projections. Whereas the inherent goal-directed behaviour in flow beckons us to fuse with the moment and become one with our thoughts and the task at hand. In flow, there is no gap between thinking and doing – we are absorbed in the task; anything that is not relevant to the task at hand must fade from awareness. In flow, the mind is acutely judgemental of what to attend to or not, and we may use the past and future to assess our decision-making in the present, such as strategising potential future moves while playing chess. In other words, mindfulness encourages a theme of thought detachment and disengagement, while the journey to flow incites deep engagement and connection with the task; one might summarise the differences as diffusion versus fusion.

Mindfulness can certainly be a helpful preparation for flow, as it helps us to detach from negative habits, re-centre and gain back control of our thoughts and subsequent reactions. However, being too mindful or being mindful for too long will not help us revel in the actualisation of our own ability and become immersed

How to Find Flow

in intuitive action. Being mindful is ultimately an act of conscious control and, as you will learn later in this book, being in flow and performing at our best requires us to step out of these controlled and comfortable states. Instead, the notion of 'think less, *be* more' is to discourage our incessant need to overthink, and instead trust ourselves to *be* in the moment more. As I will describe shortly, to achieve this, we need to work with our innate biology to rewire certain systemic habits.

EVOLUTIONARY ERRORS

In my pursuit to understand optimal functioning and experience, I have spent over two decades cross-referencing research within neuroscience, physiology, psychology and philosophy to find clear intersections and identify overlapping explanations that can shed light on why we think more and become less, and sometimes falter or flounder instead of clicking into flow.[44] What is clear is that there are three key aspects of our evolved biology and psychology that help to explain how we get in our own way. To explain and help overcome what I call our 'evolutionary errors', we will now look at the science behind 1) our cognition: how our brain processes events and decisions; 2) how we biologically respond to perceived threats; and 3) the brain's natural desire to control and predict our future.

Reset for Flow

Battle of the brains

Humans have evolved and survived by developing cognitive functions that allow us to critique, reflect and refocus attention towards planned goals consciously. These higher executive functions are often considered to be the apex of human intelligence, allowing us to coexist in relative peace and develop logical solutions. Accordingly, much of education and societal messaging sponsors the need to think more and sharpen these higher executive functions in the hope of being better and advancing our communities.

Anatomically, this higher executive thinking is carried out in the prefrontal cortex (PFC) located at the front of the brain, just behind the forehead. As you think, the PFC, specifically the medial and lateral components, light up. While this thinking part of the brain is active for most of our waking moments, it is only associated with one of two cognitive operating systems within the brain. The scientific trend is to split our cognition into two systems, known as dual-cognition. Depending on the specific sub-specialism, such as whether someone is studying memory or emotion, neuroscience or psychology, scientists refer to this thinking brain as our 'cold system', 'explicit system', 'slow system' or 'system 2 cognition'. For the purposes of this book, and to avoid confusion, I will continue to refer to this part of our dual cognition as the Thinking Brain.

In terms of performance, many would presume that,

How to Find Flow

because the Thinking Brain is responsible for our most 'advanced' brain functions, helping to separate us from other animals, this area would be supercharged when in flow. Right? Wrong. While our greatest evolutionary asset has helped us build skyscrapers and wear branded clothes instead of fur pelts, it does have its shortcomings and causes some unintended drawbacks. Contrary to what we might expect, consciously thinking about something is actually more likely to impede our performance than help us excel. Whether it's thinking about not hitting the golf ball into the bunker, listening to your inner critic before speaking or thinking about trying to fall asleep, this Thinking Brain readily gets in our way. Moreover, studies show that, during our most optimal states of functioning, this prefrontal area of the brain is virtually offline.[45] In one of the first psychophysiological studies to examine optimal functioning in an activity that you might expect to be driven by the rational Thinking Brain, Csikszentmihalyi and colleagues found that the PFC of elite chess players became downregulated (i.e. deactivated) rather than upregulated (i.e. activated). Why? Although boasting reflexive and rational abilities, the Thinking Brain has a very limited processing capacity – it processes events in a linear and slow manner. Despite the advantages of self-awareness and critical thinking, this Thinking Brain activity is actually burdensome when it comes to application. If we want to access learnt behaviour in an instance, act fast, be intuitive or process

Reset for Flow

information in parallel, the Thinking Brain, by design, will inherently slow us down.

Despite these shortcomings, the Thinking Brain is continuously promoted as the preferred operating system to manage our moment-to-moment experiences in daily life. We have become so accustomed to its promotion and subsequent governance that many rarely escape its 'cold iron rule', suggests Edward Slingerland, a distinguished university scholar at the University of British Columbia.[46] So much so that the transient relief of self-concern, for example, can feel like ecstatic liberation in a modern age. Anecdotally, we feel the elated freedom from our Thinking Brain when people describe the joys of their brain 'switching off' or when commentators remark about athletes 'playing out of their mind'. For example, the writer Edna O'Brien said, 'My hand does the work and I don't have to think. In fact, were I to think, it would stop the flow. It's like a dam in the brain that bursts.'[47] Nick Troutman, World Champion and five-time National Champion kayaker, describes:

> 'When I performed my run [to become World Champion] I felt like I wasn't thinking, I was just reacting. I was reacting so quickly ... it was just like bam-bam-bam. I wasn't thinking, "Oh, I'm going to do this and that", there wasn't time to think, I just kinda did it ... sometimes it feels like my brain just shuts off and I'm better when it does.'

How to Find Flow

In these moments of liberated action, our mind remains mildly conscious but not consciously thinking – it feels acutely in control without the need to be in, or force, control. To say our brain switches off is obviously inaccurate – we are seeing more, processing more, making more decisions and executing skills more competently than usual. More accurately, we feel like our brain switches off because we switch cognitive modes.

While we might feel strongly differentiated from other less cognitively sophisticated animals, the American Museum of Natural History states that 98.8 per cent of our genetic make-up overlaps with chimpanzees.[48] In fact, our brains share more similarities with other animals than they do differences, and for good reason. Humans are just sophisticated wild animals. Just like other animals, we live out the same pre-coded instructions in our genes to survive and seek out the fulfilment of our basic needs in the hope of advancing our sub-species and the information encoded in our DNA. We also share, and thankfully so, a more primary operating system. This second system, or second brain, is perhaps more relatable to the same brain that facilitates a lion to pounce on its prey when hungry. In contrast to the Thinking Brain, this brain is super-fast and responsible for much of our effortless, intuitive and automatic behaviour. While it is often referred to, depending on the specific sub-specialist discipline, as our 'hot system', 'implicit system', 'fast system' or

Reset for Flow

'system 1 cognition', I will refer to this part of our dual cognition as the *Being Brain*.

What the Being Brain lacks in reflexivity it more than makes up for in processing capacity. It is hardwired to our motor cortex, basal ganglia and sensory acuity, respectively enabling instant physical responses, direct access to our behavioural blueprints and more sensorial bandwidth to receive and process incoming information during each moment. It is why we can walk and not spill our drink without thinking about it, yet, when trying to be cautious (activating the Thinking Brain), we are more likely to spill it. While the Thinking Brain starts developing in early childhood and doesn't reach biological maturity until we are in our late twenties, the Being Brain is the brain's first cognitive system to develop as babies.

To contrast how these two brains work, let's look at how they would each respond to the task of climbing a tree. The Thinking Brain would initially ponder the best ascending strategy: analyse the route, create a plan, foreshadow possible problems and perhaps give ourselves a pep talk or philosophically ponder the point of the task. Consequently, the approach is rationally calculated, and the application glacially slow. In stark contrast, the Being Brain would approach it much like a squirrel scampering up a tree. Using intuitive action and trial and error to guide its actions, the Being Brain would race to the top of the tree. While the odd strategic error might occur, the Being Brain's parallel processing ability

How to Find Flow

far outshines the Thinking Brain's linear processing, and would allow it to reach the top before the 'thinking' brain had even finished analysing the route.

Andrew Newberg and Jeffrey Satinover, professors at the University of Pennsylvania and Yale University, suggest in the film *What the Bleep Do We (K)now!?* that, while our Thinking Brain can handle about 2,000 bits of data per second, the Being Brain dwarfs this ability by handling over 400 billion bits of information per second.[49] Even if these numbers vary greatly from person to person and from task to task, it clearly demonstrates the vastly different cognitive capacities and why our conscious thinking may be downgraded during optimal states of functioning. In summary, the trade-off for prioritising our seemingly 'advanced' Thinking Brain is a reduction in processing power, speed and application. In a personal interview, Arne Dietrich, neuroscientist and professor at the American University of Beirut in Lebanon, the theorist behind transient hypo-frontality theory, explains:

> 'Not only will thinking about movement be of little use, but it will also mess up the movement itself. Powering up your explicit system [Thinking Brain] and pondering the meaning of life when you are being chased by a grizzly bear is not something that will help you contribute further to the gene pool! Optimal performance of a real-time sensorimotor task is associated with maximal implicitness [Being

Reset for Flow

> Brain activity] ... This is one of the main reasons flow feels flowy – because any brain structure [such as Thinking Brain activity] that would hamper rapid-fire decision-making is literally shut off.'

Once we wrap our minds around this cognitive neuro-scientific intelligence, it becomes obvious that optimal states will always demand that the slow and energy-expensive Thinking Brain is replaced with the fast and more efficient processing of our Being Brain. Flow emerges not by supersizing our executive brain functions but from a radical alteration in normal brain function – by inhibiting our most recent evolutionary bio-cortical asset. Put simply, it is an efficiency exchange. We're trading the energy that is usually used for higher cognitive functions for heightened attention, awareness and movement response.

In the movie *Top Gun: Maverick*, the veteran aviator, played by Tom Cruise, must prepare a team of flight school graduates for a mission that will require them to rip through a narrow canyon at about 800mph while under fire from surface-to-air missiles. His main advice? 'Don't think; just do.' We hear these messages all the time, because when optimally engaged in a task, our cognition goes through a depleting 'onion-peeling' effect of unnecessary Thinking Brain activity. The more our attention is super-focused on the present demands, the more susceptible other higher executive functions that might otherwise slow us down become.[50]

How to Find Flow

In a personal interview, Lauri Järvilehto, author and intuition researcher at the Helsinki Academy of Philosophy, explained that it is only by restraining the Thinking Brain that other advanced forms of humanity, such as embodying intuitive action, is allowed to occur. Experientially, you may have felt this when riding a bike, skiing down a mountain or driving fast. During normal high speeds, our Thinking Brain wrestles to manage the high demands of the situation and you have to slow down to squeeze through the tight gap. The experience feels effortful, as you try to remain in control and avoid uprising dangers. There comes a point, however, when we go so fast that the Thinking Brain is simply not equipped to respond to the increasing risk and demands, nor capable of making decisions at such a fast speed, and it has no choice but to shut down. Objectively, it may look like we are flying by the seat of our pants, seemingly 'out of control', but the experience is just the opposite. The usual struggle and strained application that comes with difficult challenges disperses. Instead, we sense an unusual ease to our actions and feel more in control than before. As we become forced to trust our innate capabilities and slip into intuitive action, our mind becomes clear of the usual thoughts that distract our attention and our innate ability is allowed to actualise – we race through the tight gap with better precision, often left feeling surprised and in awe of our ability, wondering how we did it.

It is not just performance that gets amplified during

Reset for Flow

Being Brain dominance, but also creativity. When the cold iron rule of our Thinking Brain surrenders, our otherwise suppressed intuition is free to grapple with the demands of the situation and send creative answers bursting to the surface of our consciousness. This is no more obvious than in patients with permanent brain damage or frontotemporal dementia who display unusual creative abilities. Without access to the higher executive anatomy of the Thinking Brain, these patients display a greater ability than normal to dial down the rule-based and conventional processes that most brains adhere to, and instead demonstrate more novel and creative forms of behaviour.[51] Similarly, the Stanford Prevention Research Center found that participants who walked on a treadmill were more creative than those sitting down.[52] Why? Because the activation of our motor cortex simultaneously encourages Being Brain governance.

While the Being Brain is typically dominant during optimal expression, the Thinking Brain is not a switch – it does not turn off entirely. On the contrary, it is still required to help direct attention and recalibrate goals and priorities, and helpfully lingers in the background in case the task demands us to pause and engage in some reflexive thinking. In practice, the two brains are always working in parallel, not in direct competition. For example, our Thinking Brain can be engaged in a conscious self-reflective conversation, while also allowing our Being Brain to bring the coffee cup effortlessly to our mouth.

How to Find Flow

Equally, our Being Brain may be in command while playing football, and still require a minimal input from the working memory processes and executive functions of the Thinking Brain to calibrate certain strategic aspects of the game, such as formational or strategic changes within the opposition. Or in writing an email response, we may want to momentarily promote the Thinking Brain to use its cognitive flexibility to think through the complexities and consequences of our response, and then re-promote the Being Brain to continue writing the email. In most activities, the level of Thinking Brain activity that is required to amplify our performance is so negligible, especially if pre-calculated on the training pitch, that any Thinking Brain activity that is required can usually occur in unison, without disrupting or sabotaging the Being Brain. It is this exact dynamic partnership between the two brains, in which both brains work towards one end, in preference of a Being Brain captaincy, that allows us to perform at our best. The scientific name for this dynamic use of our dual processing systems is 'transient implicit-explicit synchronisation'.[53]

Captain your cognition

When the brains are not in this harmonious interplay, the natural state of order is for the Thinking Brain to be at the helm, ever trying to dominate its dominion and captain our cognition. This over-control and struggle to stay in charge during moments that would better suit our Being

Reset for Flow

Brain is exactly the friction that causes the disjointed, strained and clunky performances that so often limit our potential. This battle of the brains is perhaps most obvious during moments of frustration when we talk to ourselves, be that in response to a mistake, muttering in the shower or giving ourselves a pep talk before an important moment. What do you say to yourself after making a mistake? Go on, pause and take a moment to reflect.

When making a silly mistake, for example, we may tell ourselves, 'You idiot ... Why did you do that?' or 'I'm better than this, you're so disappointing.' But who is talking to whom? It is easy to think we may be psychotic, though we would have to label every human as such if that were the case. Rather, the Thinking Brain ('*I*') is talking to the Being Brain ('*You*'). The Thinking Brain cannot deal with the illogical nature of the act and, in this case, is telling the Being Brain that it shouldn't have made a mistake ('I can't believe it – why did you do that?!'). It is blaming the Being Brain for not living up to expectations, which is ironic as it is likely the interference of the Thinking Brain that caused the mistake in the first place. Ordinarily, we can hear the Thinking Brain flex its authority in our self-talk when it endeavours to control our Being Brain by giving it direction or commenting on and judging its actions. If you listen closely to the commentary of your Thinking Brain, you may even be surprised by how scolding, or even berating, it can become. 'You fu**ing idiot, why are you so incompetent? You're pathetic,

How to Find Flow

you're useless!', we may hear ourselves tell ourselves. If the words being exchanged in your head were expressed between two people in a real romantic relationship, for example, the relationship would likely be in tatters, perhaps even termed abusive. The more you become aware of these two entities in your psyche, the more you will realise how frequently the Thinking Brain is actually captaining your mind to control events and commentating on matters pre- and post-event. You may also start to see how frequently it interferes and undermines your Being Brain by filling your psyche with the needless noise of fear, frustration or doubt.

While the battle and discord between the two brains is not ideal, and the Thinking Brain's continuous over-reach is not helpful, we cannot blame ourselves for overthinking, just as you can't blame a cow for overgrazing its habitat. Overthinking and getting in our own way when faced with difficult challenges is almost a biological inevitability. Humans are evolving, but we are still conditioned to our innate and habitual engineering. Ultimately, we are limited by our 'human operating system' and the upgrades we have installed. To be our best in our daily challenges, we first need to look at how to work with this human operating system, which may require a different type of training than what may have got us to where we are now. Considering that artificial intelligence is quickly exceeding the capabilities of our Thinking Brain, I would argue that now is an ideal time

Reset for Flow

for humanity to recapture the assets of our Being Brain and position flow and intuitive action as prized assets worth mastering. Promoting the Being Brain may feel risky or unmeasured, but this is only true for an *untrained* Being Brain – there is also risk in trusting an untrained Thinking Brain. (More on this in Part 3.) Our Being Brain will only mature if it is allowed to learn, make mistakes and cultivate wisdom. Since creativity, wisdom and connection are fast becoming lauded as the top skills wanted in our leaders, perhaps it is time to prioritise intuition over logic, wisdom over knowledge, which all require being brain prominence.[54] In the future, we may even be forced into a new era of Being Brain education.

Regardless of where you sit philosophically in this educational debate, it is clear that it is time to stop sponsoring the battle of the brains and conflicting our cognition. In the knowledge that our overreliance on and over-promotion of the Thinking Brain in our moment-to-moment experiences is, more often than not, counterproductive, causing psychic incoherence, we can also recognise that the remedy to being more is, in fact, to *be* more, and value our Being Brain more. To change this tide, we first need to help the two brains respect each other in order for them to work together. Like any successful relationship, both parties need to see each other's strengths and trust one another to do what they do best.

For most people, the new learning here is for the

How to Find Flow

Thinking Brain to appreciate the talents of the Being Brain and let the Being Brain do what it has been designed to do. In other words, *be* more, think less. We can start by helping the Thinking Brain to take the time and attention needed to value and reward Being Brain mastery when it happens. This book will help you promote your Being Brain in your preparations and general approach to life's challenges. However, spending a few seconds every day reflecting on how the Being Brain effortlessly manages all sensory feedback, movement decisions and pattern recognition in any given second can go a long way to appreciating the value of your Being Brain and building a lasting bridge between these two captains. It is precisely the strength of this bridge and the relationship between the two brains that will allow you to choose one brain over another, and allow the better suited captain to manage your cognition when the time comes.

Taking back control

Comprehending that I had two brains, or cognitive operating systems, and realising that many of my issues could be explained by the Thinking Brain overextending itself, was eye-opening. It not only helped to explain much of the anxiety, stress, internal discord and dissatisfying experiences both myself and my clients were experiencing daily, but it also helped me to feel more in control of my experience. If I was unnecessarily promoting the Thinking Brain to captain my cognition, I

Reset for Flow

alone wielded the power to change this. While this line of thought was empowering, practically promoting the Being Brain at will was another matter entirely. Logically, I knew we all had the power to alter our thinking and inner experience, irrespective of how demanding or threatening the situation, but it wasn't until I was held up at gunpoint in Brazil that this idea truly hit home.

With eight hours to kill at a ghostly port in southern Brazil, I had naively accepted the offer of a free lift to a nearby shopping centre, from a seemingly kind and helpful local. 'I need to kill several hours before the next bus,' I thought. Before long, another man with a gun entered the car, the doors were locked and I was driven to a remote setting. We stopped, I grabbed my backpack and ran. I made it to a nearby commercial area and ducked into a shop for cover, only to be caught again on exit, thinking I had escaped. These two punks muscled me into a deserted square and sat me down at a dilapidated table.

I sat helpless, feeling forgotten and utterly disempowered. Mind racing, I was lost in my thoughts, only to surface in a fog of fear. I couldn't believe what was happening to me. Unable to think clearly or act with confidence, my whole internal world had been shaken to the core. I felt like a helpless, panicking passenger. In hindsight, I had handed over complete control of my thoughts, emotions, perspective and volition to the criminals who stood before me. But, to my surprise, it was

How to Find Flow

in the deepest depth of this despair that a great clarity revealed itself. These two punks seemingly had control of the situation, but the more I surrendered to a devastating fate, the more a strange feeling of agency grew inside me. They might have me by the short and curlies, I told myself, but they do not have to govern how I feel about the situation.

It quickly dawned on me that I was not only getting in my own way by thinking about the many problems and possible worst-case scenarios, but I had also allowed these two brutes to manipulate how I felt. Even though I was clearly out of my comfort zone, from the seedy deserted streets to being the victim of a robbery, I didn't need to fill my mind with fear, let my heart race out of control and dig my own grave with inaction. Regardless of whether they pulled the trigger or not, it did not mean that I had to disempower myself and relinquish control of my inner experience. With this newfound awareness and a renewed sense of volition, I surprisingly regained control of my inner experience. Feeling slightly more empowered, I calmed my heartbeat and quelled my panicking thoughts. My emotions instantly became less overwhelming. With all my resolve, like the start of spring, I blossomed feelings of hope and disregarded those of despair. While I had nearly an hour shackled in my own experiential prison, in only a matter of moments I was gaining clarity and perspective on the situation. I had a newfound intelligence to my experience,

Reset for Flow

and the situation. Emerging from the fog of fear, I realised that these two gruff men were after my money more than my scalp. I estimated that I could run much faster than them, and if they really wanted my scalp there was not much I could do about it. So I handed them an empty money belt that I had saved for such an occasion and ran as fast as my legs could carry me. They followed, but they could not keep up. As I hid behind a large distant rock, out of breathe and heart beating through my chest, waiting for them to pass by, I soon realised I was safe.

On reflection, by empowering the agency of my inner experience, I was able to change the contents of my consciousness and perhaps save my own life. In managing my psyche, I turned what was, on paper, a traumatic experience into something quite special.

This situation taught me two important lessons. Firstly, no one has the power to govern the contents of our consciousness, no matter the situation; and secondly, in order to self-regulate our experience and subsequent actions, we first need to believe that we have power over our experiential landscape. Even those who have been tortured or imprisoned in solitary confinement can differentiate the pain they feel on the outside to the experience they curate inside. People, places and things may trigger a reaction, but we always have the power to choose how we experience and respond to such triggers. As Anil Seth, Professor of Cognitive and Computational Neuroscience at the University of Sussex, posits, 'As

How to Find Flow

thinkers and agents, we do more than perceive our world; we actively generate it.'[55] In other words, it is our mind's response to events that determines our experience, not the situation itself. I'm sure you have had a range of different experiences when undergoing the same event multiple times, whether it's a job interview, a cold shower or a visit to the dentist. As you start to own and change your perspective of the situation, your experience changes too.

The premise that our internal world is distinct and separate from our external world is often difficult for people to fathom; it can be hard to take full responsibility for the way we feel. If we feel frustrated by encountering three red traffic lights in a row, could only a green light have saved us from this stress? No, of course not – we have all encountered consecutive red lights and not necessarily felt the same level of frustration. We blame traffic lights, events, people and situations in life because, for the most part, we prefer to give this power away. While giving our power away may result in fluctuating dissatisfying experiences, for many, it is better than holding the reins of responsibility. To take full responsibility for our inner experience we have to overcome the triggers not only of our external world but also our internal ones. Perhaps the biggest internal trigger of all, for almost any human, is the second evolutionary error concerning how we deal with threats.

Reset for Flow

Fight, flight, freeze, fawn, flop or flow

To keep us vigilant and survive the dangers of leaving our cave in search of food, back when we were less civilised, our brain developed a component to continuously scan for threats. While we have evolved to have state policing and food delivered to our front door, this brain function is still at large, scanning every moment. When a threat or conflict is anticipated, a small but powerful group of neurons in our brain, the amygdala, raises a neurological alarm bell, which simultaneously alerts and activates our neurology for action. Importantly, this reaction occurs whether the threat is falsely perceived or whether it is real; the psyche responds the same. Although this reaction can be initially helpful to make us alert and prime our body for battle, most of our perceived threats these days don't relate to life-threatening situations. Nowadays, this threat response most frequently gets triggered when our comfort or competence is threatened, such as running out of coffee in the morning or speaking to our boss.

This lingering threat response has two critical consequences. Firstly, it causes rigidity to the very physical muscles we require to be agile when performing at our best; and secondly, the continued threat unnecessarily triggers our evolutionary prized asset, the Thinking Brain, causing further rigidity in our mental functions.

To understand this first point, we need to peek into

How to Find Flow

the window of our physiology. Communication between brain and body is carried out primarily by our nervous system, of which there are two parts: the central nervous system (CNS) and the peripheral nervous system (PNS). The CNS carries out the signalling from the brain to the spinal cord, and the PNS then takes over the messaging to control our muscles. Imagine the brain as the board of directors of a company that makes all the decisions. These decisions get passed to management (CNS), who pass on instructions and messages to the workers (PNS) to carry out the directives of the board. The PNS is made up of multiple systems to help carry out these orders, one of which is the 'autonomic nervous system' (ANS) – a self-regulating system that manages the unconscious behaviour of our body, such as our heart rate and breathing. This system is especially relevant to flow as it is this system that determines whether or not we automatically carry out the orders from our brain in perfect synchronicity. Importantly, the ANS consists of two arms: the sympathetic and parasympathetic. The sympathetic nervous system works to prepare the body for intense physical activity by activating our physiology, giving it a burst of energy, narrowing our attention and helping us to stay alert and present. The parasympathetic nervous system has almost the exact opposite effect, keeping the muscles relaxed and flexible, while also facilitating maximum efficiency of the nervous system as a whole. These two arms of our ANS work side by

Reset for Flow

side to manage our arousal levels and the automaticity of our movement. Now, when a threat is perceived, the sympathetic nervous system is hardwired to respond, to alert and protect. While this has an initial helpful impact, when sustained, alertness turns into stiffness, tightness and, over time, rigidity. We only have to hold the anticipation of receiving a catch for several seconds to feel our arms getting tight. Try being alert yourself, now, for an extended period of time, and you will feel the tightness in your body. This over-alertness has a cost in subtle and obvious ways. For example, if nervous when socialising, our stressed neurology can quickly make us stiff, inattentive and clumsy as we knock over a glass. For many workers, the continuous stream of urgent tasks on the computer forces a narrowing of attention and sustained sympathetic reaction, which accumulatively leaves us stressed and fatigued at the end of the day. But this prolonged rigidity and tunnel vision is not the only issue.

In the raising of the alarm, like a firefighter rushing to put out a fire, the Thinking Brain will endeavour to control anything it can in order to quell the perceived danger and feel more 'in control', causing us to think more, just when we want to think less. In doing so, it inadvertently thinks about the many negative 'what if' scenarios that could happen, triggering further alarms and providing cyclical justification for the Thinking Brain's continuous involvement. Along with it, the brain triggers a host of distracting feelings and further sympathetic activation

How to Find Flow

and rigidity. When continued, the brain becomes locked in its own self-made hamster wheel, embroiled in a ream of threat responses and cognitive ping-pong. The net result is that our threat response will eventually lead the mind and body to fight, flee or freeze, fawn, flop or flow, unless intervened. Instead of actualising our best under this threat and finding *flow*, our psychophysiology makes us either a) *fight* through the situation as we double down on our doggedness and push on to hopefully combat the threat; b) enter *flight* mode and activate our avoidant patterns of thinking and behaviour, such as making excuses and blaming others for our mistake; c) even *freeze* up as we enter analysis paralysis and ruminate so much that we hesitate, such as flustering when unsure how to answer a question; d) fawn, such as placating and people pleasing our way through the experience, often

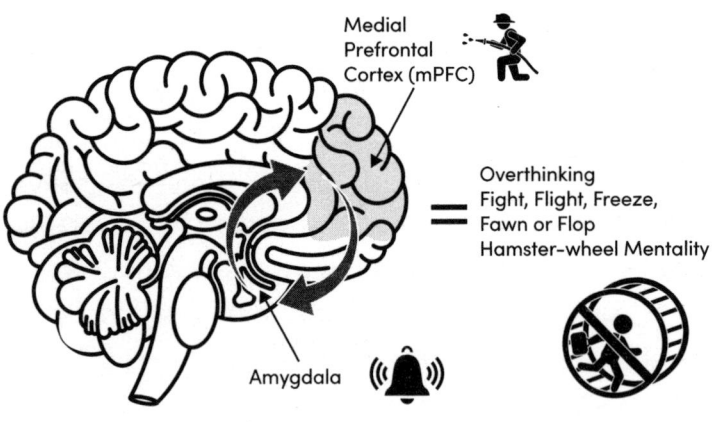

A simplified neuroanatomical diagram of the brain when in a threat response

Reset for Flow

forgetting our own values and standards in the process; or e) flop, as we protect ourself from any perceived emotional pain by completely shutting down or dissociating our emotions from the situation and other people, such as fainting or becoming disorientated.

While this biological activity may seem beyond our control, our awareness of this process can liberate us from it.

Empower your inner experience

When we are being experientially competent, we can quickly acknowledge that any perceived threat is a) probably not life-threatening and b) is a fabricated projection and doesn't require the Thinking Brain to panic and step in.

To be the person we want to be, we first have to wake up from the moments in which we do not feel in control of our inner experience. When life gets tense or busy, the importance of our moment-to-moment experience can often get discarded in favour of other short-term gains; any active shaping of how we think and feel gets shelved until the task is done. As discussed earlier, we are usually so metaphorically asleep to the active management of our internal experience that a large percentage of our waking hours is spent in automated reactive patterns of thinking and behaviour.[56] Though neglecting our internal experience in the moment – to push on or otherwise – is a false economy, it doesn't help to optimise either our

How to Find Flow

satisfaction or our performance. In fact, it is precisely our ability to manage our subjective experience beyond our automation in any given moment that determines whether we rise above dissatisfaction or stay calm in the eye of a storm to perform at our best.

Understanding the responsibility and authority I had over my own inner experience was life-changing. It gave me the foundations to turn any unsavoury situation around – no longer did I need to wait for the house to be burning down before taking action. I stopped giving absolute credence to my thoughts, and instead turned my attention towards experiences that I wanted to feel.

This capacity to manage our moment-to-moment experience must not be taken for granted. The awareness of our momentary inner experience and the power we have over our inner game is a notion I have termed *experiential intelligence*. Being numb or oblivious to our momentary experience and the power we have over it is *experiential negligence*. The ability to actively choose and embody desirable inner experiences within a given situation is what I call *experiential competence*. Whether we choose to enjoy a mindful experience by witnessing our thoughts or feeling our breath, when we intervene to manage our subjective experience with some degree of success we are, in essence, displaying competence in managing our inner experience. On the contrary, *experiential incompetence* is when we allow other people and things to push and pull or dictate our

Reset for Flow

inner experience. Experiential competence is a skill, like any other, that requires practice to master, but one that is innate in all of us.

I found that life became surprisingly less stressful, even when it was full of pressure, when practising becoming intelligent to my experience. Optimising a better experience throughout the day gave me a platform to feel better and more empowered when speaking, facing adversity or dealing with the emotional ups and downs of daily life. Now it is your turn to practise your experiential intelligence. Start by checking in with your experience throughout the day. Become aware of when your mind and body trigger your Thinking Brain because you have entered a threat response. No matter how mild or intense the experience, whether it's running late for work or facing a confronting conversation or daunting task, train your brain(s) to become experientially intelligent. Start by simply recognising your momentary experience. Then, see if you can start to sidestep the automation of your fight, flight, freeze, fawn or flop response when facing these perceived threats. (More on how to do this later.) For now, practise recognising this evolutionary error wherever and whenever you can.

Craving control

To meet our primary agenda as humans – survival – our brain has unintentionally created a third evolutional error: a craving for order and control.

How to Find Flow

The brain is the biological organ of subjective experience – we only have to take hallucinogens or psychoactive drugs that target certain brain regions to see how experience, perception and reality can become distorted. It is also why craniopagus twins, who are conjoined at the cranium or skull, can often feel the other person's reality. In any given moment, there are billions of bits of information for the brain to process. To meet this disposition for order and to feel more in control of this minefield, the mind structures and categorises almost everything into labels and creates patterns to what we see, hear and feel. It is why, without seeing it clearly, we can unquestionably label a stick with lights as a traffic light from 50m away while driving. This categorisation process increases processing efficiency and helps us feel more secure among the profusion of information we face each second. In this deciphering and organising, however, it also makes a host of assumptions, estimates and inaccurate judgements to process each moment and progress to the next. At a micro level, for example, this categorising occurs as we quickly group colours and shapes to assume whether the item before us is an apple or a pear. At a macro level, this occurs through the memes and cultural patterns that are passed on as we inherit common political, religious or cultural beliefs, values and ideologies – even if we have not examined or evaluated them properly. To make sense of all these categories and our interaction with them, the mind organises how we

Reset for Flow

view the world into self-selected psychological scripts, justified narratives that make sense to us and justify why we believe what we believe, see what we see or do what we do. When life is 'in order', most of our processing is seamless and unquestioned. The more ordered things are, the more in control we feel. It is no wonder that the German word for 'okay' is '*Ordnung*', which, when translated, literally means 'in order'.

This predisposition for order is the reason why we feel the need to create a plan for the day, find ourselves straightening the painting on the wall, organising our shoes in the wardrobe, ensuring the butter is placed in the same place in the fridge or why random notes played on the piano can be earsplittingly painful but, when the same notes are played in order, we call it music. When life is in order, we are less perturbed, we feel more in control and secure, and consequently we have a greater bandwidth to allow ourselves to be more flexible, adaptable and open-minded. We ironically get a greater sense of freedom and allow ourselves to be more creative or 'loose' when things are under control. On the contrary, the more chaotic things become, the need for order becomes increasingly urgent. When life seems in disarray, we will likely find ourselves wrestling for some order in our lives to gain a better sense of control. When something gets really 'out of control', our Thinking Brain, like a judge in an unruly courtroom, will bring down the hammer and start laying down strong instructions. For example, have you ever

How to Find Flow

doubled down on your opinion in front of others to not look incompetent? Have you ever told yourself you *must not* be emotional even though you are? Sure, we all have. We become fixed in our thinking, not because it is the best approach in that situation, but because it provides us with some sort of order and structured certainty among the chaos. This constant predilection towards order is also why the mind is continuously evaluating and judging events and behaviours as right or wrong, good or bad. For example, we may catch ourselves thinking, 'Yes, that make sense', 'This way is definitely the right way' or 'Why on earth are they doing it that way?' It is also why we may sidestep someone in the street because they look strange and unpredictable or avoid certain people when asking for feedback, because we know, consciously or not, that they may not give us the response we want – when their differing opinion is precisely what we may need. This *desire* for order affects everything we do. And while these underpinning mechanics are essential to help process life efficiently, they also unintentionally skew what we see, think and do, manipulating and sometimes blinding our attention.

Given this prominence for order, let's examine this a little further. A major cog in the wheelhouse for curating and maintaining a sense of order is a process scientists call 'Bayesian inferencing' or 'Bayesian processing'. It is a mental process of predicting the future in order to feel better positioned to act in the present. In this process,

Reset for Flow

the brain creates a prediction of the future or, as neuroscientists would say, an 'end state'. Think of it as a projected snap-shot of what is to come. The brain then cross-references these predictions with our past experiences, considers any influential present-moment variables and then concludes on how to act next. I'm sure you have projected ahead when looking at the daily calendar to work out what to wear, how to feel or how to manage your day. Our brain relies on this type of processing to deal with the plethora of information in any given moment, so much so that our constant predictions and generated end states create a self-defining framework that we attribute to being reality. Meaning, we make predictions to better prepare for the imminent future (to feel in control). The more uncertain or important the future event is, the more the brain will try to predict the future experience to feel more in control. Importantly – time to really pay attention now – in the process of predicting the future, we end up believing our own projections.

I'll say this again, as it is critical: how we predict and project subtly trains our mind and body how to think, feel and act when the time comes. Every time we make a prediction and create an 'end state', this prediction not only provides information about the future situation, but also attributes an experience to the prediction. In doing so, our psyche creates millions of neurological reactions to embody this experiential end state, attaching feelings, thoughts, sensations, a sense of volition and a perceptual

How to Find Flow

lens to the future imagined experience. Expecting this predicted experience to occur, we anchor these experiential sensations to the future event and essentially train the psyche to think and feel in this manner when the time comes. We effectively predetermine our future by creating self-fulfilling experiences. When this future arrives, instead of engaging in further energy-draining processing, it is more efficient for the psyche to simply follow the blueprint it has been trained to embody already, leading us to experience these previous projections. We essentially create our future realities through these self-fulfilling projections. How? Because once we envision something, even if it is a projection, the psyche processes it as a real event, building it into our database of past experiences. You only need to spend a few seconds imagining speaking into the microphone in front of 300 people as you begin your best man or maid of honour speech for your mind and body to react with an elevated heart rate and sequence of thoughts. Alternatively, take a moment now to imagine standing at the open door of a plane circulating at 12,000m as you ready yourself to jump out and skydive through the clouds below. Go ahead, stop, and visualise standing at the open door, as the deafening wind sweeps across your face and trickles down your spine. Have you imagined it? Did you get a psychophysiological reaction? I'm sure you did. Why? Because your psyche thinks the projection is real and is reacting accordingly. Our psyche reacts as

Reset for Flow

if it is, or could be, real, even though you may not have a wedding speech or skydive inked into your calendar. Moreover, if you imagined yourself feeling nervous tapping the microphone or standing at the edge of the plane door – creating an end state laced with anxiety – your mind will also believe that experiencing a sense of nervousness during this activity is inevitable.

Power your predictions

This predictive processing is so ever-present in our moment-to-moment processing, continuously occurring in the background of our cognition, that many would argue that the mind rarely deals with the present moment itself; rather it lives in a continuous state of projection and perceptual processing – we react not to what is in front of us but to an anticipated or hallucinated mental construct that we attribute as reality. Is your mind blown yet? In short, the brain lives in a continual process of 'reification', meaning treating a perceived abstraction as a concreate reality; we live through a hallucinated predicted version of reality. This predictive processing is so integral to how we operate that neuroscientists suggest that even our actions are in fact hallucinations, or self-defining perceptions from our predictions, as they occur from self-fulfilling proprioceptive predictions.[57]

We are going down a bit of a rabbit hole here, and I promise we'll get back on track shortly, but please take a moment to understand what is at play here, as it is the key

How to Find Flow

to deeply forming new responses and realities. Grappling with the predictive processing nature of our mind initially made me very confused; in fact, it blew my mind at the time. Importantly, it helped me to comprehend:

a) how deceptive our own mind can be;
b) how much of our present-moment experience is tainted by the veil of a previously predicted future; and
c) that, while we develop these cognitive maps to cover our present moment with a sense of order and certainty in an uncertain future, if left unattended, our mind will only ever experience biased interpretations of reality, not actual signals from the present moment, which is far from a universal transparent window into reality.

Why does this matter? Well, we all create the world in which we live by what we choose to pay attention to. How we invest this attention determines what we predict and perceive. In knowing that the brain is geared towards generating more 'order', we can also appreciate how the mind will naturally distort reality so as to make it consistent with our ideology, beliefs and self-selected psychological scripts – so that things are more in order and we can feel more in control of the situation at hand. The moment before us may feel very real, but our versions of reality are ultimately laden with biases, assumptions, prediction errors and falsehoods that are unique to each of us. We

Reset for Flow

only need to examine two opinions of the same event, as evident through many relationship issues, to see how we each see different things in any given moment. In fact, given the number of perceptual errors and skewed versions of reality we all experience, equivalent to two people picking up the same grain of sand on a wide-open beach, it is truly amazing that humans seem to agree on so much. Yet, despite the importance of these predictions and the power of our projections, rarely do people who first come to me for coaching manage and manipulate their attention accordingly.

Regardless of whether our future-projected versions of reality reflect the same thing or not, the truth or not, for all intents and purposes they are very real, because they feel real, and, for the most part, we perceive and believe that they are or could be real. While these self-fulfilling projections are helpful most of the time, if unmanaged, they can inadvertently create experiences that we may not want to have. For example, we can project a boring day at work, effectively training our psyche to expect and experience boredom when we arrive at work, only to be at work wondering why our job has become so dreary. Alternatively, we can project an end state of being nervous when performing at a future social or professional event, training our neurology to be anxious when the moment arrives. Unfortunately, for most of us, most of the time, we unintentionally predict and self-determine negative or suboptimal experiences, but rarely, if ever, project and

How to Find Flow

self-determine a flow experience. And herein lies one of our biggest barriers to flow, but also our greatest opportunity to find it. A fundamental premise of a Flow Mindset is to switch this natural Bayesian processing towards flow. Instead of continually predicting and causing us to self-generate a multitude of experiences other than flow (for example, anxious experiences, strained actions and so on), if we can place flow as the seed to our predictions, we can set in motion a self-fulfilling prophecy towards flow – a skill we will embody later in this book when building a Flow Blueprint.

The five big mistakes we all make

Understanding these scientific insights of how our own brain can work against us helped to explain how much of my anguish when speaking publicly was self-manifested through these evolutionary errors, forcing me into a fight, flight, freeze, fawn or flop response. The two brains battling for domination, the continual over-reach of my Thinking Brain during moments of pressure and the brain's tendency to unintentionally predict and self-determine suboptimal experiences highlighted how the psyche can create a perfect storm just when I want to be coherent and calm. It helped me to comprehend how even just thinking about speaking publicly would predict an uncomfortable end state, firing my amygdala and triggering a multitude of panicky thoughts, feelings and sensations. Feeling out of control, my Thinking Brain would then go into hyper-

Reset for Flow

drive in the hope of thinking its way into more order; but imagining what I would say and how others would judge my performance only triggered further imagined threats to my comfort and confidence, causing me to think even more and become more anxious. Just when I needed to stay calm, this cyclical patterning would readily distract my focus, cannibalise my attentional bandwidth and create chaos in my neurology; it was crippling.

I have come to realise that, while this was painful for me, I was not alone. These evolutionary errors cause us all to react in this manner to varying degrees. If we do not take our biology and cognition, or, as I like to say, our human operating system, into account, we will continually create the same five mistakes:

1. Our psyche will have us believe that we don't need to practise experiential intelligence: 'It is not that important, we don't need to prepare or actively manage our experience; we can just wing it.' Yet, in doing so, the result is always the same: a rollercoaster of fluctuating performances, experiences and satisfaction levels.
2. We will make predictions that include suboptimal projections, setting our course in a direction we don't want to go and training our psyche in a manner we don't want to experience.
3. When we experience a threat to our comfort and competence, triggering the neurological

alarm bells, we tend to think our way through it, inadvertently locking us into a Thinking Brain dominance, triggering further alarms and restricting our flow.
4. We relate to ourselves differently than we would to another, often talking to ourselves poorly and adopting a self-restricting leadership style.
5. Instead of *recognising* that we are getting in our own way and *resetting* our experiential landscape to *rewire* ourselves towards flow, we power on, push harder and make it impossible for the mind and body to be in flow.

To overcome these traps and set a platform for flow, we have to work with our human operating system. When we understand its limitations and the experiential cost of overriding it, we no longer have to feel the need to fight against it. Instead, we can work with it and more naturally use its assets to our advantage. To help you overcome these five big mistakes and get READY for flow, it has proved invaluable to many of my clients to practise the 'three Rs': recognise, reset and rewire. If you can recognise your state, you then wield the power to reset it, giving you the foundation to rewire your psyche towards flow.

Throughout the rest of Part 1, we will look at ways to help you recognise and rewire, but first I want to cover a fundamental skill of experiential competence that we all need to have at our disposal.

Reset for Flow

RESETTING

While understanding how the brain has developed to unintentionally get in our own way was insightful, it was not always easy to overcome this problem in practice. I noticed, both in my own practice and in those of others, that, despite the recognition and desire to alter our state, lingering distracting emotions and thoughts would re-enter the frame, making it difficult to rise above our evolutionary errors. But on one rainy, cold and dull afternoon, when working with a young athlete, I discovered something that was a game changer.

As Paul, a twelve-year-old talent who had been earmarked to be Australia's next big footballing sensation, got out of the car to join me in the rain, I could tell that he was not keen to do the session. I imagined how his mind might have created this self-fulfilling state as he projected ahead to a cold and wet session, as his parents drove him to the park in the pouring rain. After twenty minutes of standing under a tree discussing the nuances and power of experiential intelligence, I could clearly see that what we were doing was not working. Any intellectual conversation was unlikely to work, and rightly so – he wasn't even a teenager; the weather had clearly knocked me off my game too. So, to mix things up, we played a method acting game of embodying different states. This was fun initially, but when it came to acting like an angry chimpanzee, Paul suddenly started tearing up the grass

How to Find Flow

under our feet, let out an almighty burst of anger and then collapsed into a heap, letting out a little cry. In letting out his bottled-up frustrations, the underlying raw emotion that had been clouding his state was finally set free. Once ready to move on, we then danced under the tree acting like chirpy chickens. Clucking away, flapping our wings, we cackled and smiled. The dreary weather, and now damp clothes, were a million miles away from his mind. The joy that filled his entire being beamed so bright that you might have mistaken him for someone who thought that Christmas had come early.

Reflecting on the session, the realisation of how the mind and body are inextricably intertwined to the point of inseparability hit me like a spade in the face. The act of helping Paul's mind without taking his physiology into account was dating my coaching practices back to the mechanistic and disembodied approach of the seventeenth century. It was at this time that René Descartes' disembodied theory of mind spurred sceptics and, later, phenomenologists, such as Edmund Husserl, to lay the foundations for the embodiment thesis that desegregated consciousness and cognition, and helped us towards what we now call embodied cognition, premising that our mind is deeply rooted in the nuts and bolts of our physiology.[58]

For the first time, I truly understood that if we want to change our inner experience at will, we cannot simply engage in cognitive ping-pong and talk our way into a new state with more constructive thinking, as many

Reset for Flow

positive thinking books would suggest. Instead, we have to muster our entire subjective experience towards a new end. It is often easier to imagine our inner experience as just our thoughts and feelings, yet this is too simplistic. More accurately, our subjective experience is the collective sum of the contents of our consciousness; it is an ever-evolving assortment of thoughts, emotions, sensations, bodily arousal, perspectives and volition.

To use a painting analogy, in any given moment, we paint shades of volition, perspectives, thoughts, feelings, emotions and sensations onto the canvas of our consciousness that come together to depict the picture of our inner experience. Simply altering one of these colours, such as painting a lighter shade of positivity instead of a deeper shade of doubt, will not change what the picture is about. If we only change one aspect of our subjective experience, other aspects of consciousness will remain and linger in our neurology, affecting our momentary state. Clucking away with Paul taught me that working with the canvas (our overall embodied experience) can be far more effective and powerful than working with just one colour, as often happens with emotional intelligence. To completely renew our inner experience, we must first wipe the canvas clean. Then, if we can see ourselves as the painter of our consciousness, we can empower our experiential competence to paint an entirely new picture and ignite a preferred inner experience, such as being in flow.

How to Find Flow

Release sticky thoughts and emotions

No doubt you can relate to the rollercoaster of thoughts and emotions that arise during your challenges in life. Events in which the future is more uncertain or the past is more perplexing tend to cause even more evocative reactions. These internal responses can feel like they are good or bad, positive or negative, right or wrong, satisfying or dissatisfying, but really, they are all just a reaction in our body trying to distract our attention to process these future or past events. At their biological essence, these thoughts and feelings are electrical surges and neurochemical reactions that flutter through our body charged with the purpose to communicate a message. They are not as random as we might think – they emerge for a reason; after all, we created them. Typically, they exist to create change and flag something of importance in our consciousness, most often to optimise our bioregulation and maintain a sense of internal order or homeostasis (a comfortable internal environment for example).

While it might feel as though these rising reactions and surges are problematic, they are not the problem – they will quickly disappear once the intended communication is heard. Rather, it is the *denial* or *harbouring* of them that creates friction to these messages, conflicting our neurology and distracting attention. While many of us may be accustomed to ignoring, suppressing or pushing

Reset for Flow

past unwanted thoughts and feelings in the hope that they will go away, modern-day research suggests otherwise. In ignoring these messages, the neurochemicals do not disappear; they linger in our neurology, causing stagnant states. Further, more neurochemicals flood our synapses in the hope of getting the message through, clouding our neurology with excessive unwanted electrical messaging that ultimately creates an ever-increasing number of distracting thoughts, emotions and sensations. Instead, modern research highlights the importance of embracing and releasing our thoughts and emotions, even during the heat of competition, to allow uninhibited performance.[59] The logic being that, once any friction to the rising commotion is released, the emotions and sensations become less distracting, allowing attention to resume to the task at hand. Contrarily, the more they are ignored, the more friction occurs, the more energy is needed for their suppression and the more our experience and focus become fractured. This is especially evident in talk therapies such as counselling or psychology, where the intellectualisation (i.e. the felt need to rationalise and complicate what is happening) of an issue is, for the most part, seen as an avoidance technique – insofar as the Thinking Brain rumination distracts us from actually feeling and expressing the undealt-with emotions. 'Learning how to have an intimate relationship with fear is one of the best things you can do,' explains Dr Andy Walshe, ex-director of high performance at Red Bull,

How to Find Flow

when talking about how extreme athletes overcome frightening situations.[60] Even in life-threatening situations, it is evident that we need to become intimate with our thoughts, emotions and sensations so that we can effectively let them go and gain back full control of our inner experience; we cannot let go of a pen, for example, if we haven't got hold of it in the first place.

If you do not have a tried-and-tested system for being intimate with your thoughts and emotions so that you can process them, then I suggest you view any rising commotion as an incoming letter from your own body. I'm sure you have already felt the internal friction created by not opening an unwanted house-hold bill or letter, as the avoidance festers in your mind. Instead, the idea here is to recognise and read the letter on arrival to gain clarity on its intended message, paradoxically reducing its distracting impact on your consciousness. You can open the letter by sitting with the feeling, witnessing it and asking the feeling to reveal its intended message – for what reason does it exist, why is it flagging in your consciousness and what does your body or inner child want to communicate? Once the letter is opened and the message is understood – once you know why the feeling has arisen in your awareness – it is also important to actively release it and let it go. You can do this by physically shaking the feeling out of your body, shouting it out or breathing it out with three large exhales. Sigh, throw a tantrum or cry – it doesn't matter; express it and let it go. Feel the intensity of

Reset for Flow

the emotion and sensation subside as you visualise the associated neurochemicals and electrical signals dissipating. Once you have expressed and released the message, it can help to thank the commotion for its communication and then visualise the letter disappearing, going up in flames or decomposing. Keeping in mind your embodied cognition, it is important that you *embody* this process, you don't just think through it – you want to experience the message and feel the release and fading intensity of the emotion.

Taking the time to process sticky emotions and remove this conflict from your presence is essential for achieving flow. Part of being experientially competent is learning to work with our feelings, not changing our state to evade them. A common trap when seeking experiential competence is to overlook this step and focus solely on the desired state – a common avoidance technique the brain will utilise. For example, in an attempt to be positive and 'fake it to make it', we may be negating our fear of the challenge or suffering from an earlier conversation. In pushing away these feelings, as opposed to facing them, we fracture our psyche, conflict our neurology and are unable to move forward in the union that flow demands.

Clean out the cache

Once you have released any sticky commotion, unwanted feelings or sensations, it is time to wipe the canvas clean

How to Find Flow

by resetting your psychophysiology to make sure parts of your neurology are not holding on to the old state. Like my example of the chicken dance, clucking like chickens with Paul, resetting can be easy and fun. All you need to do is captivate your attention with something so shocking or arresting that, for a few seconds, all your physical and mental attention is consumed with this act. By glitching your inner experience in this manner, you clear out the cache in your consciousness and create a fresh canvas on which to paint a new picture.

In practice, it is important to have several resets up your sleeve so that you can apply different resets in different settings – a couple of quick, discreet methods while in the presence of others, and a few more powerful immersive resets that you have planned throughout the coming weeks and months. Quick resets that can often go unnoticed include pinching yourself, taking ten deep breaths, shaking your arms, clapping your hands loudly or pulling an elastic band on your wrist. If you have a bit more privacy, then you can try my favourite, the chicken dance (and don't forget to make the clucking sound), jumping up and down while shaking out your limbs, splashing your face with cold water, holding an ice cube in your hand, taking a (cold) shower or slapping yourself in the face. Alternatively try some gardening, playing a musical instrument or doing a walking meditation. Throughout the year, it is also essential to schedule in several substantial resets, such as going on

Reset for Flow

holiday, fasting, engaging in immersive activities such as adventure sports activities or music festivals, and extended periods of rest or exposure to nature.

What my clients find helpful is scheduling the yearly resets into the calendar, and then having a list of daily resets to choose from when needed. If you create your own personalised resets, just make sure that they are fun and that they truly glitch the system, shifting both your psychology and your physiology. Regardless of what reset you choose to do, don't just go through the motions. Do them purposefully and mix them up. The success of a reset is largely determined by your intention and commitment to resetting, rather than the activity itself.

Thinking less to *be* more was a constant reminder not to feel enslaved to how I was feeling and to start working with my psyche, not against it. As a result, I started to feel more relaxed in speaking situations. I no longer had to carry around the ball and chain of past experiences. Every time I recognised my mind entering a state of self-pity over a missed tennis career or cringed in memory of stuttering in public, for example, I would release and reset, and then rewire my state by painting a new picture in my consciousness. My projections to stuttering when talking reduced, and while I wasn't finding my flow when speaking, I was calmer, more confident and less stressed.

However, recapturing those moments of flow I had felt on the tennis court remained a difficult state to engineer

How to Find Flow

and harness at will. In all honesty, while I could intuitively relate to flow, thinking about flow still made me a little confused. The more I analysed it, the more questions arose. I had a better idea and understanding of flow than most from all my reading, but the elusiveness of the experience and the vagueness and variety of its descriptions still bugged me. So I set off on a quest to dive into the established science of flow in the hope of demystifying it further and gaining an understanding of flow beyond my felt experience.

LET'S RECAP

In this chapter, we have looked at a number of flow skills to invite flow into your life:
- learning the importance of promoting the Being Brain
- growing your experiential intelligence
- understanding that our projections create our future experience
- understanding that our evolutionary errors don't need to control us
- releasing sticky emotions
- resetting our experiential state

We will continue to cover more ground on how to recognise, reset and rewire in the following chapters.

Reset for Flow

YOUR CHALLENGE

Using the mantra 'Think Less, *Be* More' as I went through my day was a game changer. It helped me to become more experientially intelligent and reminded me to rise above my sometimes unhelpful human operating system. Moreover, it reminded me to be the painter of my consciousness and work towards becoming experientially competent. It allowed me to simply *be* within the experience, not think about the moment. Slowly but surely, I also witnessed my clients who utilised this mantra become more present and experientially competent too, placing themselves in a better position to find flow. I challenge you to do the same.

Over the next three days, check in and observe your inner experience. Then repeat the mantra, 'Think Less, *Be* More'. I suggest setting a reminder for every waking hour to help your brain; but do what you can do. It doesn't matter if you are stressed, at peace, overthinking, anxious or grateful at the time. The point here is to become more attuned to your momentary experience, more experientially intelligent. If you find yourself in an unwanted state, release it and reset. Once reset, remind yourself to *BE* more.

Chapter 3

DEMYSTIFY FLOW

SO FAR, TO BECOME 'READY', WE HAVE COVERED HOW important it is to become intelligent about our inner experience, as our moment-to-moment experience dictates how we later perceive, think, feel and act. Hopefully, you have observed your mind engaging in reams of unhelpful thoughts, as you become more aware of how the Thinking Brain captains your cognition. When reflecting on your inner experience, it is common to witness your experience being less than optimal most of the time and, for many, readily dissatisfying. In fact, you may suddenly feel that life is getting worse when, in fact, you have just become more aware of your inner experiences. If so, this is absolutely fine – the aim up until now has been to become more experientially aware of the quality of your momentary experience, not necessarily competent in changing it towards flow; this will come with time.

Demystify Flow

In this chapter, we're going to go deeper into understanding flow, so that we can better refine what we are aiming for. I will share my findings from my PhD on flow and simplify the experience of flow into three core components to help clearly differentiate it from other states and better equip our minds to find it.

UNDERSTANDING FLOW

I grew tired of hearing flow used flippantly in everyday life, none more so than the saying, 'Just go with the flow', which, with a better understanding of the topic and the importance of intuitive action within flow, might be considered a direct antithesis to flow, since it encourages suppressing one's own intuition in favour of the status quo. Further, the pseudoscience and commercial communication of flow was making the clarity surrounding flow even murkier. Bestselling books and self-proclaimed flow experts all had different representations of flow, often using the attractive outcomes of flow, such as performance results and happiness, as interchangeable definitions to better suit their commercial agendas. I knew this wasn't right, but I couldn't blame them if I was still grappling with flow myself. My integrity demanded more – I knew I needed greater clarity, so I jumped back into the pool of academia.

How to Find Flow

The godfather of flow

Csikszentmihalyi's presentation of flow had given me a language to a feeling, an experience, that had previously been unexplainable. He had an amazing way of communicating complex ideas so that simpletons like myself could understand them. One such approach he used to conceptualise flow utilised terms that had previously most commonly been used in metaphysics. Csikszentmihalyi talked of the contents of our consciousness either being in a state of chaos, 'entropy', or a state of order, 'negentropy'.[61] *Entropy*, the dissolution of order into redundant randomness, is seen as a natural default characteristic of consciousness for most humans, apparent through much of the random thoughts, distractions and conflict that echo through the halls of our consciousness every day, and exaggerated when humans become isolated or put in solitary confinement. The focus and coherence so evident in flow is, conversely, negentropic. Instead of chaos, there is clarity; instead of disorder, there is order. It is in this state of negentropy that humans are allowed to get creative and dance with novelty, because so much of consciousness is already structured and in a harmonious order.

In his earlier writings, Csikszentmihalyi suggested that flow can occur during moments of complexity,[62] the logic being that complexity demands our focus and deep engagement. He defined complexity as describing a

Demystify Flow

situation that required both differentiation and integration – 'differentiation' referring to the degree to which a system is composed of parts that differ in structure or function, and 'integration' referring to the extent to which parts communicate and enhance one another's goals. A human cell, for example, is both differentiated from other cells, processing activities independently within its cell membrane, and integrated, as it works in unison with neighbouring cells to share resources which together form part of a larger organ. When something is both differentiated and integrated, Csikszentmihalyi posited that it reaches a state of complexity. He suggested that our metaphysical world is always in a state of either entropy, creating change towards disorder and conflict, or negentropy, creating change towards harmony. Once a human's psychic energy coheres into a negentropic state of complexity, flow is possible, meaning that, if we face a complex situation and our mind is in a state of harmonious order, such as completely committed to one end, then we have the perfect recipe for flow. While this approach is perhaps more esoteric, it helps to highlight both the required harmony and the complexity that allows flow to sit at the zenith of human experience.

In Csikszentmihalyi's psychological research, he posited that there were nine dimensions to a flow experience:[63]

1. A balance between the challenge and skill levels.
2. Action and awareness merging: there is no thinking

How to Find Flow

about something that has happened or might happen; we are instead completely absorbed in the task at hand.
3. Clear goals.
4. Unambiguous feedback.
5. Concentration on the task at hand.
6. An absolute sense of control.
7. Loss of self-consciousness.
8. Transformation of time.
9. An autotelic experience, deriving from the Greek words *auto* (self) and *telos* (goal); the experience itself is so rewarding that it is a goal in its own right.

These descriptive dimensions gave me so much food for thought, terms that I could certainly relate to at times, across all my personal flow experiences. His profound words, timeless as they are, however, still invited so many unanswered conceptual and technical questions that were bursting out of my head. With no obvious answer to quell the curiosity, it just made me even more curious.

THE THREE KEY DIMENSIONS OF FLOW

Questions surrounding the definition, accuracy, consistency, relatability and measurement of these dimensions felt important to answer, though how to achieve this and shortcut decades of isolated research, I wasn't quite sure,

Demystify Flow

until I was on a work trip in America, coaching part of the USA junior rock-climbing team in San Diego. During my time there, I was able to sit down with the owners of Mesa Rim Climbing Centers – one of whom was Bob Kain, former vice-president of the company Molecular Dynamics, and Illumina, which today has about 4,000 employees worldwide and a market cap of nearly $30bn. In discussion about how he engineered success in business, Bob attributed the breakthrough successes to moments in which all the different specialists working for the company were united under one roof to advance specific agendas. It was in the bringing together of expert opinion that the differentiation and integration of their specialisms forged complex ideas and innovative solutions, fast-tracking their collective understanding and intelligence. Inspired by this meeting, a vision was born to bring all flow researchers into one room, metaphorically speaking, through their research and literary works, and conduct the largest ever review of flow science – this notion of synthesis and integration is continued up until this day in the biennial gathering of the Flow Conference.

This review branched into over sixty far-reaching niche research disciplines, such as neurochemistry, positive psychotherapy, physiology, pharmacology, human computer interfacing, artificial intelligence, economics and philosophy; and a plethora of domains, such as leisure and tourism, sport, music, business,

How to Find Flow

workplace, scholarship, emotion, health, technology, learning environments and many more. What I found was fascinating. To my surprise, flow had no gold-standard definition, and only 46 per cent of the literature used Csikszentmihalyi's nine-dimensional model. While I found the variety of conceptual nuances awe-inspiring, it also felt disruptive to a collective understanding of flow. These great works were incomparable, and with every self-interpretation of flow, it watered down the meaning and application of flow. Determined not to add to the problem and produce another self-opinionated piece, like a boy on a quest to decipher a treasure map, I kept examining flow through these different lenses to identify a core experience and language that could be utilised across all scientific disciplines and domains.

My research, together with colleagues Ben Jackson and James Dimmock, led me to identify a conceptualisation of flow that represented the simplest model with the greatest explanatory power and addressed the many inconsistencies made apparent by prior researchers. I proposed a definition of flow: **'an intrinsically rewarding state of absorption in a task in which a high sense of control feels more effort-less than usual'**, which encompassed three main dimensions to the experience: absorption, effort-less control and intrinsic reward.

Demystify Flow

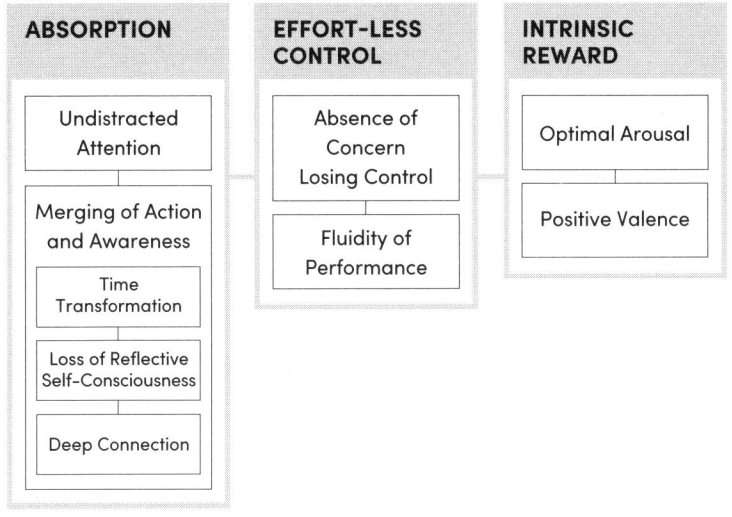

The three core experiential dimensions to flow[64]

Absorption

The most obvious characteristic of flow is an individual's *absorption* within the task. It is this deep state of concentration characterised by focused and undistracted attention that permits the immersive experience so apparent in flow. As discussed in Chapter 2, in flow, the usual felt dualism of thinking and then doing disappears, action and awareness merge, and we think less and become more. It is this characteristic of being absorbed into the task that causes many to refer to flow as a fortified altered state of consciousness, such as being 'in the zone' or 'in the bubble'. Depending on the intensity of the flow experience and the context of the activity, certain nuanced experiences also become apparent, such as a distorted

How to Find Flow

sense of time, a loss of self-reflective consciousness or a deep connection to another person, equipment or item central to the activity – apparent when we work deep into the night as we lose track of time, feel deeply connected to other members of the choir or feel that the paintbrush is an extension of our hand.

How does this happen? Well, the usual functions of the brain that are otherwise busy monitoring time, reflecting on self and delineating the boundaries between ourselves and others (or other things) become progressively downregulated the more absorbed we become. As touched upon earlier, a depleting 'onion-peeling' effect of our higher cognition occurs as mental resources deemed momentarily surplus to requirements become increasingly shut down or reallocated to the demands of the moment. The higher the intensity of the situation, the more cognitive layers are peeled away, and the greater the absorption becomes. For example, in high-speed sport, the Thinking Brain becomes inhibited, as it is too slow to deal with the moment; as a result, we don't think and then do, we just do. When deeply engaged in writing a story or studying, there is no need for our continual monitoring of time – this would be a distraction; as a result, hours can seem to fly by in what feels like minutes. In certain deep states of flow with continued absorption, a deep sense of connection can prevail because the cognitive functions that usually install the boundaries of self become depleted – and the

Demystify Flow

brain can only assume it is at one with the other dancer, or the racquet we are wielding. More on this, and how to recreate it, later.

The depleting 'onion-peeling' effect of our higher cognition and downregulation of the Thinking Brain that are central to this state of absorption also help to explain why flow experiences are initially so difficult to detail or recall immediately after they occur. As highlighted by fumbling artists and athletes in post-event interviews or catching a falling wine glass during dinner, it can feel perplexing, as if we can't explain what just happened or how we did what we did. This is because, in flow, the Thinking Brain is benched, making it near impossible for the Thinking Brain to articulate to the interviewer what just happened. The Thinking Brain is confused because it wasn't there. The Being Brain was in charge. Which is why the detail of the event can only be recalled on reflection when re-living it in our mind; in this manner, we allow the Thinking Brain to witness the Being Brain's memory. As neuroscientist Arne Dietrich describes, 'the two parts to our dual cognition each have their own database, for want of a better analogy, which are physiologically encapsulated from each other'.

Effort-less control

Absorption alone can also account for non-flow experiences, such as watching a movie or being momentarily hypnotised by someone's beauty. What separates flow

How to Find Flow

from other forms of immersion is the high degree of control we wield, specifically the unusual felt ease to this high degree of control. This high sense of control in which the task feels less effortful than usual is commonly characterised by a fluidity of performance and an absence of concern over losing control. Our actions feel fluid, our movements feel smooth and there is a sense of effortlessness in our performance even during effortful acts, as if every cell in our body is working together in harmony towards one aim. There may still be a sense of effort attributed to the task, especially in physically demanding acts like running, which is why it is *effort-less*, and not, effortless, control.

In contrast to other controlled experiences, the high sense of control felt in flow does not come from a conscious grip over the experience – we are not forcing or holding on to control. Rather, in line with one of Csikszentmihalyi's original descriptions of flow, there is a paradox to the control in which a high degree of control occurs from letting go of the concern about being in control. It is not that we don't care about the performance; rather, we know that our capacity to wield the moment to meet our end game is possible, in principle. Because there is no fear of losing control, it is as if doubt never existed. We let go of the Thinking Brain's incessant need to trigger our threat responses and instead trust our innate abilities to deal with the unfolding reality, acting spontaneously. Without the usual distractions and conflict that holding

Demystify Flow

on to control precipitates, the messaging between the brain and nervous system is more coherent or, as we say scientifically, a greater cortico-muscular coherence is realised. With greater efficiency comes faster responses and greater neural capacity to better calculate outcome probabilities and act more effectively.[65]

Further, when in flow, the reduced threat reactions allow the parasympathetic arm of our autonomic nervous system (see page 86) to better curb the rising sympathetic activity that naturally occurs in pressured situations. Instead of our neurology escalating to a mild or severe fight, flight, freeze, fawn or flop response, still aroused and alert to the situation at hand, it softens and becomes agile and acutely responsive instead of rigid, allowing us to feel sufficiently aroused yet calm within the eye of a storm. Technically, we call this process 'parasympathetic-attentional interaction'; our muscles are allowed to be flexible even under pressured and effortful acts, facilitating the automatic and effortless feelings we experience in flow during immense stress.[66]

Intrinsic reward

When this state of absorption and effort-less control come together, a high degree of *intrinsic reward* occurs. The experience becomes innately rewarding, not like the pleasure of self-indulgence or the satisfaction of our expectations being met, but rather because a) we experience a rare sense of psychological harmony and

How to Find Flow

physiological cohesion, and b) because playing with the complexity and novelty of the moment makes us feel that something surprising has occurred – the interaction has resulted in an inner discovery.

The dimension of intrinsic reward is often confused with a measure of enjoyment, but while flow is enjoyable upon reflection of the experience, after the experience, the feelings of enjoyment, pleasure or joy involve a conscious Thinking Brain reflection of the moment to exist. While this is very much a technical detail, it is an important one, because it upholds the experience of flow as being absorbing; we are too immersed to be distracted by reflective thinking or feeling. In the experience of flow itself, any feelings just come and go as they flow through consciousness – we do not become attached to them; rather, our psyche is informed by them helping to direct our intuitive decision-making without being distracted. It is not until the experience of flow finishes that self-reflection and the subsequent injection of feeling, such as enjoyment, surprise, creativity or satisfaction, rise in our consciousness to distract us. Most consistently noticeable, a sense of positive valence (i.e. positive attraction to the experience) and arousal may trickle through the experience, allowing the experience to continue, but it doesn't linger, or we do not stop to consciously capture it and reflect on it.

The felt sense of reward in flow that involves a high degree of positive valence and optimal levels of

Demystify Flow

arousal are mirrored by a cascade of neurochemical reactions. Most noticeably, dopamine (which packs a bigger pleasurable punch than morphine, a drug commonly administered in hospital) is released in volume, urging the experience to continue. The effortlessness and absorption experienced in flow is literally blissful. This heightened dopamine count is responsible for much of the emergent motivation that keeps us coming back for more. In fact, the correlation between flow and dopamine is considered so strong that a few scientists have suggested that proneness to flow is anticipated to be somewhat genetic – those with more adaptable dopamine receptors in the striatum

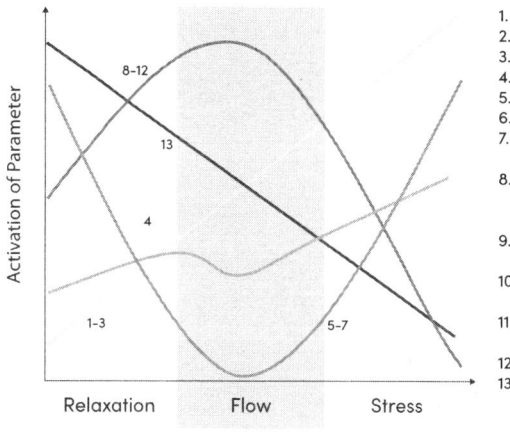

The neurophysiology of flow. (Advancing on Peifer and Tan's six factors of optimised physiological activation during flow[157])

(Note: The line curvatures are not precise but aim to reflect low and high levels.)

How to Find Flow

(a key brain structure, part of the basal ganglia, involved in motor control, reward processing, decision-making and habit formation) may be better able to produce and process dopamine, choose intrinsically rewarding activities and be more prone to experiencing flow.[67]

Now that we have demystified flow, in the next chapter I want to take you through a more practical model that incorporates what we have learnt so far and has helped countless clients adjust their mindset to find flow.

> **LET'S RECAP**
>
> In this chapter, we have sliced and diced the concept of flow to understand that flow:
> - is a state of ordered consciousness – aka negentropy
> - can be thought of as an intrinsically rewarding state of absorption in a task in which a high sense of control feels more effort-less than usual
> - has three core dimensions: absorption, effort-less control, intrinsic reward
> - has a neurophysiological signature

Demystify Flow

YOUR CHALLENGE

Every time we identify and celebrate flow in our lives or in the lives of those around us, we build our metacognition around flow, meaning we deepen our understanding of flow and develop an underlying belief that flow is a) achievable, b) valuable and c) worthwhile attaining again. So my challenge to you is to celebrate every time flow occurs in your life. Make a ritual out of it, give yourself a pat on the back, pump the air or release a proud smile. Let your brain and body know that you are grateful for the experience.

Chapter 4

PRIORITISE FLOW

THERE IS A MYTH AROUND FLOW – THAT IF WE FOCUS on it, we get further away from it. But as Mihaly Csikszentmihalyi once stated, 'optimal experience is something that we make happen'.[68] In fact, in a review of flow research studying athletes, 72 per cent of athletes reported that finding flow was in their control and 81 per cent reported that they could restore states of flow after disengaging momentarily.[69] In my own research examining the effects of educating people on flow within feasibility and single-case studies, results consistently showed that participants' flow and performance scores increased by over 30 per cent when putting flow first.[70] Why? Because the more we understand flow, the more we see it, label it, value it and create signposts in our brain to prioritise it and recreate it.

In this chapter, we will cover how to prioritise flow in your life by changing the way you approach challenge

Prioritise Flow

and complexity. I will guide you through the Flow Model and explain how it can help you develop your experiential intelligence.

PUTTING ON THE FLOW MINDSET

A surprising finding from my research on performers was that most participants knew flow was attractive yet didn't prioritise it. Rarely, if at all, did they purposefully try to engineer flow; rather, their attention was predominantly focused on achieving an outcome. A second important finding was that there was a common misconception that the flow state was reserved for the performing elite; 'you needed 10,000 hours of training to achieve mastery, and only then, if you were lucky, flow may appear during the throes of a heated battle', they thought.[71] So most participants felt flow was outside their daily reach. In helping them to understand that flow is simply a natural state of harmony, which is permitted by our own internal synchronicity, participants were better able to relate to, and therefore create, flow. It is often a surprise for people to hear, as it was for my participants, that flow is most commonly experienced by children at play, and not related to IQ scores or cultures of origin. Instead, the journey to flow is more to do with reducing distraction and conflict than attaining something astonishing. Flow may feel special and turn the ordinary into the

How to Find Flow

extraordinary, but flow is a subjective experience and no more irregular than any other subjective experience.

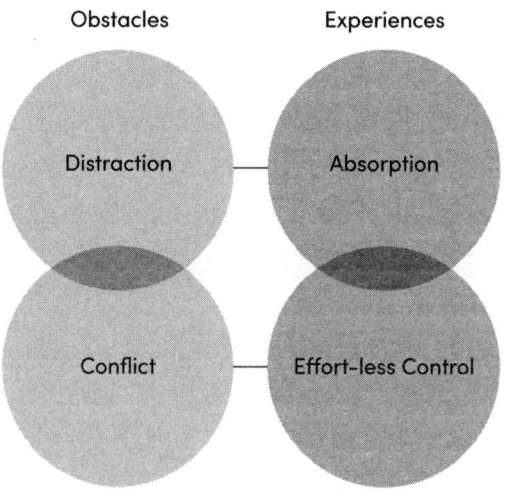

Barriers to flow

Making flow seem more attainable led to remarkable results. By participants simply putting flow first, as analogised by putting on a metaphorical hat to embody a Flow Mindset, participants evidently felt better, performed better and reported more flow in their lives. For example, Dave was a successful entrepreneur and CEO of his own company. While he was a face of excellence on the outside to his staff and clients, internally, he was secretly worried and distressed. When examining his approach to achievement and success, it was clear that his dogged and results-driven approach, while drawing some success, had also resulted in a gradual accumulation, even normalisation, of overthinking,

Prioritise Flow

anxiety and stress that was heading towards burnout. Dave just needed a new way to perform. As the well-known car manufacturer Henry Ford supposedly once said, 'If you always do what you've always done, then you will always get what you always got.'[72]

Once Dave grew in experiential intelligence and realised that his internal world did not have to be dictated by the events and pressures of his external world, he assessed how the inner experience of flow appeared in his work and life. He quickly realised that flow was absent from not only his work performance, but even the day-to-day quality of his life in general. In realising how far he was from his best, Dave became diligent about putting on his Flow Mindset every morning and before every meeting. Prioritising his inner experience in this manner and giving his compass a new heading – flow – he quickly gained back control of his moment-to-moment experience. He stopped overthinking every situation, anxiety and stress reduced, and, in time, his personal performance improved. His experiential competence paid dividends. Dave became a more powerful CEO and enjoyed a richer quality of life. A noticeable reality for Dave, as it is for all those who embody the notion of a Flow Mindset, was that the pursuit of flow was as valuable as finding it. Putting flow first exposed the inner and external distractions and conflicts that were causing a hindrance to flow, which were not only pertinent to his leadership, but also transferable to

How to Find Flow

many other aspects of his life, helping him not only to elevate his personal performance at work, but also to flourish through life in general.

When discussing human performance, mindset training is becoming an increasingly popular topic in changing rooms and offices, over the ever-increasing conversations of technique, nutrition, fitness and strategic changes – which is a good thing, as it is always the star of the show, the cog that turns all the wheels. When it is discussed, however, people frequently confuse adopting a new mindset with achieving a new outcome. Importantly, our mindset underpins *how* we perform or our *approach* to what we do, not what we do. For example, I might have a growth mindset when playing tennis, but I'm still focused on hitting the ball with pace and power in the moment. Therefore, when you place flow at the helm and put on your Flow Mindset, it is essential to remember that flow is not a goal to occupy our moment-to-moment focus – that will ultimately distract your attention from the task. Rather, it is a notion, an approach or something that you want to achieve during the task. When putting on your Flow Mindset to write, for example, don't focus on finding flow with your fingers as you type; still intentionally aim to find flow, but, in the moment, focus on the message you want to convey.

Another common mistake many people make when first coming across the Flow Mindset is to confuse prioritising flow with simply having more fun, enjoying the

Prioritise Flow

process, or being more relaxed. While these aspects may be helpful in finding flow, they should not be confused with the entirety of adopting a Flow Mindset. Flow is a rich experience, an optimal experience, one of deep engagement and self-actualisation, that may be at odds with having 'fun' or a state of relaxation. When prioritising flow, the intention is to be deeply engaged and intensely present, which is very different from simply enjoying the journey more.

OK, it's time to examine this Flow Model I keep talking about and see how it can help you move towards a more flow-orientated approach.

THE FLOW MODEL

For my clients, the idea of placing flow as the central ethos behind their mindset was having great success as an antidote to the stresses that blight modern lives. To fix the application of flow alongside more traditional approaches, however, I knew I needed to develop a proven model that people could relate to without the accompanying time-consuming education. After many years and a collaboration with educator John Hendry OAM, we developed a more performance-based model, which seemed to penetrate, and, after feedback from experts, many revisions and testing on countless willing subjects, the Flow Model was born:

How to Find Flow

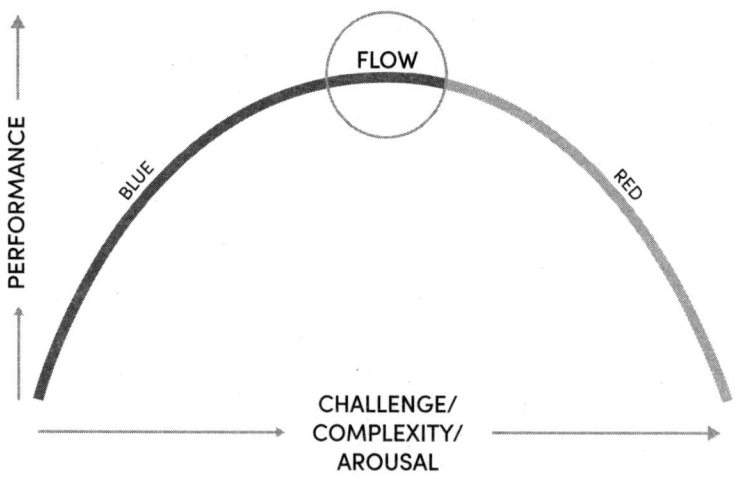

The Flow Model: An optimal experience (Norsworthy & Hendry)
(Note: The bell curve shown does not account for inter- and intra-differences, meaning the curvature may skew left or right, to varying levels of challenge/complexity depending on the task and individual. For example, flow may require lower challenge/complexity/arousal levels when playing chess due to the cognitive load than required when running. Equally, lower levels may also be apparent if the individual is fatigued, for example. The notion of an 'optimal' level still exists.)

The model positions flow at the apex of performance in which a perceived optimal level of challenge or complexity is reached. If there is too little or too much difficulty, then performance suffers, along with the absorption, effortlessness and optimal physiological arousal levels required for flow.

Either side of entering or exiting flow, we experience a multitude of felt experiences. From left to right on the model diagram, as the richness of complexity or the difficulty of the challenge rises, we move from feeling

Prioritise Flow

bored to relaxed, then in control and composed, to feeling playful and on the precipice of uncertainty. In these more advanced states, our engagement increases, confidence flourishes and resilience naturally develops; our performance and well-being have opportunities to thrive. On the contrary, if the level of challenge or complexity is too difficult, then the inherent stress becomes distracting and inhibitive. As doubt, conflict and apprehension ensue, our focus becomes splintered. The more anxious or worried we become, the more strained we feel physically and the more distressed we feel emotionally – and, consequently, the lower our performance and subsequent well-being.

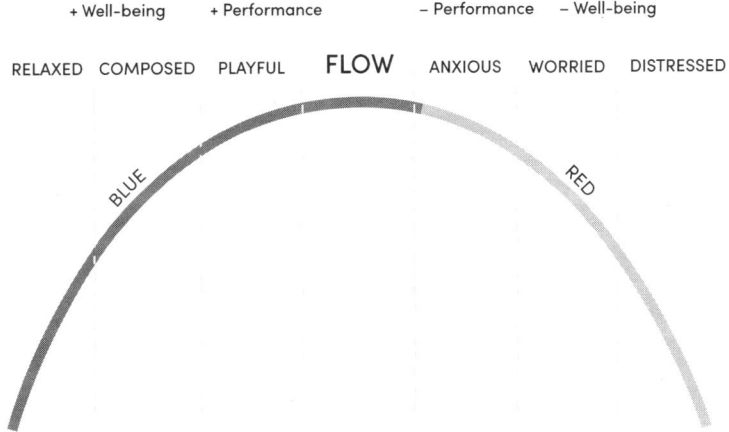

The Flow Model: Experiential variation when facing challenge and complexity

How to Find Flow

To take it one step further, in any given experience, there are a number of experiential components, such as *emotions*, *sensations*, *perspectives*, *arousal*, *volition* and *behaviour*, that make up this subjective experience. For example, when in a state of distress, our behaviour may be reactive, our mindset fixed, our thoughts distracted, our feelings worried; we will likely perceive the high degree of physiological arousal to be negative and feel a victim in the situation. See if you can recognise how the components in the next figure show up in your life.

	RELAXED	PLAYFUL	FLOW	ANXIOUS	DISTRESSED
	BLUE			*RED*	
BEHAVIOUR	Receptive	Responsive	Enactive	Responsive	Reactive
MINDSET	Fluctuating	Flexible	Focused	Rigid	Fixed
VOLITION	To Me	By Me	Through Me	By Me	To Me
THINKING	Disinterested	Helpful	Engaged	Unhelpful	Distracted
FEELINGS	Ambivalent	Excited	Calm	Anxious	Worried
AROUSAL	+Arousal	++Arousal	Optimal	-Arousal	--Arousal

The Flow Model: Experiential components

Throughout this book, we will explore the Flow Model in greater depth and, more importantly, with greater practicality. The Flow Model is here to help you recognise where you might be in any given moment. Do not get caught up in recognising each aspect of your experience or cross-referencing your experience with every aspect of each figure; this level of experiential intelligence is not necessary to self-lead towards flow. The figures are

Prioritise Flow

here to serve you. They are all meant to be tools in your toolbox to help you practise your experiential intelligence and self-assess where you are in relation to flow.

CHANGING YOUR APPROACH TO FLOW

The injuries that prematurely ended my tennis career were stifling. Over the years, I had tried everything I could to overcome the pain and limited ability – from surgery to spiritual healing, experimental acupuncture to years of regular physio – but nothing had made significant strides to alleviate the daily aggravation. Regular yoga and massage seemed to be my only tonic, yet they were limiting in their effects. So I learnt to live with the daily pains of tennis elbow in both arms and refrained from participating in activities that demanded a strain on my arms. However, determined to move beyond the languishing, feel more meaning and still find flow in my life, I discovered a love of free sports: adventure sports free from the structure and outcomes of competition. Free sports such as skiing, kitesurfing and scuba diving, to name a few, gave me a new lease of life. They were immersive, fun and nature-bound. It soon became obvious that the environments, contextual conditions and inherent risk within free sports were ideal contexts for producing flow. They challenged my ability and, without the focus on winning, my mind felt liberated.

Buoyed by my ability to find more flow, I lived for the

How to Find Flow

days in which I could fly down mountains, sail across the seas or explore the ocean depths. Despite the seemingly hedonistic gains, these sessions were incredibly meaningful. They became my lab for experimenting with flow and, perhaps for the first time in my life, I felt like I had met my tribe. To my surprise, I didn't feel alone anymore, for everywhere I went there seemed to be others on their quest to find flow, knowingly or not. It wasn't just me who had uprooted their lives, moved country and developed careers in uncharted domains if it provided them with a path to find their magical moments in Mother Nature's back garden. Like me, many of the athletes were not in it for the thrill-seeking adrenaline kicks or sensation-seeking possibilities that are often associated with the pursuits of the weekend warriors. Rather, they were looking to repeatedly explore their own capabilities and taste the fruits of flow. For the many athletes who grew up next to the ocean or in the heart of the mountains, these sports were their after-school activities, and they never looked back. Not only was flow the main reason for returning to their sport, but it also seemed to be a lifestyle pursuit. It was a way of life for them.

Being in flow was just as apparent outside the activity as it was in it. The way they talked to each other and challenged each other while hanging around the campfire seemed more engaging, more playful and more effortless than what I was used to. They interacted not to be better than one another, as it was in tennis, but

Prioritise Flow

to connect and revel in each other's stories of finding flow. What also struck me was that these characters I met on the road and in far-away flow cathedrals were often practising contrary principles to what most performance experts would advise. Specifically, their mental approach to their activities was wildly different from other athletes participating in more traditional sports. They were not partaking to be better than others or grinding out performances just to win a medal or receive praise. Instead, they turned up because they loved participating in the sport. The hullabaloo of winning seemed nonsensical, as everyone just wanted each other to find their flow. If another raised their game and landed a new trick, everyone celebrated. A competitive nature seemed to be replaced with a collaborative mastery, and the usual doubt and anxiety that fill the air of sports arenas was non-existent. Even in elite competitions, while everyone wanted to take home the trophy, it felt like a team effort, everyone pushing each other to go that one step further, applauding creativity and rejoicing in the mastery of the sport and the opportunity to be where they were. These athletes were not only some of the happiest people I had ever met, they were actualising the very peak of their performance abilities day after day. Surfing 30m waves or free diving with no breathing apparatus to a depth of 214m, they were accelerating the progression in their sport at a rate that far exceeded any other performance context – and

How to Find Flow

defying much of the performance literature that I had thought to be true.

Why did this happen? Because the combination of their mental quest for flow and the innate intensity of the activity was forcing them into flow. Nick Troutman explains:

> 'It almost forces you to go into these fight, flight, freeze or flow situations ... once you peel out of the eddy and approach the rapid, there is no turning back, you're in the lion's den. You have to come out victorious, or something horrible is going to go wrong. When people ask why I love kayaking, I would explain that it's to some extent the love of nature, which is a part of it, but mostly it is the forced decision-making. You're forced into flow to make extremely quick decisions and execute creative manoeuvres; anything else just wouldn't work. I love these moments. It is what I live for.'

Finding flow was more than just a performance benefit for many of these athletes; it was a lifestyle pursuit. As professional surfer John John Florence said to me while chatting about the experience of flow in the athletes' tent before his heat at the Margaret River Pro leg of the World Tour, 'you're describing my every day, man'.

While recent years have seen an injection of money entering these sporting arenas, diverting many people's focus away from the participation and process and

Prioritise Flow

towards results and outcomes, the original free sport spirit of questing flow, doing it for the stoke and celebrating participation and creativity, is still very much alive in the action sports space.

This affinity with flow in adventure activities and action sports is one of the main reasons I have spent so much time coaching in this arena. The stories are scintillating, the research ripe, and I'm able to practise the sports that I love too. In contrast, when working in other domains, I was constantly surprised by the resistance most would have against this flow-orientated approach. People and businesses seemed so entrenched towards achieving results through a combative and dogmatic competitive approach that adjusting to anything other than gritting your way to results seemed off-kilter, too good to be true. Suggesting that their true north could point to being their best, not the best, was clearly going against the grain and often put in the luxury or fanciful basket of ideas. Athletes and businesses alike had their feet firmly on the pedal to outperform their competitors and didn't have time to implement any overarching changes. Other than intellectual interest, they seemed accepting of their fate to take the hard approach, creating friction with each step, wondering why there was so much 'success tax' and doubting whether these efforts were worth it. The rhetoric was that burnout and staff turnover was part and parcel of success. Entrenched in their evolutionary errors, they lived and breathed a dissatisfying, stressful

How to Find Flow

and, at times, unhealthy battle towards success, interested mainly in small, quick wins to bear the brunt of their exhausting struggles. It was as if they were filling up their Ferrari with the dirty, cheap fuel from forty years ago, because they were used to it or knew no better. Too busy and stressed to assess the cleanliness of the fuel they used every day, they kept driving, wondering why the car was not performing at its best, and occasionally having to go to the mechanic for a quick fix.

Have you ever questioned what you are doing, or how you are doing it, when the cost of your success or failure has become unbearable? Sure, we all have, but it doesn't have to be this way.

Renounce the red

While no doubt preferable, positioning oneself in the blue area of the Flow Model (on the left-hand side), so that we can be composed and playful instead of anxious and worried, can prove practically troublesome. As explained in Chapter 2, we conditionally limit our opportunity for flow because we are cognitively and physiologically predisposed to be in the red (on the right-hand side of the Flow Model) and become distracted and stressed when faced with too much difficulty. In working with hundreds of clients using this model, what I found was that, in almost every single instance, if someone was in the red, this was because they were prioritising outcome goals that were ultimately extrinsic or egoic, at some level

Prioritise Flow

of their psyche. For example, athletes focused on winning were riddled with stress, nerves and poor sleep before the competition; executives who were worried about keeping their jobs, earning more money or what their colleagues or boss would say lived with the daily residue of anxiety and distress. Why? This happens because when our attention starts to value the outcome, our psyche tries to self-determine these outcomes, inadvertently generating expectations and apprehension about not achieving these self-prescribed outcomes. Since outcomes are rarely in our full control, and are dependent on other people or things we cannot control, our brain senses a threat, and triggers the evolutionary errors we talked about earlier.

Stuck in a cyclical threat response, stress accumulates, mildly or intensely, but often, committed to the end goal, we push on. This approach not only creates psychological friction to the task at hand, but also creates physiological friction. In this combative, expectation- and apprehension-driven approach, the body inevitably gets flooded with cortisol and stress-related reactions. The amygdala, hippocampus and limbic areas of the brain go into overdrive, and we become emotionally sensitive, anxious and fearful of what is to come, despite our best efforts, because there is simply too much cortisol running through our veins. In the misleading hope of feeling better, our Thinking Brain enters a realm of inaccurate and unreliable comparisons. In competitive or relational settings, this often results in us comparing how we feel

How to Find Flow

on the inside with what another appears to be feeling on the outside, to which we conclude that we are either inferior or superior to others when equality stares us in the face. Directly or indirectly, our consciousness becomes filled with fear-driven thoughts of, 'What if I don't win or meet my expectations?', 'What will others think of me?', 'How can I get by without losing face?', 'I'd better not make a mistake' ... and so on. We end up overthinking the situation, triggering doubt and distraction. In an attempt to overcome this conflict and feel more in control, we force results, over-control the situation and become rigid in our psychology and physiology with the false hope of protecting how we feel. The more pressure, the more fear. The more fear, the more perceived conflict. The more conflict, the more distress. The more distress, the more effort is attributed to our actions to overcome the conflict. The more effort exerted, the more tense and inhibited our performance. Regardless of the outcome, this approach makes the journey (to both our long-term goals and the immediate challenge) feel effortful and stressful. Ultimately, the journey becomes arduous, so much so that we may notice avoidant-based thinking entering our minds to ease the pressure – we make excuses, blame something or someone, or, at extremes, disengage and walk away. Even if we do overcome this friction and accomplish the goal, it is met with relief that the journey is over, as it has been innately dissatisfying. While a momentary sense of pride or accomplishment

Prioritise Flow

can be felt for overcoming this internal/external adversity, it is always somewhat marred by the inner knowledge that our limited performance and shackled version of our potential fell short of our best.

In some cases, the experiential cost or success (or failure) tax of this approach is immense. Poor sleep, emotional breakdowns, twitches, headaches, lost relationships, impulsive spending, injury, skin conditions ... you name it. When high levels of cortisol, unnecessary stress and tight neurology become the norm, our mind and body will eventually suffer or break, in one way or another. We can try to fool ourselves, but the body never lies.

The Flow Model: The experience of being in the red

How to Find Flow

Move beyond winning

This friction-based approach is no more apparent than in the 'winning mindset' mentality that is so rife in sport, business and popular culture. With so much cultural attachment to obtaining outcomes and 'winning', it is no surprise that the desire to win and create 'winners' has become ingrained in the lives and behaviour of so many of us. 'Win at all costs', 'Win ugly if you have to' ... society and the media have become obsessed with the notion of winning, as sporting scores dominate the news and winners are put on a pedestal to be idolised. As a result, traditional performance coaches have used a 'winning mindset' as their bedrock, and books about 'winning' are abundant. For decades, these outdated messages have motivated people to work harder, force a win and fight for the goals that seemed so important when originally conceived: 'Work till you drop', 'No pain, no gain'. But the net result is rarely one of joy and flow, and rather is one of stress and burnout; and when achievements do occur, while a level of pride about the persistence may exist, relief that the journey has ended dominates the experience. Before we know it, the Thinking Brain has quickly moved on and attached itself to a new, shinier goal to take its place.

To the surprise of many of my clients who come to me expecting to learn better coping skills to handle a more entrenched stance of 'winning is all that matters', I often have to help them to see that this dogged outcome-

Prioritise Flow

driven approach is an antithesis to finding flow. While it may be widespread, it is ultimately a *coping* strategy not an *optimal* strategy. It may have helped us to get by, and persist, but will this approach bring out the best in us? No. That is a biological and neurological certainty. Even if we clawed a result, could we have been even better implementing another approach? Most likely. A winning approach, contrary to what it promotes, doesn't even necessarily demand high standards; after all, we can win by some margin and still be far off our best or any marker of excellence. While this forced approach to be better than others may, at times, help to whip compliance, drag us over the line or, at best, clutch a shot in a gritted manner, it comes at the cost of deeply satisfying experiences, undistracted focus and optimal performance. Many ancient teachings, such as that of Laozi, a contemporary of Confucius from the school and religion of Taosim, even suggest that it is precisely this consciously forced, effortful approach that so many of us adopt to strive towards our goals that is the source of all human suffering and the world's ills.[73]

On reading or hearing these words, a common response I receive is, 'So, you're telling me not to dream big or have outcome goals? Not to fight for my dreams, and strive to win?' However, it is not the forecasted outcome that is a problem. On the contrary, an outcome goal can focus our efforts and be a valuable metric and benchmark for feedback. Rather, it is the fixation

How to Find Flow

towards this outcome that produces the distracting expectations and conflicting stress. It is problematic when the outcome goal supersedes or becomes a higher-order goal than what is in our complete control – a pursuit of personal excellence, for example – and distracts our moment-to-moment attention. In this pursuit for the outcome, expectations to be 'better than another' or 'achieve a win' arise, and our mind naturally anticipates the converse, radiating fear, distraction and conflict in our psyche.

Another critical aspect as to why this 'winning mindset' fails to actualise our best is because it is intricately linked to a discompassionate style of self-leadership that further entrenches us in this suboptimal coping position. When mistakes are made, the outcome seems further out of reach, and the brain cannot help but feel like a failure. To feel better, we try harder, double down and become even more competitive. The Thinking Brain, not wanting to look like a fool or feel like a failure, blames the Being Brain for the mistake. 'Why did you do that?', 'You're such an idiot', 'I'd better not make another mistake', 'I'd better not embarrass myself again', 'I must do better!' We inadvertently become discompassionate to our self in the hope that it will shock us into better behaviour. However, like telling a kid off for doing something they don't really understand, what really remains is a sense of shame and imprinting of failure. As a result, we play safe, shy away from future risk, look for shortcuts to avoid the pressure

Prioritise Flow

and focus on avoiding embarrassment. The net result is that our psyche is more concerned with doing enough to get by or not making a mistake than it is on actualising our ability and being our excellent best. While some might argue that this gritted fear- and outcome-driven approach may help to initiate short-term compliance and eject us from the sofa, creating urgency and discipline in the process, it indisputably undermines our continued performance and satisfaction, and creates detrimental patterns to achieving flow.

In light of this knowledge, I often ask my clients to self-assess their self-leadership – a question I now ask you. Are you actualising your ability or restricting it with the way you approach a challenge? If you are finding yourself in the red, then you are likely being a 'restrictor'. We will now look at what it takes to be an 'actualiser' and rewire your psyche to lead yourself into the blue.

Be in the blue

The journey of putting flow first and adopting a Flow Mindset is one that values intrinsic experience and prioritises personal excellence and our own capacity for growth in the moment. In line with many leading theories on human behaviour, when we put flow first, above the agendas of winning and looking good, we set in motion a different cascade of thoughts, emotions and behavioural responses, empowering our performance and ability to flourish. Whether it is self-determination theory, enactive

How to Find Flow

learning theory, goal achievement theory or a 'growth mindset', all motivational and goal-orientated research roads suggest that when we focus on our intrinsic goals and innate capacity for growth, and optimise our moment-to-moment actions towards being our optimal self – flow – we allow unrestricted performance, continued engagement and well-being.[74] Akin to ancient Eastern spiritual teachings of mastery that emphasise the continuous excellence of being, prioritising flow centres our focus on being *our* best rather than being *the* best. When walking the journey of a Flow Mindset – inviting the challenge, curious to the moment and motivated by the intrinsic rewards of participation – we activate Mihaly Csikszentmihalyi's idea of an autotelic personality. We generate helpful arousal, or what stress theorists call 'eustress', that actualises rather than restricts our systems for optimal performance.[75] Ultimately, putting flow first bypasses the usual expectations, apprehension, comparisons and mind games that come from focusing on outcomes. We can dare to risk and prospect rather than retreat and protect. (When prospecting, we see opportunity and become open to the possibility or likelihood of success. On the other hand, we protect when we sense failure and negative fear.)

When pressure does come knocking, if flow is pinned down as our true north, we can invite it in and view pressure as a privilege rather than a problem, as we know that pressure creates flow, as well as diamonds. It

Prioritise Flow

is this exact pressure, or eustress, that enables us to be optimally challenged, crystallises our ability and allows us to step into flow.

Flow Mindset

The Flow Model: The experience of being in the blue

With a Flow Mindset as our underlying notion for engaging in the activity, we not only give our psyche permission to prioritise a flow response when under pressure, but we also inherently alter our relationship with stress. We don't just change the level of satisfaction drawn from a single event, but also diminish the cumulative felt stress in daily living. When flow is the highest-order goal, our mind doesn't have to be consumed with the

How to Find Flow

accumulative daily mental stress of trying to control events and achieve results; instead, it can stay agile, curious and open to the moment as it unfolds. Instead of our physiology having to spend energy and resources to deal with the friction we create and handle the excess of cortisol in our system, we can enjoy the helpful arousal and instead simultaneously create the natural delights of dopamine – further increasing our motivation to engage. When faced with a mistake or 'failure', we don't have to scold our performance and shame our Being Brain in the process, as success and failure is not our focus. We naturally see mistakes not as 'failure' but as interesting feedback, helpful information to advance our growth. In this manner, we inherently become self-compassionate, as this is the best way to enable learning and pivot towards flow. We form a natural source of resilience, as adversity is not met with friction – we don't see problems or difficulty, we see puzzles and complexity. Rising issues become exciting opportunities for growth, as it is precisely this complexity that is needed to progress into flow. As a result, we innately invite life's challenges, shedding our avoidance routines and creating helpful patterns of thinking and behaving to our goals and dreams. Changing our approach and the way we relate to challenge and complexity makes us more adaptable to stress. It fundamentally changes how our PFC (specifically the medial and ventromedial PFC) operates under stress.[76] Instead of triggering the amygdala and the

Prioritise Flow

hypothalamus (specifically the hypothalamic-pituitary-adrenal axis) to raise the alarm and flood our autonomic nervous system with unnecessary cortisol, respectively, we can side-step the usual fight, flight, freeze, fawn, or flop response and open a window for flow.

In competitive situations, a Flow Mindset enables us to enjoy an entirely different relationship with our opponents. We turn a combative approach to competition into what I call 'collaborative competition'. If flow is routed as our true north, then our opponents are not combative to our progression; rather they are essential collaborators to our own excellence. Without them, we would not have the complexity we require to grow and find flow. As Jason Dorland, Olympic rower, points out, the Latin root word of 'competition' is *'competere'*, which means 'to strive together'. Dorland elaborates:

> 'In sport, in the crucible of the contest, my opponent and I are striving together to perfect our individual athletic craft. Without our opponent, without the contest, without the game, we can never know what we are capable of in the practice of our sport. I've often said we should love our opponent more than our teammates, because without our opponent there would be no game and no way to excel and enjoy our sport. We need an opponent to drive us both to the doorstep of, and often into, these transcendent states of being [flow].'[77]

How to Find Flow

The greats of any domain know this implicitly. Would Ferrari be what it is without McLaren? Would Microsoft be as developed and refined without Apple? We also see this approach in great athletes who pass the test of time. For example, Phil Mickelson, a legendary golfer who, for many years, would have been a world number one if Tiger Woods' high performances had not been so consistent, was interviewed after a day's play at the 2012 AT&T National Pro Am at Pebble Beach. When Mickelson was asked whether Tiger Woods' return to golf after injury was a threat to him winning tournaments, Mickelson replied, 'I love playing with him, and he brings out some of my best golf. I hope that he continues to play better, and better, and I hope that he and I have a chance to play together more in the final rounds.'[78] Mickelson was looking forward to competing with Tiger, even if it meant potentially losing, as he knew that his biggest competitors were his greatest collaborators, helping him to bring out the best in his performances and better master his craft.

APPLYING THE FLOW MINDSET

While this flow-orientated approach might seem preferable from an armchair perspective, it can be difficult to adopt when the going gets tough. The greater the pressure, the greater the perceived threat, and the more the Thinking Brain likes to take control and default

Prioritise Flow

to older, more engrained conditioning. For example, all the work behind growing the Flow Centre led to an increased profile and a growing number of speaking invitations. I knew continuing to accept these keynotes would advance the organisation, but I also couldn't help but feel petrified. Though, deep down, the disingenuous rumblings could be felt, I knew I had to face the discord I felt inside, not only for the growth of the organisation, but for my own peace of mind and overall ability to find flow. I also didn't want to be a hypocrite when advising others to find flow within their fears and difficulties. So, despite the act of public speaking being my Mount Everest, I accepted every opportunity. In most talks, I got by and did enough to satisfy the client. My stammering became infrequent, though I knew that my performances were a little wooden and somewhat strained. To remedy this, I levelled up on public speaking tips and tricks, which certainly helped to structure an engaging talk and divert attention when needed, but I was mainly in the red of the Flow Model when speaking, and finding flow was sporadic. Most talks were forgettable, except this one that I will never forget.

Jet-lagged and not on the top of my game, I found myself on stage about to address close to three hundred senior executives. I had been invited to speak and run a two-day training seminar for a company's annual general meeting. I was standing in the middle of a wide-open stage big enough to showcase three bands.

How to Find Flow

My hands felt cold, and a shiver ran down my back. 'Is my willingness to deliver these talks a form of masochism?' I wondered. 'Surely there is someone better placed than me to do this job.' My Thinking Brain's inner critic was on a roll: 'Sure, I know a lot about flow, but I have never worked in a large corporation; who am I to motivate and train these people?' The negative thoughts compounded. I was far from home and my usual professional context. While I enjoyed working with CEOs in person, at that time I was used to talking to a room full of athletes, not corporates.

I scanned the room to help myself feel better, but all I could see were progressively impatient faces. The boardroom in my mind was full of chatter, as if a hostile group of directors was having a debate. One director was ridiculing what I was about to say, another was implying that I should have never been invited to speak in the first place, and a few others were hypothesising the many possible negative outcomes of my speech. 'What if I stutter? ... I'd better not stutter ... just do enough to get this over and done with.' These fictitious directors were talking at such a pace that I couldn't keep up, let alone contest the arguments. This internal self-talk was literally paralysing. My stomach churned. I grasped for some last-minute confidence, but found nothing. The very threat response that I was going to talk about was now occurring in full force, inside me. Heart beating, palms sweating, I had lost all experiential competence; the tie

Prioritise Flow

around my neck felt like a noose. Whichever version of myself had agreed to speak had clearly done a runner.

Unfortunately, it was time. The room was quietening. In an attempt to embody the speaker inside me and take control, I reached forward and fumbled for the microphone in front of me. The feedback screeched loudly, awakening the room to my impending words …

So how did I get out of this pickle? Well, it started with putting on my Flow Mindset and then adopting the tips that follow to stop it from falling off.

Remember, it's innate

While putting flow first may feel quite foreign, the flow approach is a natural way of operating that is already deeply embedded in your psyche. It may feel new, but, more accurately, it is just forgotten. This approach was everyone's default approach when growing up as a child, and you have likely adopted it in your recent past when feeling safe and confident. The principles of growth, mastery, agility, trust, effort-lessness and optimal functioning are already being actualised inside you, by your physiology. Whether your physiology is circulating blood to all areas of the body, maintaining a state of homeostasis or healing a cut on the skin, it does not get distracted by egoic or extrinsic gains. It simply does the best it can in any given moment, working continuously towards optimal levels of functioning. You simply need to attune the mind to the same song – after all, your

How to Find Flow

brain is just another organ in the body. Remembering that this approach is already part of your very fabric, psychologically and physiologically, can make the Flow Mindset seem far more natural and attainable.

Repeat 'learn, grow, flow'

Research on mantra usage suggests that repeating the same phrase repeatedly can help to install an intended message – even better with music.[79] Rapidly repeating a mantra can also help to preoccupy the Thinking Brain, while the Being Brain gets on with what it needs to do. The mantra 'Learn, Grow, Flow' synthesises the ethos behind prioritising flow into a distinct, repeatable phrase. By focusing on learning, we grow, and it is in this growth that we find flow. So, when a mistake occurs or your expectations are not met, ask yourself, 'What can I learn here? How can I use this information to grow and progress? Now, how can I get back to focusing on flow?' Brainwash your mind with 'Learn, Grow, Flow'.

I personally used this mantra to great effect when learning to play tennis with my non-dominant hand. After sitting on the sidelines unable to play tennis with my right arm because of my injuries, I decided to try playing left-handed. My footwork and fitness were still on point, I just lacked the coordination. Each time I stepped on the court, the Thinking Brain would go into overdrive: 'You can't even throw a ball left-handed, what are you doing trying to play tennis? This will take you

Prioritise Flow

years; you're just making a fool of yourself.' Determined not to be a *restrictor* and bow to these false limitations and insecurities, I chose to embody a Flow Mindset instead. With every mistake, I would repeat the mantra 'Learn, Grow, Flow', brainwashing myself to let go of the mistake and instead draw any learnings and redirect my attention to being in flow for the next shot. Off the court, I would stand in front of a large mirror hitting forehands and backhands, repeating 'Learn, Grow, Flow', confusing my brain as to which arm was my right arm in the aim of using neuroplasticity to map over the neural habits of my right arm to my left arm (we'll talk more about neuroplasticity in the next chapter). When on court, I rarely focused on the outcome of my shots; I just looked to optimise each mistake and find the fluency within my strokes. To my amazement, in just under a year, I was playing at the top level for my club.

Overcome outcomes

When working with clients, they often resist letting go of their fixation to outcome goals – most commonly, this is because it is what they know and has seemingly helped them to get this far. However, goal-setting should come with a large 'Warning' sign, as outcome goals, if used inappropriately, can be very counterproductive, producing distracting expectations, stress and friction in our performances. If it overrides our process goals, it will eat up our attentional bandwidth, and make us less likely to reach the desired

How to Find Flow

outcome. Whether it's quitting smoking,[80] saving money,[81] losing weight[82] or achieving almost any difficult goal,[83] research suggests that outcome goals frequently have the opposite effect. 'We get so emotionally attached to a goal that we're setting ourselves up for failure and disappointment,' explains author Stephen Shapiro.[84] Lisa Ordóñez, Dean of the University of California at San Diego's Rady School of Management, who has studied goal-setting for over two decades, states that the over-prescription of outcome goals has led to 'a narrow focus that neglects non-goal areas, distorted risk preferences, a rise in unethical behavior, inhibited learning, corrosion of organizational culture, and reduced intrinsic motivation'.[85] Ordóñez gives the example of a call centre that set a goal for its employees: keep the average call time under two minutes. The result? Employees would call a number and, when the person answered, hang up immediately. They met their goal, but the outcome-oriented goal radically limited their performance. The workers didn't take the time to learn or discover the best methods because they were focused on achieving the goal – and, as a result, they didn't do very well. In business and sport, principles are continuously tossed aside in order to achieve short-term gains, regardless of the ethical or long-term detriment. Shortcuts are targeted, using others as stepping stones becomes acceptable, once-held strong values are compromised and cheating to win can even be overlooked if it is a means to an end. In short, once

Prioritise Flow

goals have helped forge a vision, then all the fruit that they will offer has already been dropped from the tree.

As discussed earlier, a common first mistake people make when wanting to find flow is making a Flow Mindset a fixed outcome and inadvertently slipping into the red side of the Flow Model. Working with a tech entrepreneur called Peter, for example, I could not fault his enthusiasm and commitment to finding flow. He was motivated and proactive. He went over and above with his homework in between sessions, but, frustratingly, fell short of finding more flow in his life. In discussion, it soon became clear that Peter was chasing flow as he had been his past goals. In treating the attainment of flow as an outcome-focused approach, he simply exchanged one problem for another. He would rate his flow attainment each day and started to get anxious, stressed and competitive when his scores were low. While he put flow first, his approach was deeply in the red, and flow became more distant. It wasn't until he pitched the quest for flow as an *intention* for engagement, a mindset on *how* to achieve his goals, not *what* he *had* to achieve, that he was able to refocus on the task goals he was engaging in and his flow training gained traction.

It is helpful to remember that flow is a subjective experience, an actualised process, not an outcome in and of itself. We can use flow as a focus for our mindset and as an approach towards a task, a deeper intention for our overall engagement, but to be in flow we need to be

How to Find Flow

100 per cent focused on the task at hand. You don't want to be focused on flow when singing, for example – you want to be connected to the song.

Choose to move beyond coping

Despite good intentions, a common hindrance for adopting a flow-orientated approach is the attachment people have to their egoic-, extrinsic-, fear- or outcome-driven approaches. Even if we logically agree with the flow approach, if we are still emotionally attached to and holding on to other approaches, then, given their historic prominence, they will take centre stage when it comes to the crunch. When our back is up against the wall, our mind will always default to our deeper conditioning. If the red approach is deeply embedded in your psyche, it can be helpful to remember that it is ultimately a coping strategy, which you probably adopted in the past because you modelled others operating in this manner at the time. It remained to this day, as it obviously provided some level of escape or success. But just because it 'worked' in the past, doesn't mean that it is right for your future. Now that you are open to being your best and not just doing enough to get by, you can let it go; you have a new approach to model.

Like leaving a dysfunctional relationship, it can be difficult to let go of an approach that has served you for so long. In this case, it is helpful to *thank* this old approach for protecting you in the past and say your goodbyes by

Prioritise Flow

embodying the more empowered blue approach. While coaching a professional taekwondo athlete, for example, I witnessed how his outcome-driven approach was fuelling his perfectionism. The stress of needing everything to be as expected was crippling for him – it had even stopped him from participating in the sport he loved and hamstrung his learning at university. When I challenged him about his perfectionism and how he treated himself when not living up to his high expectations, he defended his approach. He doubled down on being exceptionally hard on himself, and not forgiving himself until the mistake was corrected or the goal was achieved. He stated that it was precisely this approach that had helped him get this far and rise above the thousands of other athletes. He was blinded to alternative approaches. I outlined that it was also precisely this approach that had caused him to burn out, not enjoy his training and under-perform at the Olympics. Unable to deny this fact, he was trapped in a contradiction. Holding on to his old truth was crippling his present ability. In time, he finally came to believe that he had to surrender his old approach, choose to move beyond coping and take a leap of faith. To do so, he actively had to thank and abandon the red approach daily and put on his Flow Mindset to fill the void.

Adopt continuous compassion

Many years ago, I coached a surgeon, Janelle, who struggled to operate at the level she knew she was

How to Find Flow

capable of. Janelle was stressed about each operation and the inevitable interaction that she would have with her peers post-theatre. The stress was so consuming she was close to quitting. When we met, it was clear that she had all the skills to sustain a high-performing lifestyle, she had all the technical skills and acumen for her job, and she even excelled in her research. Yet Janelle couldn't get past the plethora of personal distractions that occurred when faced with conflict. Seemingly competent in many self-regulatory skills, she was able to focus for hours on end. As soon as a criticism or technical mishap occurred, though, she would be her own worst critic, continually beating herself up and stamping on her own self-regard. This low self-regard affected not only her operational performance but her social interactions, at work and outside. Expecting the worst of herself grew into expecting the worst of others, skewing the words of others and misinterpreting feedback or comments. It wasn't until I asked her to adopt a radical level of compassion in her self-relationship that her feelings, perceptions and actions started to change. In moments of compassion, she could evade the usual story that had otherwise become so normalised she didn't ever question whether the rhetoric could be true or not, helpful or not. Through her self-compassion she was able to open a window to change. We then used her imagination to revisit past moments of flow when in theatre to help her feel confident and regarded once

Prioritise Flow

again. Embodying this momentary state of self-regard, she was then able to forgive her mistakes and move on. Janelle committed to using this strategy to intervene every time her old story surfaced. Slowly but surely, she grew in confidence, her self-regard remained and she was able to operate in theatre as the surgeon she had once dreamt of being.

A common inhibitor to being READY is when the manner in which we treat ourselves doesn't allow us to learn and grow or move beyond our embedded coping patterns. The relationship we hold with ourselves, our self-leadership, underpins everything we do. If we are to change old habits, then we need to treat ourselves in a way that allows for change. As outlined in the story just told, a common self-leadership many motivated or achievement-orientated people possess is the uncompassionate approach to failure – 'This is not good enough', 'Pull your socks up', 'You're such an idiot', we may say to ourselves when under pressure, unknowingly disempowering our ability to change. They become a self-limiter, a restrictor. In contrast, being self-compassionate allows *hope* to be restored and a natural resilience to surface. 'Being compassionate allows us to *for-give* ourselves, in order to *give-for* future psychological flexibility, agility, learning, performance and progression. In forgiving, we are *giving-for* the future relationship,' as my friend and colleague John Hendry always says to me. A self-compassionate and forgiving style of self-leadership

How to Find Flow

allows us to feel safe and secure, seek feedback, process mistakes, learn from them and integrate the growth into future practice – there is no need to protect, blame and avoid. Being compassionate doesn't threaten our confidence or bully ourselves into playing safe, not risking another mistake, like a discompassionate self-relationship does. Instead, it allows us to risk more and shoot for standards higher than before.

It's time to examine your self-relationship. In your activity, or life as a whole, are you creating friction to stress or using it to find flow? Are you a *self-restrictor* or *self-actualiser*? Of course, you may flip-flop depending on the task or context, but if you're struggling to find flow, it is likely that you are in the red, creating friction and self-restricting your actualisation. If you are unsure, one of the easiest ways to unpack the relationship you have with yourself is to examine your self-talk. You need to look for a common story, a repetitive message that you hear your Thinking Brain say to yourself, one that shapes how you perceive things. It can help to periodically write down your self-talk over several days, and the story that you are telling yourself will eventually become clear.

It doesn't matter what the story is – we all have a unique story relative to our background and upbringing. Importantly, try not to judge what comes up – this will only make the truth harder to unearth. For example, your story may be one of:

Prioritise Flow

- *diminishing worth*, evident by your inner commentary, 'I'm useless', 'They deserve it more than me', 'I'm not really worthy of this affection/success'
- *self-inflation*, highlighted by the self-talk: 'I'm better than them', 'I deserve it more'
- *victimisation*: 'Why don't people listen to me?', 'It always happens to me', 'It's just not fair'

I have helped people unpack a whole variety of different stories that they tell themselves. These three stories are just examples; you may not relate. See if you can identify your own story. We all have one.

Our self-narrative consists of the stories we tell ourselves, and they are neither good nor bad, they just are; some may be helpful, some unhelpful. These stories may feel deeply entrenched, fabricated in our youth. If so, it can help to think of them as old statements about the past. Once we highlight any unwanted story that narrates in our consciousness, we can choose to frame it as an old statement – the past doesn't exist anymore – and then adopt a new and preferred story that aligns us with finding flow. For example, a common narrative of people who are stuck in the red is: 'I'd better not fail or embarrass myself … I must do well … I need to do well to impress others … How can I be worthy if I don't achieve?' In this instance, they have an inner script that has attached their self-worth to achievement, and they can

How to Find Flow

take a moment to recognise that this script is not serving them anymore. On recognition, they can then work towards a more helpful story and narrative, such as: 'I'm worthwhile regardless of the outcome ... This challenge is interesting ... I'm curious about the complexity ... I can't wait to get stuck into the crux of it ... There is no failure, only feedback!' And so on.

Replacing the stories we tell ourselves with more helpful stories or scripts is a common intervention within yogic practices, psychotherapy and many ancient teachings to move oneself towards a more progressive path of self-actualisation; actualising flow is no different. While I strongly advise that you workshop these stories and new scripts with a Flow Coach, so that it is a) done properly and b) not sabotaged by your own blind spots, I also suggest you get started today by examining how you treat yourself throughout the rest of today.

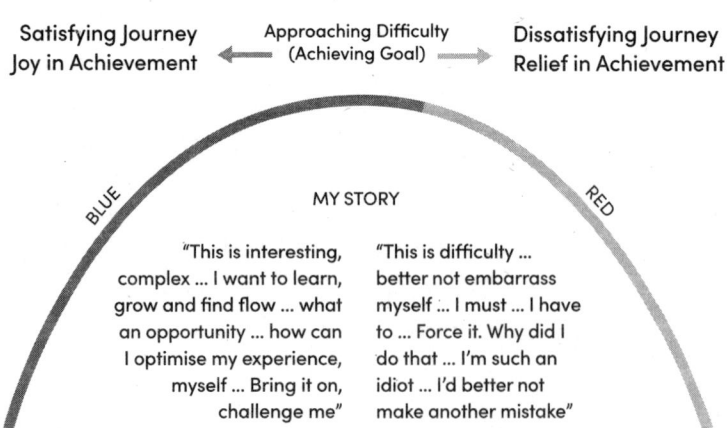

The Flow Model: The story we tell ourselves

Prioritise Flow

While this book hopes to give you the playbook to find flow for yourself, it cannot be a substitute for the personal and emotional work that many of us need to do to remove the inner conflict that so often restricts our flow – namely, the deep work that may be needed to rewire deeply embedded patterns of thinking and behaving. Over my time Flow Coaching, I have become acutely aware that the more secure an individual is, the less inner conflict ensues to derail ambitious plans. The more fulfilled our mental and emotional needs become, and the more secure our self-construct (self-worth, self-identity, self-esteem and self-regard), the less inner conflict we are likely to suffer and get distracted by, and the more likely we are to prospect rather than protect, collaborate rather than combat, see success rather than failure. Our insecurities and undealt-with trauma are continuously processing behind the scenes, using up vital psychic energy. These insecurities seep into the relationship we have with ourselves and others, limiting the level of trust we can embody and restricting our commitment to the task. Children who endure a hard upbringing, neglect, abuse or turmoil, for example, are often subconsciously so preoccupied with combatting these issues, they burn much of their psychic energy to prove their worth for love and attention – so much so that they may not have the psychic energy left over to self-care, wonder about self-discovery or ever actualise the self.

Unless it disrupts our daily lives, the development of

How to Find Flow

self, and what therapists call our 'inner child', is often deprioritised in favour of more 'urgent needs', such as achievement, power, money or affirmation. If you can dedicate the needed time to process and let go of your inner conflicts then you will remove or diminish much of the foundational distraction that restricts your flow. If you need to deal with personal trauma or unhelpful childhood scripts that still linger in your mind, please act on the available support. Taking the time to assess our attachment styles through the lens of attachment theory, for example, can give great clarity as to why we often get in our own way and allow our fears to drive our actions. Psychodynamic work, when done properly, can liberate us from these inner conflicts that sabotage our internal synchronicity; it can help us better relate to ourselves and others, and better foster both sustained moments of flow and increased frequency of flow. This work is advantageous not only for yourself but also for society as a whole. Ignoring our own dysfunction only creates conflict in the present and passes down this avoidance script to future generations in our behaviour transference, dispositions and genes. Once we realise that the best thing we can do for our children, neighbours and society is to free ourselves from our own conflict, prioritising this work no longer needs to feel like a selfish pursuit.

It is helpful to remember that self-actualisation is a journey not a destination. The more secure we make ourselves feel along the way, the more likely we will be to

Prioritise Flow

step into the position of an *actualiser* – and the easier it will be to adopt a Flow Mindset.

BE READY

Returning to my moment fumbling the microphone in front of hundreds of senior executives, it was precisely the Flow Mindset that got me out of the hole I had dug. By recognising that I had prioritised the outcome of the talk and, by default, abandoned the quality of my internal experience, I intervened and re-cognised my approach. With a breath of experiential intelligence and self-compassion, I reset and forgave the self-crippling leadership style that had taken hold. Instantly, there was a release of tension across my mind and body. I moved from a restrictor to an actualiser. In this newfound space, I noticed the blue and red arc symbol printed on the piece of paper in front of me. Realising that I was deep into the red, I repeated the mantra 'Learn, Grow, Flow' under my breath. My mind instantly focused towards embodying a Flow Mindset, and being READY to be in flow. Now unhinged from my previous entrenched position, my attention shifted from wanting to impress the audience towards the meaning behind my opening statement and the fluency of my breath. The directors who had been grappling for control in the boardroom in my head seemed to have walked out of the room. Feeling the need to loosen my body, and not just my mind, I took off

How to Find Flow

my jacket, shaking out my arms in the process – initiating another personal reset to ensure I was cleaning out the cache. Coming back to the microphone and seeing the room, I remembered the phrase situated on my one-pager (you'll get one of these at the end of the book as well – see page 360): 'pressure is a privilege'. With these words, I suddenly felt the expectant audience change from being an unhelpful room of judges to a collaborative energy that was going to springboard me into flow. Trusting the innate brilliance of my psyche that had got me here in the first place, I launched into my opening line feeling like a different person from only moments before.

You may not be able to relate to my personal story of speaking in public, though I'm sure you have your own examples in which you overthink and get in your own way, causing anxiety or stress to prevail. Whatever your domain, if you want to be READY, it is your responsibility to intervene – recognise, reset and rewire. Thankfully, in this last speaking situation, I had the knowledge and practice of applying a Flow Mindset prior, allowing me to shift my approach on demand. Now that you have this knowledge and are hopefully practising your experiential competence, you can also begin to shift your approach into the blue to not only restore a disastrous performance but turn a good performance into a great one.

I see the Flow Mindset become a self-fulfilling prophecy for all those who embody it. Those who believe

Prioritise Flow

in it, and truly adopt it, are liberated from the doubt that they are both worthwhile and able to achieve it. For example, in working with a budding young cricketer, Kai, I was amazed to watch his adoption of a Flow Mindset foster not just better focus, performance and activity satisfaction, but also habitual change towards other aspects of his life. Within several months, he went from not wanting to bat and face a cricket ball to being excited by the challenge of each ball. By relentlessly moving his intention towards flow, Kai naturally moved his subconscious focus away from the outcome and expectations that brought him so much anxiety and dread. Before every ball he faced, Kai proactively embodied his Flow Mindset, by challenging the bowler to bowl his best ball, in the knowledge that it would bring out the best of his batting. Instead of batting, putting pressure on himself to hit fifty runs or, more often than not, hoping to avoid getting out, Kai focused on learning from every ball he faced and leaving the crease a better batter than when he arrived. Slowly but surely, by applying the 'Learn, Grow, Flow' approach he learnt to optimise his own experience with each ball he faced, and revelled in the challenges of first-grade cricket.

To my amazement, Kai arrived at a session one day buzzing. While I expected another story of his new-found cricketing success, I was surprised to hear him recall how much he had enjoyed the challenge of a recent exam. In our session, we hadn't talked about his

How to Find Flow

approach to challenges outside of cricket, yet he seemed independently able to transfer this flow approach from cricket to finding flow at school. Kai not only surpassed his own expectations within sport and school, but, months later, he was also unlocking performance and satisfaction in how he interacted with girls he was attracted to. Kai had not only changed how he thought and felt, he had changed his whole outlook on life. 'He is a completely different person', remarked his father.

In this chapter, we have examined how to prioritise flow through recognising your experience using the Flow Model, changing your approach to challenge and complexity, and the beginnings of adopting a Flow Mindset. Now that you have some of the skills to recognise, reset and rewire, in Part 2 and the next chapter, we will take this approach one step further and explore how we can use flow as a guiding star to our preparations before important events.

LET'S RECAP

In this chapter, we have looked at a number of factors to invite a Flow Mindset into your life:
- embodying all the lessons in this book by putting on your Flow Mindset
- using the Flow Model to help self-assess your immediate experience – are you in the red or the blue?

Prioritise Flow

- understanding your body is already congruent with a flow approach
- taking responsibility for your self-relationship – becoming an actualiser not a restrictor
- letting go of your outcome and egoic agendas with 'Learn, Grow, Flow'
- being compassionate to yourself and forgiving your mistakes to give-for your future flow
- choosing to be in the blue – taking action with the three Rs: recognise, reset, rewire

It is now over to you to put on your Flow Mindset and embody these trainings into your daily life.

YOUR CHALLENGE

Being READY is the foundational part of a Flow Mindset. Before we move on to the application of being STEADY and entering FLOW, I suggest you consolidate all the nuances that you have learnt so far.

To help yourself become READY, place the arc in the next figure as a visible symbol that you can see every day to crystallise all the lessons in this book, starting now.

How to Find Flow

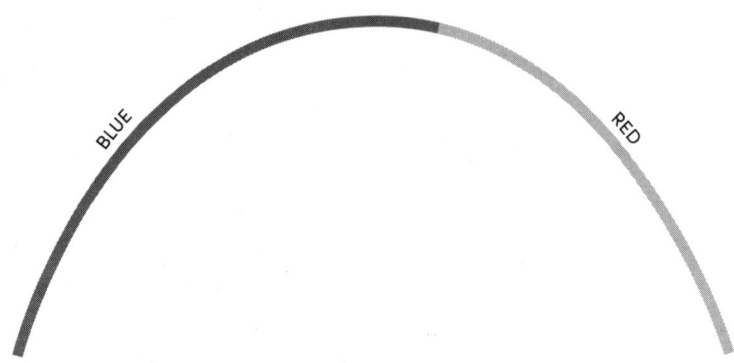

The Flow Model: Red and blue zones

It can help you not to overthink where your mind is at, but rather to simply and quickly self-assess whether you are in the red. It also works well for teams in which you might need to quickly address the team's mentality without distracting the session with too much detail. As long as there has been an initial education on what the red and the blue areas mean, one quick question can trigger a number of lessons for the individual to help get them back on track. 'You seem to be in the red, what can you do to get back into the blue?', for example. Referring to the red zone or blue zone is also less confronting than calling someone out for being egoic or combative, helping the team members to feel safe and empowered to recognise, reset and rewire.

Remembering to self-intervene and be READY with your Flow Mindset in the throes of the daily chaos can easily get forgotten, so it is helpful to externalise the arc and put it in places where you will naturally see it as you

Prioritise Flow

go about your business. People have drawn the blue and red arc on the back of their hand, stitched it on their gloves and even made stickers to fix on the back of their helmets, equipment or work folders. Most commonly, people print it out and place it around the house, on the mirror, on their desk and in their kit bag. Regardless of how you do it, if you place this arc in front of your eyes, you will automatically be reminded to self-assess your momentary experience and optimise your self-leadership out of the red and into the blue.

Part 2
STEADY

IT IS NORMAL FOR US ALL TO DO AS LITTLE AS POSSIBLE to get the job done, so after putting on your Flow Mindset and getting READY, it is easy to think that entropy will turn into negentropy, chaos into cohesion or friction into flow. But our time, attention and energy are finite. While getting READY is a good start – after all, it is the foundation we need to curate and sustain flow – we need to address how to deal with the many distractions and conflicts that arise just before important events or in mild doses throughout the day when facing life's difficulties. If we are not proactively tailoring this limited bandwidth towards flow, then we may not create the pre-conditions to flow or stay READY.

While prioritising flow is certainly a solution to these distractions as it deals with the underlying catalyst, I knew that my comprehensive cartography to flow needed a number of self-regulatory skills to curb the turbulence most people would feel leading up to an event – skills that would help people prepare better and STEADY the flow of consciousness from the frenetic 'noise' that would regularly push and pull attention from remaining READY. So I set out on a quest to experiment and test such skills.

Steady

Although I was hired to help my clients, the truth is that they were my secret heroes. I would often use myself as a guinea pig, experimenting with research and practically testing ideas. However, I would also learn from them in the process, as they had decades of experiences and a multitude of unconscious practices already installed. While many of these self-regulatory habits were unhelpful superstitions, like tapping their racquet against the ground before serving, not having sex the night before a game, wearing their favourite socks or always sitting down after the client in a meeting, elite professionals are very creative at finding ways to bind pre-event anxiety to an action they can control.

Over the years, it became clear that no magic milkshake or new fancy skill was going to hack their consciousness. While fashionable tricks circulating in high-performance circles gave momentary relief, and were certainly sexy from a marketing perspective, they were often not self-sustaining or, indeed, were another attempt to push through the red zone. What did become evident over time, however, was that, in order to stay STEADY for flow, they needed to proactively reinforce the principles of flow into their preparations.

In this part, you'll learn a number of skills to ensure you are targeting flow precisely. You will also learn the self-regulatory skills you need to stay STEADY and stop your evolutionary errors and old habitually entrenched mindsets and reactions from taking back control.

Chapter 5
BUILD A BLUEPRINT

IMAGINE A FUTURE CHALLENGE THAT YOU WILL FACE in the coming weeks. Put down this book, close your eyes, if you feel comfortable doing so, and visualise the event for ten seconds.

Imagined it? OK, I'll assume you have. Now, in the imagined event that you just visualised, what was your experience? Were you nervous, confident? Did you succeed or fail? More importantly, did you imagine yourself performing the specific challenge in flow? If not, why not?

Next, imagine a confronting or challenging conversation that you need to have with a parent, partner or friend. Ready? Put down this book, close your eyes, if you feel comfortable, and envision the confronting conversation for ten seconds.

Did you imagine yourself having the conversation in flow this time? Were you completely absorbed and effortless in action?

Build a Blueprint

If you are like most people, then you may have forgotten to encompass the experience of flow in your visualisation, even though I gave you a second chance. If this is the case, do not worry – your flow training has only just begun. Hopefully, this quick exercise emphasises how your brain is not conditioned to prioritise flow in your life, and how important it is that we change this.

Some questions I like to ask all my clients, and now you, are: what would need to change inside you to start prioritising flow for your future self? What needs to happen to move flow up the priority ladder? And if not now, when? And one more question if you'll let me: what would life look like if you did?

In this chapter, we will attempt to answer these questions, and I will guide you in how to use your predictive processing to your advantage to train your brain to be in flow when the time comes.

THE POWER OF PROJECTION

If you do not give your brain the idea of flow, then how can you *expect* it to respond in flow when the time comes? To understand the importance of including the experience of flow in our future projections is also to understand the importance of prioritising quality over quantity, and the impact our projections have over our future performances.

Every time we act, train or work, we build neural

How to Find Flow

pathways in our brain directing our brain to act in the same manner when confronted with the same situation. Our nervous system is constantly firing electrical signals through our body to initiate thoughts or to move our muscles. When we repeat certain signalling, our neurons will literally fire and wire together, creating a stronger neural pathway, allowing the electrical signals to travel more efficiently, resulting in better communication.[86] To increase the speed of these messages, our neurons also create a myelin sheath around the body or axon of the neuron, almost like forming a rubber coating around a wire. This myelin helps to increase the speed at which the electrical signal travels down the axon, ultimately affecting the speed of our responses. The more myelin strings wrapped around our neural axons, the faster our neural processing and efficiency potential. Dr Douglas Fields, Chief of the Nervous System Development and Plasticity section at the National Institute of Child Health and Human Development in the US, suggests a fully myelin-wrapped circuit can increase velocities by up to a hundred times faster than an uninsulated fibre.[87] Wow! This development of our neurological pathways not only increases the speed of our neurological activity but, in doing so, also promotes the future use of this pathway and improves the associated skill or action with each layer produced. With every intentional action, therefore, we literally self-direct the neuroplasticity of our biology, embedding more efficient habitual ways of operating as

Build a Blueprint

we go. 'Practising a trick ten times perfectly is much more valuable than doing it fifty times poorly. In fact, training poorly just trains our neurology to do things incorrectly – it makes imperfections more permanent', explains world-renowned aerial artist Jochen Pöschko. As Jochen points out, the saying 'practice makes perfect' is misguided and should more accurately be positioned as 'practice makes permanent' – something to be mindful of when training for an event.

While the quality of our actions is impactful, our thoughts and visions are equally important. As we saw in Chapter 2, the psyche does not always distinguish between what's real or imagined. Neurologically speaking, much of our biology responds in the same way whether something is imagined or occurring. Whether we are *imagining* ourselves doing something or *actually* doing it, our neurons still fire, neurochemicals are still produced, thoughts and feelings still occur, our perspective is still consolidated and an experience is still formed; we effectively react in exactly the same way.[88] It is why scientific studies show that people who only visualise lifting weights still increase their muscle strength. For example, in a 2004 study at the Cleveland Clinic Foundation, researchers divided thirty participants into three groups.[89] Two practised guided motor imagery – visualising finger or bicep movements as vividly and realistically as possible – while the third served as a control. Remarkably, they found that simply visualising

How to Find Flow

the strength training led to a measurable finger strength increase of 35 per cent and bicep strength of 13.5 per cent, despite no physical movement. This is also how Cliff Young, an Australian potato farmer from Victoria, defied logic and expectation and became known to many as the 'Young Shuffle'. In 1983, Cliff surprised those around him by entering the Sydney-to-Melbourne Ultramarathon at sixty-one years of age. This race is no ordinary race. It is a gruelling 875km long; impossible for most fit people to complete. Generally, athletes who took part were elite runners half his age, yet Cliff had other ideas. The media soon took an interest in his story and quickly made fun of his usual footwear: the gumboots he wore to round up his sheep. Defying professional advice and pressure to withdraw, the other competitors left Cliff for dead at the start line. The most successful strategy employed to win such a race had previously been to run for eighteen hours, sleep for six hours, and then repeat the cycle for several days until the finish line was crossed. Cliff, however, wanted to show the world that the 'tortoise could really beat the hare', and kept running at a slow pace. During TV interviews, Cliff was resolute that he would continue to the end of the race without sleeping, saying, 'It's not easy, it's tough, pressure is there all the time ... but you gotta keep going ... I just imagine running after my sheep and trying to outrun a storm.'[90] Leaving scientists at the time baffled and eating their own words, Cliff continued to shuffle for five days, fifteen hours and

Build a Blueprint

four minutes, winning the race and breaking the record by two days! He achieved the seemingly impossible by imagining that he was protecting his sheep from an impending storm. The brain believed it, and his body responded as if it were true.

We have so much more power over our future experiences than we may otherwise realise. In fact, most future experiences will already be pre-programmed by the time we arrive at them. As explained in Chapter 2 – and I will say it again in case you skipped it – at a deeper level, we have often already decided how we want to think, feel and act when the time comes from the hundreds of imagined dress rehearsals. In the moment, our brain simply follows the blueprint we have laid out. As Muhammad Ali said, 'The fight is won or lost far away from witnesses – behind the lines, in the gym, and out there on the road, long before I dance under those lights.'[91] When the pressure is on, and your neurology and physiology is under stress, your brain, actions and experience will default to what has been imagined – what it has been directed to do by your previous projections: the only real training it has of the event.

To find flow when it matters most, we need to prioritise the quality, precision and intensity of the flow experience within the *end state*, or projected vision. For an important upcoming event, the mind will likely project to this future experience, each time creating and fostering a specific end, hundreds of times. It may only be for a split second,

How to Find Flow

but, sure enough, we will think about the future event, attaching an experience to it, many times over. On each of these occasions, we effectively train our psyche to respond in this manner when the moment arrives. If we imagine that we will be excited about this upcoming event hundreds of times, then our biology will be trained and triggered to become excited when the time comes. If we imagine being nervous hundreds of times, then we will train the brain to be nervous when the time comes. If we imagine being in flow, then ... I think you get it.

While many people who consider themselves to have a strong mental game might imagine a positive outcome or confident performance, this is not enough. We need to capitalise on our brain's incredible natural predictive processing and insert flow into the equation.

Let's try this again. Put the book down and for several seconds imagine an upcoming event.

I'll assume you have finished. Now, did you visualise yourself experiencing a state of flow during the act? Hopefully, you nailed it this time. If not, don't worry. As you proactively put on your Flow Mindset throughout the day, this new habit of creating future flow blueprints will naturally seep its way into your projected end states and envisioned future, training your brain and making it natural for you to experience flow when the time comes.

Build a Blueprint

Install flow blueprints

There will be times when you'll want to take a few minutes to pause and proactively visualise the future event in flow. There will also be times throughout the day when you'll need to intervene halfway through daydreaming about an ordinary or negative future experience and reshape it to being in flow. Regardless, the very act of cultivating your future experience by taking ownership of it in the present is an advanced skill of experiential competence. By proactively shaping your end state, you give your psyche a blueprint to act. As Wayne Rooney, ex-football striker for England and Manchester United, once recalled:

> 'I lie in bed the night before the game and visualise myself scoring goals. You're trying to put yourself in that moment, to prepare yourself; to have a "memory" before the game. I don't know if you'd call it visualising or dreaming, but I've always done it, my whole life.'[92]

I have used the tool of creating blueprints for flow to great personal and professional effect. Academically, I was involved in one study that helped tennis players, who already rated highly in their flow scores, to use this very skill to increase their intensity of flow by 29 per cent and the accuracy of their tennis serves by 22 per cent.

How to Find Flow

Simply visualising themselves in flow prior to the act gave their brain a blueprint to follow.

Whenever I think about creating a flow blueprint, one memory always comes to mind . . . Years ago, a tennis player once challenged me to walk the walk and prove that visualisation really works. Not wanting to diminish her belief, I found myself readying to hit a serve at a small can on the other side of the court, which was positioned just inside the far corner of the service box. The can was about 30cm tall and 10cm wide – a relatively small target to aim for.

I could hear the self-doubt and excuses flood in: 'I'm not warmed up; I've hardly hit a ball all day; my elbows are still injured; this is totally unrealistic; you need at least five ... ten ... twenty attempts to hit it; if you don't hit it, she won't respect you.' The chatter continued. I bounced the ball to bring myself back to the moment. Bounce, bounce, bounce ...

I played the movie over and over in my mind's eye. I imagined myself throwing the ball high into the air, leaping up with a spring and contacting the ball at the optimum height. The ball would sail over the net with a perfect trajectory, destined to hit the target. Sure enough, in my imagination, the ball smacked the target and sent it spinning into the air, spraying balls around the court. As I pumped my fist and turned to see my student's jaw drop in disbelief, I could see her clapping her hands in delight as her mind removed any

Build a Blueprint

lasting limiting belief that visualisation wasn't helpful.

This movie in my head was almost perfect – far clearer than the last one, but still not flow-like. It looked good, had great results, but didn't feel flowy. 'One more time,' I thought. Bounce, bounce, bounce ...

I focused on the target and replayed the movie again, but, this time, I visualised a felt effortlessness to my actions. The vision felt smoother than before – there was more fluidity to my swing. As the ball hit the can on the other side of the net, the vision felt so real that, for a split second, I believed that I had just hit the target in real life. Everything felt complete, and the task suddenly seemed surprisingly easy.

So, without delay, I threw the ball high into the air and simply reproduced my blueprint. As I watched the can of balls fly into the side netting, I felt a strange sense of gratitude. Then, as the outside world merged back into my awareness and I became consciously aware of what had just happened, I entered a mild state of shock. Did I just hit the target?!

As the teacher wishing to instil confidence in this scenario, I managed to contain my excitement and maintained an air of calm. 'Your turn,' I smiled.

Over the years, I have discovered several important tips to building a flow blueprint.

The first factor is to believe in the power of visualisation and the control you have over your experiences. Secondly, when envisioning yourself in flow, it is critical that the

How to Find Flow

imagined future experience is firstly an experience, and not merely a projection of the practicalities, technicalities or outcome, and that it is specific to the environmental and contextual realities of the actual event – or as close as you can get with the information you have. For example, when doing a talk I always arrive early to see the location, so that I have time to build a blueprint of flow that includes the exact stage, microphone, lighting, audience capacity and what I am wearing. Further, and hopefully I am not boring you with this vital message by now, the experience needs to be one of flow, containing the absorption and effort-lessness associated with flow. If you find yourself activating the Thinking Brain in the visualisation or envisioning an experience that isn't in flow, such as a strained performance, that's OK, simply stop and start again.

For important events, it can also help to create a snapshot of the projected flow experience – a picture or symbol that will represent the blueprint when wanting to insert or reflect upon the blueprint quickly. For example, you may want to take a snapshot of the visualisation as if taking a photo of yourself in flow and associating the future experience of you in flow with this picture. You may choose to add colours, sounds, smells or a physiological feeling to this snapshot or mini movie. Don't force a particular snapshot – allow one to intuitively arise by asking yourself to take the most impactful snapshot. Once you have a snapshot, trigger it whenever forecasting to

Build a Blueprint

the future event. Every time your brain naturally projects to the future event, insert the envisioned blueprint on demand by bringing the snapshot to the forefront of your attention. See it, feel it, breathe it. The more you use it, the more you will believe it is possible. Visions are like plants. If we give them space to exist and keep them well fed, they will grow and weather life's storms.

For important events, the mind will continuously try to project. The more you become aware of this happening, the greater your opportunity to own your future experience. It is not uncommon to end up inserting your snapshot hundreds of times before a major event. My experience is that the further out from the event you create your blueprint and use your snapshot, the less your mind will feel uncertain and need to project. When working with clients for a major championship, for example, we will create the blueprint months prior, sometimes even years in advance, as it affects not only the event itself, but also how they train.

When you spend time to cultivate and refine your flow blueprints, they will become one of the most powerful flow tools in your arsenal. It is my experience that the more we insert the snapshot before an event, the more we train and brainwash our psyche to feel and act like it when the time comes, and the less intervening we need to do in our preparations and during the actual event. As one teacher, Eric, states:

How to Find Flow

'Every morning I imagine the day ahead in flow. I insert my snapshot at breakfast, when getting my kids into the car and multiple times when driving to work. By the time I get to the school, my brain believes that the snapshot will happen. I walk in less stressed, more present and look forward to welcoming the noisy mob. The more I see the snapshot in my morning routine, the better day I have – it's that simple.'

While this may seem like a bit of extra 'work', the more you experience success with this tool, the more you will believe in its power, and the more you will want to build your own flow blueprints.

I encourage you to go the extra mile with your method acting when creating your flow blueprint. In the past, skiing clients have been dressed up in full ski gear, including skis, with a fan against their face in their hotel room to help trick their mind that the vision is real as they embody their line down the mountain. The more real you can make it, the more senses you can invite into the projection, the more the blueprint will stick.

Create mini blueprints

Building a flow blueprint for larger projects, such as getting a promotion, building a business or competing at the Olympics, can become overwhelming and will require a more piecemeal approach to help you feel more in

Build a Blueprint

control or, more aptly, enable you to let go of the need to worry about losing control.

Over time, I have found the use of Short-Term Achievable Flows (aka STAFs) to be very helpful for both myself and clients alike. By this, I mean breaking down the bigger goal into a series of short-term achievable goals in which you can see yourself finding flow – stacking a series of mini flow blueprints. For example, when coaching Pau, a lawyer looking to pass his final exams, the final stretch of studying was so overwhelming that procrastination and stress were stifling. Qualifying as a lawyer had been a life goal that had already taken over a large part of his life. He had the skills and motivation, but months of studying full time on top of an exhausting and demanding working week seemed insurmountable. The challenge was too big, too much to handle all together, forcing him into the red each day.

By breaking up the study curriculum into smaller parts, mapping it across a timeline, and then creating smaller process goals for each week, Pau could finally see himself achieving success. Further, creating smaller blueprints of flow around these process goals not only allowed him to feel that the journey was achievable, it trained his psyche to be in flow for each task. For example, Pau imagined himself in flow practising past exams as he studied at home; he imagined actually being a legal ethics advisor to better absorb the information when studying the practical ethics of barristers … in flow. Collectively,

How to Find Flow

the STAFs increased his belief that he could enjoy and not endure the intense schedule ahead, and eventually *invite* the challenge of the written and oral assessment. Instead of thinking about the overwhelming task of passing his exams and the sheer volume of work he had to cover over the proceeding months, Pau focused on finding his flow every day in a series of manageable STAFs.

Creating STAFs may seem most pertinent for big life challenges, but they are just as relevant for single events. When I deliver a keynote speech, for example, I always break my initial flow blueprint of the speech into multiple STAFs. I imagine myself adopting the Flow Mindset prior to going on stage, generating a feeling of gratitude for the opportunity, beginning the speech with an impactful line, inviting audience engagement within the first few minutes and ending each image shown on the big screen behind me with a simple and poignant insight – all while being in the experience of flow.

Sarah Hendrickson, World Champion ski jumper, remembers her winning run:

> 'When I'm waiting at the top before it's my turn to jump, there is a lot of time to think as jumpers before me take their turn. Having these smaller preparation steps is really important for me. I also do the same ritual in practice … Just having that same physical and mental repetition is key to managing the mind

Build a Blueprint

and body with what to do next – it stops the mind getting distracted and disrupting the body. In the championship jump, I simply focused on my smaller visions and, before I knew it, I got to the bottom of my jump, and had won. I don't know how I performed to that level with that much pressure. It was like something else took over my body. I just said to myself, "Okay, you know what to do, I've already imagined it, so just focus."'

So the next time you have a big goal or a significant event that you want to nail, see if you can break it up into a series of process goals – mini steps that need to happen in order for the bigger goal to be realised. Then, take each of these smaller goals and create mini flow blueprints for each one. I advise not to do too many STAFs, otherwise it can be overwhelming. Do enough so that your focus is on something smaller that feels achievable. Alternatively, take one step at a time. Create a blueprint and STAFs for only the first step of the bigger goal; you can create secondary blueprints for later steps after nailing the first step.

Now that you know how to create a flow blueprint, the next chapter will examine how to engineer the pre-conditions of flow to ensure that both your blueprint and your preparations are targeting flow.

How to Find Flow

> **LET'S RECAP**
>
> In this chapter, we learnt how to build your very own blueprint for flow. Remember:
> - visualisation is one of the most powerful tools at your disposal
> - your brain is always projecting to your future events, predetermining how you may feel
> - you can intervene in this predictive processing by imagining yourself in flow
> - make your flow blueprints real: use visuals from the actual location, make it a sensory experience
> - above all else, make sure your projections include the absorption and effort-less control of flow
> - after creating your flow blueprint for a specific event, take a snapshot of the vision to insert into your mind when in a hurry
> - break up your blueprint into mini STAFs
>
> It is now over to you. Build your blueprints and see how they help shape your experience.

YOUR CHALLENGE

Ready to give it a go? After all, this is *experiential* training; you are not just collecting knowledge. Read the following

Build a Blueprint

passage all the way through and then stop, put the book down and build your flow blueprint for a specific upcoming activity or event.

- Take a moment to become present and close your eyes, if you feel comfortable doing so. It can help to focus on the temperature difference of the air going in and out of your nose.
- Once present, cast your mind towards the future event in which you are performing in flow – fully absorbed and effort-less in your control.
- Looking through your eyes, seeing what you see, feeling what you feel, become aware of how it feels to be absorbed in the act, effort-less in your actions. Notice how intrinsically rewarding the experience is.
- Make the experience more real by including additional senses, such as sound, smell, taste, temperature or bodily balance. Live it, breathe it and experience the event as if you are experiencing it for the first time. If it is a static image, turn it into a movie; make the changes you need to bring the experience to life.
- Allow yourself to sense the feeling of being in flow. Place your attention on where the feeling of flow is inside your body. For example, do you feel it in your chest, shoulders, head, blood flow or cells?
- Now, it is time to create a snapshot of this event. Ask your psyche to pick a moment that sums up

How to Find Flow

   this experience of flow. Don't force it or judge it, let it manifest.
- Once you have a clear picture, appreciate it, frame it or simply store it somewhere back in your body; imagine placing it in your belly, head or chest. Know that this snapshot can always be called upon when you prepare and project to the event.

I suggest proactively repeating this exercise, not just the snapshot, a few times in the days and weeks preceding the important event to build a stronger bond with the blueprint, making the entry to flow easier. If the blueprint changes over time, that is OK. Allow it to evolve and become more meaningful. Ensure that you use it as part of your preparations. When the event happens, simply place this snapshot at the forefront of your attention and allow the same feelings and neurological responses to transpire.

If you want to take this exercise to the next level, externalise your snapshot, so you can be reminded of this flow blueprint daily. Draw it, paint it, sing it; do whatever you want to do to create an externalised version of it. It doesn't have to be perfect, just something that reminds you of the flow blueprint. Each time you dream it, speak it, sing it, you will effectively be training your neurology to manifest this experience.

Chapter 6

INVITE THE INTENSITY

FLOW RESEARCH OUTLINES THAT THERE ARE TWO main pre-conditions to flow.[93] For flow to exist, we need to have a high level of motivation and an optimal level of challenge or complexity. Regardless of whether we are entering flow through a difficult challenge, such as trying to create a new song on the piano, or through non-achievement-orientated situations in which the complexity captivates our attention, such as a conversation that suddenly sparks our interest, to sustain the deep level of focus that is required to maintain a level of absorption, we need to be highly motivated. Why? Because motivation is the fuel of our attention; it directs our focus. If our motivation wanes, so does our focus and concentration; we become distracted and disengaged. Conversely, if the motivational force towards the act is high enough, we can align all aspects of our psyche with its end, propelling us into a state of flow. The strength of this internal cohesion

How to Find Flow

determines the extent to which our attention is distracted or becomes conflicted – and whether we actualise flow or not, and sustain the experience once in it.

As Dr James Oschman, professor, author and president of the Nature's Own Research Association puts it, 'The performer at the peak of his or her "game" is an individual who is able to achieve total cooperation, coordination, and participation of every tissue, cell, molecule and atom with his or her body to produce every aspect of the desired performance.'[94]

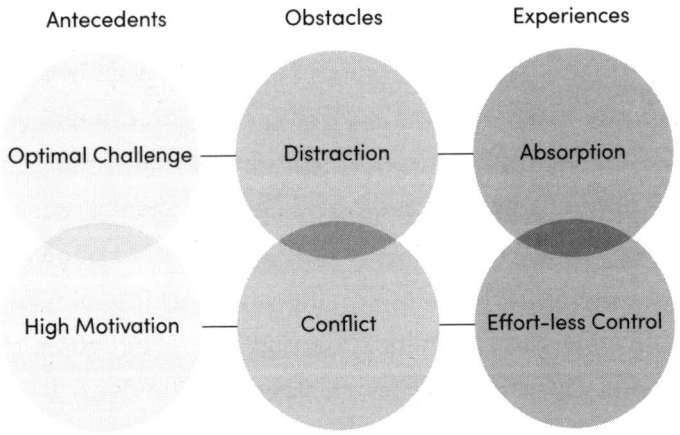

Pre-conditions, barriers and experiential components to flow

Occasionally, the task is so challenging or complex that even if we didn't want to do the activity in the first place, such as a daily work task, a high level of motivation can emerge during the act, helping to keep our attention on point. However, for the most part, finding flow intentionally

Invite the Intensity

requires us to manage our motivations to ensure we are highly engaged.

As discussed, when facing challenge or complexity, any friction with the rising tension will create conflict and distraction, restricting our level of absorption and effortlessness in the act, flipping us out of flow. Importantly, to reduce this friction, we not only have to embrace it as we face it head on, we need to go one step further and *invite* it. In this invitation, the difficulty is expected. We don't need to grapple with the challenge and complexity. The friction that otherwise conflicts our neurology and distracts our attention subsides. The more resolute the invitation, the more unwavering the Flow Mindset – and the longer we remain in the blue. The challenge or complexity then becomes a stepping stone into flow as the brain knows we are knocking on flow's front door.

In this chapter, we will discuss exactly *how* to invite the challenge and ensure the intensity level of this invitation is pitched appropriately to find flow.

IGNITING INSPIRATION

People who find flow frequently love their work more than what it produces and are dedicated to their work regardless of the outcome. They are inspired individuals who will not compromise on their interests. They are able to progress faster and deal with intense situations

How to Find Flow

more effectively, as their decision-making has become simplified. They have already made deeper principled decisions based on their interests long ago. In the moment, they only need to decide which of the options before them is best aligned with these interests, rather than continually assessing each option in its entirety. They have found the true north to their internal compass and manage their external world to align with this. In this manner, finding flow therefore becomes more natural because, internally, there is less conflict and more coherence.

Tom Carroll, World Champion surfer, once told me that when he enters the ocean, no matter how good the waves are, he goes home. Not literally, but metaphorically. His love for the ocean started when his mother gave him a surfboard at the age of seven, just before she passed away. Tom subsequently built a strong relationship with the ocean, knowing that, every time he entered the water, he was one step closer to his family. Regardless of what happened on the water, Tom was still motivated to surf. How good the waves were, or how well he did on them, was less important than just surfing. The act of surfing was inherently satisfying; in scientific speech, it was 'intrinsically rewarding'. Daniel Coyle, the *New York Times* bestselling author, similarly found that it was not the luxurious facilities or access to exceptional coaches that the world's top talent centres shared, but the high level of motivation or emotional rocket fuel that caused

Invite the Intensity

performers to treat bare bones practice areas as if they were cathedrals.[95] As Matthew Whitfield, Lieutenant Commander and Senior Flying instructor for the Fleet Air Arm of the Royal Navy, told me:

> 'The selection to be a pilot in the Royal Navy is fiercely competed, 40–50 slots available each year, with over 6,000 applicants all wanting to live their dream as a Naval Fighter Pilot. The training takes over 50–60 months and costs between £5M and £6M [in 2017] per person. There is a lot of pressure, and those who are able to find their flow, perform under pressure regularly, and pass this rigorous and sometimes bone-shaking training, are ultimately the ones who have the deepest desire and self-motivation to fly and be a wingman.'

Or as Steve Jobs, co-founder of the tech company Apple, said, 'Do what you love ... Have the courage to follow your heart and intuition.'[96] In short, it helps to love what we do and to do what we love.

Think about the activities in your life that probably brought you to this book. Start by spot-checking your motivation levels for your top activities – on the line below, mark your current level of motivation.

Low ══════════════════════════════ **High**

How to Find Flow

To ensure that you are not running up the wrong direction of the escalator, let's look at several skills to increase your motivation.

Develop intrinsic drivers

Let's take a look at your life. This past week (assuming you are not currently reading this book while sipping cocktails on holiday), of the 168 hours that have just passed, how much of this time has been spent doing activities which you love, which you find enthralling, where you would not want to be anywhere else? Go on; take a moment to work this out.

For most people, the fraction is small. Many of us are often busy doing what we have to do, what we should do, and even approach activities that we once loved with a feeling of duty rather than inspiration. This type of motivation is called 'extrinsic motivation'. We are motivated by factors that are external to our inner passions and inspiration. In essence, we engage to satisfy others or for external reasons, such as money, affirmation, duty, peer pressure, fame, fear, avoiding negative consequences, protecting our reputation and so on. On the contrary, when we are 'intrinsically motivated', we do what we do because we want to or love to. We are inspired, and we want to engage regardless of the outcome. In essence, we engage to satisfy our intrinsic desires for learning, love, belonging, curiosity, meaning and autonomy.

Invite the Intensity

I like to think of these two styles of motivation as energetic fuel tanks: intrinsic goals and drivers that create clean fuel, and extrinsic motives that create dirty fuel. Both types of energy will create action, but one will lead us into the blue and one into the red. I'm sure you can guess which. For instance, you may go to work because it pays the rent, society tells you that you should have a job and, if you don't, you'll get fired (extrinsic motives). *And* you may also go to work because you enjoy being challenged and like the banter with your colleagues (intrinsic motives). The fine print here is that we do not have to abolish all extrinsic drivers, as this may not be possible. Indeed, we all have dirty fuel driving many of our activities, whether we like it or not. Instead, the key is to focus on and prioritise your intrinsic motives and create more clean fuel. In this scenario, if you place your attention on the extrinsic motives, then your experience will always be one of friction. Yet if your core driver is to be challenged and to connect with your colleagues, for example, suddenly the driver of money doesn't become a consuming primary driver that reminds you of the bills you have to pay. Without this friction, you can become less distracted, more engaged and intrinsically motivated.

My challenge to you is to respect your internal engine and increase the cleanliness of your fuel – become more intrinsically driven. Spending time on doing activities that we love is not selfish or indulgent; it is fundamental

How to Find Flow

to a happy and prosperous life – essential if we want to find flow. Equally, honing your attention on the intrinsically motivating factors of your activity is a skill of psychological flexibility that is entirely within your control. We do, however, need to be creative with the time and space we have. As John Galsworthy, who won the Nobel Prize for Literature in 1932, stated, 'Life calls the tune, we dance.'[97] Taking charge of the steps you take on the dance floor and actively making decisions that enhance your intrinsic fuel is crucial to experiencing flow frequently. Before we move on to some other skills to increase your motivation, what changes do you need to make in your life so that you can dedicate more time to activities that inspire you?

Activate autonomy

Finding flow may be easier in activities that we love, but this does not mean that we cannot find flow in those everyday tasks that we 'have to' or 'ought to' do. Ultimately, we always have a choice as to how we do what we do, even if we cannot choose what we do. The ability to self-determine our workload ignites a level of inherent satisfaction – it makes us feel like we have a choice. Which is why almost all motivational theories include autonomy, agency, self-governance or choice as major factors to motivation, and if organisations can capitalise on this then employees will pay it back, and then some. It is why Google allows 20 per cent of employee time to be

Invite the Intensity

spent on autonomous projects,[98] and Patagonia allows its teams autonomy in their own schedule.

So how can you take back control of what you are doing and find a bit more autonomy? How can you do your activity differently to feel more empowered about your engagement?

Identify interest

In my research, the most prevalent factors of being highly motivated include the individual's level of interest and the subjective value they attribute to the activity. For example, in a meta-analytic review of flow and learning, the level of interest in the content and subject was found to be an integral element for finding flow.[99] 'Acting on intrinsic interest alone, individuals seize opportunities to learn, read, work with others, and gain feedback in a way that supports their curiosity and serves as a bridge to more complex tasks,' explains Dr Shernoff, Associate Professor of School Psychology at Rutgers University.[100]

Let's help you to become more interested in the activities where you want to find flow. See if you can relate to any of these statements:

- I have the opportunity to build a skill.
- I engage with people I like surrounding the activity.
- There is information or components that are interesting.
- This activity is a stepping stone to a wider purpose.

How to Find Flow

- This activity enables me to do something else that I want to do.
- I will feel good on completion.
- I like the result of what this activity provides.
- I am doing the activity for others that I value or care about.
- I am good at this activity.
- This activity aligns with my value of ...
- This activity aligns with my belief of ...
- This activity helps me in the long term.
- This activity helps me in the short term.
- I have the opportunity to learn and grow in this activity.

If you can relate to one of these, then you have a thread of interest or subjective value that you can hold on to and hopefully foster.

Nurture your needs

If you have discovered that extrinsic goals, such as money, fame, fear, guilt or rewards drive you, don't panic. You may *not* need to make any drastic changes. Many people make the mistake of quitting activities too early, as they initially feel that their motivations towards it will never change. Many even change careers, countries and relationships, only to regret these decisions years later. Let me give you an example. A long time ago, I coached a young male swimmer called Michael. He was tipped for stardom.

Invite the Intensity

He was passionate about swimming, but begrudgingly engaged in the early mornings and long weekends of training that life as a competitive swimmer demands. Michael was eating, sleeping and training correctly, yet lacked the spark that had led him to dominate the State championships the previous year. Family life, school and most of his life seemed to be in order, yet there was an obvious drop in performance and he certainly was not finding flow in training or competition.

While he was answering one of my questions, I unexpectedly had a breakthrough. I suddenly became aware that I had approached the whole coaching session with the same focus on finding a solution to his problem with which he and his parents had approached me. So, instead, I asked him to describe what he loved about all the different areas of his life (i.e. I examined his intrinsic and autonomous motives). It soon became obvious that there was a clear mismatch in his passion for socialising and the time that was currently available for him to do so, given his intensive training regimes. Although Michael loved to swim, this conflict within him, of which he had been unaware up to this point, was slowly eating away at him like a mild poison, unconsciously distracting him every time he performed. As a part of his life was unfulfilled, he was incomplete, and anything else he did became a burden. Over time, his beloved activity had become a chore, and soon enough he was turning up to practice in order to please his coach, his parents and his

How to Find Flow

former self. A once intrinsically driven activity had turned into something quite unpleasant, all because other needs were not being met. As a result of this realisation, he left the session pumped with a new source of energy, as if he had been reunited with a lost part of himself. He finally had clarity that if he fulfilled these unmet needs, then his intrinsic motivation for swimming would likely come back. As a result, Michael took time to satisfy his social needs, as slowly his performances began to return, and several months later he was again competing at a national level.

Unanimously, motivational theories suggest that when our basic psychological needs as individuals are met, we are more likely to make decisions that are intrinsically motivated.[101] So let's take your temperature. On a scale of one to ten, how fulfilled do you feel in your need for each of the following:

- security
- meaning and purpose
- intimacy
- receiving attention
- giving attention
- privacy
- status
- control and autonomy
- community
- mastery and achievement

Invite the Intensity

If any of these are below an eight out of ten, then I suggest you pay it some attention. Set yourself up for success not stress, and ensure your psychological, emotional, physical and spiritual needs are met, or on the rise.

Now that you have the skills to *invite* the intensity, let's make sure you are inviting the right level of intensity.

CREATING AN OPTIMAL INTENSITY

As Mihaly Csikszentmihalyi explained, 'The best moments in our lives are not the passive, receptive, relaxing times ... The best moments usually occur if a person's body or mind is stretched to its limits in a voluntary effort to accomplish something difficult and worthwhile.'[102] It is precisely the depth of difficulty or richness of complexity that provide the stepping stones into flow.

Importantly, as is often misunderstood in research and practice, it is the *subjectively perceived* optimal level that enables flow and not an *objective fit* between skills and difficulty. As the Flow Model points out, too much challenge/complexity and we become distracted, anxious and conflicted. Too little challenge and we will never be aroused or absorbed enough to find flow. But just the right amount and we become stretched beyond our comfort zone, and both flow and an optimal level of performance prevail (see page 137). Why? It is precisely the uncomfortableness of being optimally challenged or facing a stimulating degree of complexity that creates

How to Find Flow

the necessary eustress (helpful stress) and uncertainty for flow to occur. This is an important point, because we want to aim to feel slightly unearthed, like jumping from one jagged rock to another; we may be unsure if we will make it, but we are confident enough to give it a try. Creating an optimal level of challenge and being uncomfortable go hand in hand – if you're too comfortable then your intensity is too low. 'If you aren't in over your head, how do you know how tall you are?' asked poet T.S. Eliot.[103] It is precisely this positive risk of becoming slightly unearthed that helps us move from being playful to being in flow.

Presented novelty demands our full attention and ignites a neurochemical cocktail that pulls us into the present. Neurochemically speaking, it is precisely the inherent risk or uncertainty involved in a challenging situation that triggers the neurochemical norepinephrine that alerts our nervous system and heightens our attention, and the neurochemical dopamine that helps to amplify our pattern recognition and decision-making capability, and acetylcholine which transmits signals from our nerves to our muscles to trigger the voluntary muscle movement and memory processing required for exceptional performance. The higher the risk (as long as we don't go into the red), the greater the gravitational pull into the moment; and with the help of these neurochemicals our system really comes alive.

Invite the Intensity

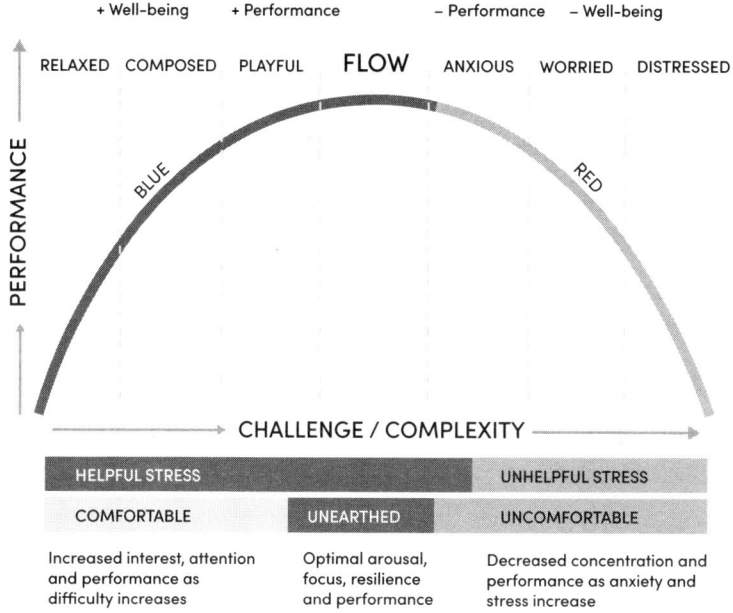

The Flow Model: Relationship to stress

When we peek under the hood of what a perceived optimal level looks like, we find three important components that must be in place for it to exist:

1. *Clear task goals* facilitate focused attention. If the task goal is not clear, then our psyche cannot fully commit all resources to one end. If the goal is an outcome rather than a process or task goal, and a heightened degree of pressure exists then the mind will fall into the red. We may not know exactly what needs to be done, such as in the case of innovation or how to take an opponent's queen in chess, but a central idea or task goal exists to

How to Find Flow

shape our moment-to-moment decision-making. Importantly, this task goal is specific to the task at hand and within our control. The bigger the task, the vaguer and more open to external influence it naturally becomes. The more specific you make your task goal, the clearer it will be and the more within your control. When studying, for example, the goal is not to pass the exams (outcome) or study hard (overall process), but rather is specific to the momentary task, such as writing a full page of notes in the next twenty minutes.

2. *Immediate and unambiguous feedback* is essential to sustain the clarity of the task goal and the optimum level of engagement. If we don't get immediate feedback on our actions, the brain doesn't know if our previous actions have been successful or not, whether we are on the right path or not, and the challenge becomes non-optimal. If the feedback we get is ambiguous, either because there is too much noise to decipher the feedback or the nature of the feedback is unclear, the challenge/complexity level becomes non-optimal.

3. To perceive ourselves as capable of meeting the demands of complexity or the highly challenging situation, an adequate level of *self-efficacy* or confidence must exist to enable effective execution. A void of confidence in our ability will likely push us into the red zone.

Invite the Intensity

If any of these three components cease to exist, then the door is opened for distraction or doubt, the perceived challenge level becomes suboptimal, we disengage somewhat and the level of absorption required for flow is not going to occur.

When examining your purpose or goals for your activities, ask yourself the following questions:

1. Is the task goal of your activity clear (don't overthink it; a task goal of replying to unread emails, for example, is sufficient)? If it is not clear, make a clear goal now for your task that is entirely within your control *and* optimally challenging or complex. Remember, you want to stretch your ability, so you need to challenge yourself.
2. What additional or differentiated feedback do you need in order to have absolute clarity on your direction? Is the feedback you are getting immediate? Is it ambiguous? What can you do to improve the quality of your feedback?
3. Do you feel confident in your ability to perform the task? Do you believe that you can find a way to deal with an arising issue?

Once the task is set up to be optimally challenging and a high level of motivation exists, a beautiful intensity is created that, on engagement with the task, demands absorption. The high level of intensity of the moment

How to Find Flow

stretches our ability as we look to find cohesion with the moment – a level of integration within the differentiation that's required for flow, as discussed earlier. However, holding this intensity or steadying this stretch of our capacities so that we keep a window open for flow is an art form that is important to learn to master. It is not to be confused with creating tension or struggle points that would otherwise be effortful and mentally distracting, causing neurological discordance or conflict. Once a high level of intensity is realised, we typically go in one of two directions. Most commonly, the Thinking Brain, unable to fully control the situation, wrestles for domination, precariously triggering the biological threat alarm, and we move into the red zone. Alternatively, our Being Brain overrides the Thinking Brain, and we harmonise with the intensity as we slip into flow.

Getting this follow-on right is tricky – a game that will have us falling into the red occasionally. It's worth noting that, when you tip into the red, as your mind tries to over-control the situation and you become slightly tense, in mild doses it is not the end of the world – you may be closer to flow than you were ten minutes ago. While the ideal position is to build the intensity and enjoy the stretch when you get there, maintaining the high degree of intensity without adding friction takes practice. To help you learn quicker, here are a few tips collated from countless clients and my own experience.

Invite the Intensity

Use the mantra 'challenge me'

Don't fight it, invite it. To help keep the intensity steady, I suggest adopting the phrases 'challenge me' or 'bring it on'. When embodied, they can help to evoke greater complexity when needed or move you back into the blue if the difficulty level has otherwise pushed you into the red. Whether it is an exam, presentation, work meeting or cleaning the house, you can use the phrase 'challenge me' to turn nerves into excitement, boredom into interest. When returning a tennis serve, for example, I repeat to myself 'challenge me' and mentally invite the server to serve their best serve, knowing a good serve will force a good return, while a great serve will beckon a great return and bring out the best in my tennis. I use the mantra 'challenge me' to invite in and become comfortable with the intensity.

Change your relationship with failure

Successful people do not simply perform well all the time, but continuously fail, and consequently develop resilience to failure that becomes second nature. For example, Michael Jordan, voted ESPN's greatest North American athlete of the twentieth century and probably the best basketballer of all time, said:

> 'I've missed more than 9,000 shots in my career, I've lost almost 300 games. Twenty-six times, I've been

entrusted with the game-winning shot and missed. I've failed over and over and over again in my life. And that's why I succeed … True failure is not trying in the first place.'[104]

If we are placing ourselves in the lion's den to stretch our abilities, exposure and bravery alone won't consistently lead us to flow; accidently tipping into the red can decrease confidence. To repeatedly stay in the blue when inviting intensity, we need to be OK with failure. As touched on earlier, when we see failure as feedback, we can start to invite it, knowing that it is a chance to learn and grow. Like the entrepreneurial tech circles that have the saying 'fail fast', we will develop stronger if we see failure as a natural course of development. Even multiple-time world champions get nervous and feel challenged, but the difference is that they rely on it to help reach their optimal state of intensity and step into flow. They continuously put themselves in a position to potentially fail, as they know it is their greatest opportunity to be their best and feel the flow.

Increase the intensity little by little

Never had I underestimated someone so badly. My assumptions when working with accountants, up until this point, was that they were conservative or cautious in their approach. However, this accountant's risk radar was all over the place. Having explained the idea of stepping

Invite the Intensity

out of our comfort zone to create optimal challenges in our last session, I was surprised to hear that my coachee, Anton, was feeling burnt by his exposure to taking positive risks. Naturally introverted and diligent, I had previously worked hard to help him take steps outside his comfort zone, to let go of needing to be in control. So to see him bereft of confidence, based on my advice to challenge himself, was not what I imagined. After a long discussion, however, it became evident that once he took a step across the comfort line into the unknown, Anton didn't know how much risk or intensity was enough. Because this was unknown territory, he aimed high, backed himself and then hit a wall as the challenge level became too much; instead of using a scaffolding approach and progressively upping the challenge level in incremental and manageable doses, he raced into the lion's den. Workshopping a few scenarios with him, it soon became clear to him that biting off more than he could chew was only going to make him backtrack into his comfort zone to protect himself and lose faith in the whole process. 'OK, so I need to increase the challenge and intensity level, little by little,' he stated. To help him remember this lesson, I replied with the Spanish equivalent, '*Sí, poco a poco.*'

While understanding that being uncomfortable is essential to entering flow, it is important to embrace these difficulties in a manner that ensures the task still feels very much achievable, so it doesn't overload your psychology and burden your physiology – triggering

How to Find Flow

unnecessary threat responses, denting your confidence and cannibalising your ability to find flow. When you try to amp up the intensity in your activity to initiate flow, do so in incremental gains. Increase the difficulty levels slowly. Aim for goals that feel achievable and then progressively take more positive risks. Your psyche and neurology will thank you and be far more resilient when it matters most.

Pitch your perspective

We cannot always change the task or goal before us, but we can always change our perspective of the situation. How we interpret the challenge determines the level of perceived threat and the severity of the stress reaction and our evolutionary errors. In other words, the optimal level of challenge or complexity required for flow is a *perceived* subjective phenomenon; it is dependent upon our perspective. It is important to remember that all the challenges we face are filtered through our perceptual lens – a lens that is not only fickle, at times fluctuating at the whim of a feeling, but also highly malleable.

When I coached tennis, players would often find themselves too stressed to find flow when returning serves. They felt rushed and would tighten up, bracing themselves for what's to come. To intervene, I would serve a bucket of balls to them from halfway down the court – this closer distance significantly reduced the time they had to prepare, anticipate and hit the return. This naturally made them feel even more rushed but, once they adjusted

Invite the Intensity

and started to loosen up under the increased intensity, I returned to the baseline – where servers would normally be positioned. The players immediately felt like they had more time. Nothing had changed technically; they were still returning a normal serve, but the new perspective helped them feel more composed in the challenge and made the challenge level feel more optimal.

The action here is take the time to pitch your perspective of the situation so that it helps you to become optimally challenged or/and highly motivated. For example, I have had the privilege of coaching women to find their flow when giving birth. Unfortunately, the plethora of movies painting a picture of pain and suffering cause many people to perceive childbirth as a gruesome, negative experience. When we change our perspective to see childbirth as an optimal human challenge, one that the body is designed to perform, then we can invite the intensity of the performance – we can see it as a different type of marathon. With a bit more reframing, we can see the physical intensity as pressure, not pain, natural surges of the body releasing the baby from the womb. Instead of tightening, causing any number of complications, we can work with our body and let it happen, creating an amazingly positive experience – not despite the intensity, but because of it. It is a privilege I have also witnessed first-hand with my wife giving birth in this manner, twice. The net result, two magnificent experiences that are a highlight of her life.

How to Find Flow

Turn nerves into excitement

Coaching elite performers is a challenging business – it often involves managing a lot of unnecessary drama. When people have spent months, even years, training for an event, the stakes are high. Nick was a golfer who certainly loved his game, but struggled with staying in the zenith of the Flow Model, always tipping into the red during big events. Playing in front of the TV cameras turned his stomach inside out. His knees would shake, and he would get what athletes call 'the yips'. In his mind, this was a catastrophe, a waste of decades of hard work. He asked me whether I could ease his nerves. To his amazement, I told him that the physiological stress he was feeling, which had been debilitating up until this point, was not the issue. 'In fact, once you are able to get your mental game under control, you will rely on this same physiological arousal to dial into flow,' I said. Slowly he learnt that these physiological responses helped him to galvanise his senses and sharpen his attention to relevant aspects of the task at hand, amplifying his state of presence. Rather it was the psychological anxiety or mental stress that came with his physical arousal that was hindering his flow. Helping him to separate his physical (somatic) and mental (psychological) arousal became a game-changer. Once he had learnt to calm his Thinking Brain and reduce the mental arousal, while keeping his physiological arousal, he was able

Invite the Intensity

to turn what had once been distress into eustress, friction into flow.

Contrary to how we may feel sometimes, it is always possible to calm our mind while capitalising on the benefits of 'physiological stress'. For simple tasks that require only learnt behaviour, such as running, there is almost no such thing as detrimental physical arousal. Even if our knees are shaking or we can't keep still, by managing our approach towards flow and trusting our Being Brain to perform, we can use this physical activation to supercharge our body and leapfrog us into the zenith of an optimally perceived level of challenge. If tasks are cognitively or technically complex, however, such as a game of chess, business negotiation or ice skating, then too much physical arousal can limit our output potential.

It is helpful to remember that, physiologically, there is little difference between nerves and excitement – the body is producing the same amount of arousal. By changing how you perceive arousal (bodily flutters, increased heart rate and alertness) – from an onset of nerves to an arrival of excitement – you can use the arousal to your advantage, to increase your motivation and focus to keep you at an optimal level of intensity.

So, if you are facing a task and you feel a sudden rush of nerves, before changing the goal to reduce the intensity, try to use the physiological stress to your advantage.

How to Find Flow

Embody your strengths

Many of us take time to warm up to our best, though we may not always have this luxury. When expectant faces are waiting for our response or the deadline is looming, we must act. In these moments, it is helpful to lead with our strengths. For example, if you are at a cocktail party and an attractive person walks up to you, talk about something you like to talk about; if you are serving to stay in a match and the intensity gets too much, hit your favourite serve; if you are starting a new job, begin with tasks that you know you are good at. Craft your actions around your strengths. This is the basis of job-crafting or life-crafting. If you don't know what your strengths are in your particular activities, take the time to do a strengths test or ask those around you for input. Knowing what your strengths are will help you lean in to the challenge and complexity knowing you have a few arrows in your quiver.

Set effective expectations

Our expectations can become obstacles towards creating optimal challenges. How we feel going into a challenge, the resultant confidence and joy we take from adversity, and our general state of happiness in life largely depends on the ratio of expectation to success. If we have expectations in proportion to our achievements, we will likely feel good about the challenges ahead and garner a higher self-esteem than when we have

Invite the Intensity

unrealistic expectations. It follows that the higher the self-esteem, the less likely we are to feel the need to set unrealistic expectations. If our expectations are too high, it instantly creates a neurological discord, triggering our evolutionary errors. Even if a working parent juggles both a job and full-time parenting duties, for example, and is doing a good job parenting and hitting targets at work, they may not derive a sense of achievement and self-esteem if their expectations are to excel at both jobs – this is a common reality for many working parents.

So if you feel that you are overstretched or spread too thin, check your expectations. Ask yourself, 'Are my expectations too high?', 'Are my expectations in line with what can sustainably be achieved in this circumstance?' If not, dial them back to a more exciting and realistic level; trying to be a superhero is not going to help you find flow.

Respect recovery

We cannot *revel* in a challenge or stay curious in deep complexity if we do not have the psychic energy to deal with the intensity. To put it another way, if our batteries are depleted, our body will naturally go into safe mode to conserve energy. Nick Troutman explains:

> 'I've learnt over the years that I can make promises of rest to my body and push it to its limit, but if you don't keep those promises of recovery and keep pushing, then there are always consequences.

How to Find Flow

> My annoying injuries have always been when I've known I was too tired and feeling sore, but I pushed anyway, and then something breaks down. I say to myself, "I'm just going to do one more ... I'll rest tomorrow", and that's when I get hurt. Over the years, I've learnt that proactive recovery is an important part of my training.'

In my experience of working with high achievers, the value of recovery is notoriously overlooked. People seem to think that simply working or training *harder* is the way to advance – that to get ahead, they have to *do more*. This is so common that working on minimal sleep and operating while energy is depleted is commonly lauded as some kind of eminent sign of success; superhero status is often given to those boasting the most extreme work-hard, play-hard lifestyle. But this approach has drastic consequences that often go unseen, affecting our neurology, stamina, motivation, engagement levels and ability to commit 100 per cent of our psychic energy to a task. If we do not actively pause to restore then fatigue can manifest into all sorts of issues, such as distraction, low motivation, disengagement, relationship miscommunication and, at extremes, burnout, ill-being, unregistered learning, neurological decay and, in the long term, neurological conditions. Aside from actualising moments of peak performance, rest and recovery are essential for brain development and the synaptic pruning

Invite the Intensity

required for neuroplasticity to occur. Decent sleep is researched to improve nerve cell communication, boost immune functions, aid memory retention, remove toxins from our brains, consolidate learning, install muscle memory and help to process the day, emotionally and mentally, so that we can clear our attentional bandwidth and ready ourselves for tomorrow.[105] As I often say to my coachees, 'There is no point building a Formula One car if you are going to run it on low-grade gasoline, let alone pungent fumes.' Maintaining high levels of energy and vitality should be an important part of anyone's day-to-day management and yearly planning.

To meet the exuberant necessities of flow, it helps to make the distinction between physical rest and psychic recovery. We can be fully rested by getting enough sleep and fresh blood into our muscles, but we can still feel unrecovered. *Recovery* is not just about securing rest, it is also about adding balance to our life, reducing conflicting stressors, releasing unwanted thoughts and feelings, and invigorating other parts of ourselves that may not see much light of day. Lying on a sofa may be restful, but may not leave us feeling zestful. Contrary to what we might think, restorative activities often require us to be active. For example, yoga can be very active, yet also a highly restorative practice. Holistic recovery comes from engaging in an array of activities that typically oppose what we commonly do. If you are stuck in an office all the time, you may need to let loose for a night out, visit the

How to Find Flow

sauna, do some gardening or climb a mountain in order to feel revitalised and recovered. The *quality* of these acts is critical. Spending time with friends or family who add stress to our life is not great recovery. Equally, we can be doing a restorative activity, but if the intention is not to recover, it will not get the required effect. For example, being in a sauna or doing some gardening while thinking about our stresses will not recover our psychic energy. Recovery involves activities that are replenishing and invigorating; we should leave the activity with more vibrancy than when we arrived.

While a rest and recovery plan should be unique to your situation, you can get started by doing what many of my clients do:

- *Mini recovery sessions multiple times each day.* These may include practices such as belly breathing, thought diffusion, gratitude or body relaxation techniques. Whether it is taking one minute every hour or breathing deeply in between email replies, set yourself up for success with recovery routines that you can adopt in a matter of seconds.
- *Regular sleep of over seven or eight hours a night.* While many people may claim that they only need five or six hours' sleep a night, only people with a certain genetic disposition can generate the same neurological recovery and performance potential on fewer than eight hours. Furthermore,

Invite the Intensity

it is my experience that clients who have physically demanding lifestyles find that they are mentally, emotionally and physically at their optimum when consistently getting eight or more hours of sleep. Quality of sleep trumps quantity. If you are unsure as to how rested your system is or the quality level of your sleep, wear a biofeedback device for a few weeks. Until then, I challenge you to prioritise sleeping for one extra hour every night to see how it affects your ability to invite an optimal level of intensity into your day-to-day.

- At least *one full day away from your primary activity* each week, in which you engage in recovery-focused activities.
- A *two-day mini recovery holiday each month*, at a minimum.
- A *full week's recovery holiday* every year, at a minimum.

Fitting all this in can seem impossible at times, especially for parents, carers or those working seventy-hour weeks. In some cases, you may have to pick and choose wisely, be creative or do it with your dependants. For elite athletes, quality sleep and recovery are starting to top the charts of their training regimes, with physical-, technical-, nutritional- and performance-based demands built around it. My question to you is what would you have to sacrifice to prioritise your rest and recovery and fully

How to Find Flow

charge your batteries? Of course, you can get away with less – most people do. But ask yourself, are you at your optimum every day? Are you doing a good job or being your best? If you don't respect your rest and recovery, what you may be unknowingly sacrificing is your own flow.

Next up, in this last stage of becoming and staying STEADY, we will discuss the most valuable asset you own – your attention, and how you can use it to steady your state in your preparations.

LET'S RECAP

Once you have put on your Flow Mindset and built your blueprint for flow for an upcoming event, you can invite the upcoming intensity by a) increasing your motivation, best done through choosing intrinsic motives; acting with autonomy; identifying your interest; and taking time to fulfil your emotional needs; and b) creating and sustaining the *optimal* level of intensity that is needed to slip into flow.

To help you, we have covered the flow skills of inviting the challenge:
- changing your relationship with failure
- scaffolding your challenges
- optimising your perspective
- leveraging your arousal
- leading with your strengths

Invite the Intensity

- managing your expectations
- respecting your recovery

YOUR CHALLENGE

Staying STEADY is not a philosophical approach like getting READY. It involves active and continuous participation to steady your consciousness. The more important or triggering the event, the more you will need to be proactive in your preparations. If you are not managing your mind, it will manage you. The advice I give all my clients is to develop these mental skills into habits as quickly as possible, so that they are installed for when you need them most.

I now challenge you to spend a moment prior to engaging in your activity to repeat the mantra, 'challenge me'. Take a moment to get excited for the event and then invite an intense experience. If painting, remember your love for art and then challenge your self-expression. If singing, enjoy your autonomy and then challenge your commitment to the song's intention. If returning a serve in sport, remember your love for the game and then challenge the server to hit their best serve. If building a business, take time to fulfil your emotional needs and then utilise your strengths.

Chapter 7

SHAPE YOUR STATE

ONCE WE ARE READY, HAVE CREATED A FLOW blueprint, amped up our motivations and invited the intensity, this may be enough to slip into a state of flow. There are times, however, when our consciousness still gets hijacked. We may wake up one morning, ready to find flow as we juggle getting ourselves and our kids ready, for example. We have envisioned how it might go and feel steady when taking a calm, peaceful shower. Then, as we are swiping the trickling shampoo out of our eyes, we hear a scream. Within a few seconds, we have two demanding kids fighting over who has the green towel and who has the blue one. As we intervene, barely able to see through the shampoo, our arm accidentally moves the shower lever to the coldest setting, and the onset of freezing cold water suddenly takes us aback. Shocked and unsettled, we bark at our kids to leave, only to feel a sense of frustration or shame in how we responded.

Shape Your State

I'm sure many a parent could add any number of follow-on stories to how, in one moment, they can feel calm and on course, and the next, left sweeping up the contents of their consciousness from the floor.

In flow, thoughts, sensations or emotions may emerge, but we quickly accept them for what they are and then refocus our attention to what is in front. Since there is no friction to them, they disappear as quickly as they arrive; we remain present. In the lead-up to flow, when we are not deeply engaged in the task, however, the frailties of our attention are continuously at the whim of any internal and external noise or turbulence. It is important, therefore, that we learn how to self-regulate in the moment. This chapter aims to give you a few more tools for your toolbox to help steady your state from rising distractions and keep the contents of your consciousness aligned with flow.

(Note: By 'consciousness' I mean awareness – what we are psychologically conscious of. While at times this may include a higher spiritual connection to a greater interconnected felt consciousness, for the purposes of this book, think of consciousness as your awareness.)

ATTUNING YOUR ATTENTION

Caring about what we attend to is probably the most powerful skill any human can learn. How we choose to spend and form our attention affects everything. If we place our attention on our anger, then anger will consume

How to Find Flow

our consciousness and actions. If we place our attention on the beauty of the world around us, we will be filled with optimism and gratitude. If we place our attention on the to-do list, productive actions will follow. Whatever we place our attention on will become important, even if it is unimportant. Ultimately, what we do, think and feel, and the meaning and satisfaction we draw from life, is a direct result of the quality of our attention. It is the gateway to our consciousness. It is why our attention is the most valued gift we can give to ourselves, and to others.

It is also important to value our attention because it is limited. Neuroanatomically, the PFC, the part of our brain responsible for directing our attention, cannot be 'fully switched on' all the time; instead, its level of engagement varies throughout the day, with peak performance limited to a few focused hours.[106]

Manipulating our attention is not often at the top of the self-development list, because it is a meta skill, meaning a skill that underpins many others. In this case, attentional regulation reinforces many more well-known skills, such as thought management, mindfulness or goal-setting. When we start to proactively attune our attention to prepare for flow, it is helpful to understand some of the levers we can pull.

Initially, our focus can be either *internal* or *external*. If the torch of our attention is focused internally, we may be more aware of how we feel or what we are thinking. If our torch is focused externally, we may be consumed

Shape Your State

with watching a butterfly flap its wings, the mark on the basketball hoop we are aiming at or the facial expression of the person that we are talking to. At times, it may be helpful to direct our attention internally, if we need to put on our Flow Mindset or self-regulate our feelings, for example, but when we get to the action and are engaging in the activity, it becomes more helpful to externalise our attention. For example, we may want to focus our attention internally as we assess and amplify our motivation while walking to our desk, but when starting to reply to emails, we want our attention to be focused externally on what we are reading and writing.

While our attention can be calibrated internally or externally, it can also have a *narrow* or *wide* focus. When stressed, for example, our attention will naturally narrow to try to limit the information we are processing so that we can feel more in control of the situation. This focused attention often forces the mind to become rigid and our vision to be limited. It is why it is difficult to innovate or see alternative perspectives when distressed, as our attention is busy picking out isolated information – often reinforcing our position. It is also why the extended use of focusing on a screen during work is causing so many stress-related issues. Conversely, when calm and open-minded, our attention is softer and wider. We have greater access to our peripheral vision, helping us to see more of the situation.

How to Find Flow

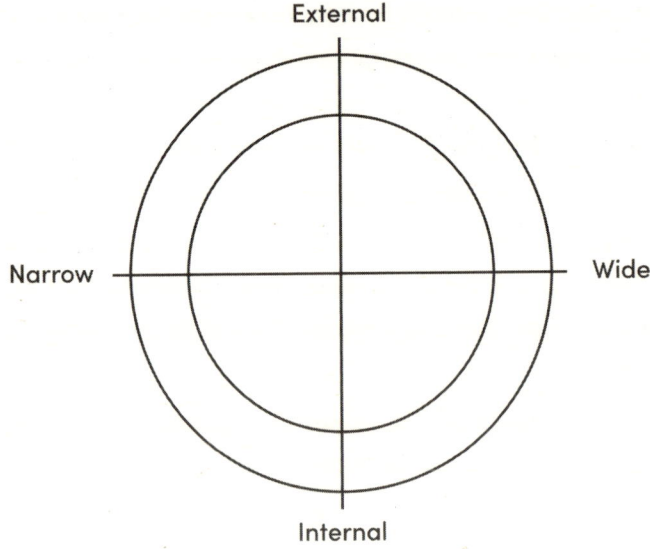

Aspects of attention

If shooting basketball free-throws, for example, it would be most beneficial to regulate our attention towards an *external narrow* focus, as the task is very specific, and we want to zone in to a single act. If the task is more reactive, such as welcoming people at a cocktail party, then it would be most beneficial to have an *external wide* focus. Alternatively, an *internal narrow* focus may be suitable for unearthing personal trauma in a counselling session, and an *internal wide* focus would be best when staying relaxed during a physical warm-up.

Flipping between focusing our attention internally and externally, wide and narrow, is a skill called attentional flexibility, which requires practice, like training any skill. So, before we move on, put the book down and practise

Shape Your State

switching your attention from internal to external, narrow to wide. Witness what it does to your experience.

Evoke helpful emotions

One powerful attentional tool at our disposal is the ability to elicit certain feelings and emotions. We all know how powerful emotions can be when unwanted, as we blush, cry or throw a tantrum when they cloud our consciousness. It is my experience that, when people apply emotional intelligence, it is generally when things are unsteady or 'wrong', like processing an unwanted emotion. Rarely do we actively harness the power of our own emotions when things are going well.

Just as a pianist selects a sequence of notes to bring a song to life, we too can select a sequence of feelings to quell the tyrannical rule of our Thinking Brain and actively prepare for flow. Chris 'Douggs' McDougall, World Record Holder and World Champion base jumper and skydiver, explains:

> 'Before I enter flow, I generally smile because I'm actually really relaxed … in this calm trance-like state. Everyone thinks I must get this big adrenaline rush when I jump off cliffs and fly low to the ground, but I don't. Instead, I help myself to be super calm and really tranquil. If I'm too scared or amped up, it becomes very dangerous.'

How to Find Flow

We may all have an inclination for what gets us 'in the mood' for flow, based on our preferences and the task at hand – some want to rap aggressively, while others prefer to be Zen-like and peaceful – but the important point here is to proactively create 'the mood'.

To curate helpful feelings, people commonly turn to external noises, such as listening to music or talking to other people. While these common techniques may work temporarily, it is more powerful to develop the internal skills to attune our attention and create the emotional landscape we want to embody. Over time, I have noticed that the feelings that seem to be the most helpful to the widest variety of people are *curiosity*, *playfulness* and *gratefulness*. These feelings seem to activate the parasympathetic nervous system, open our minds to new experiences, increase the coherence of our heartbeat (more on this later) and help us invite upcoming challenges or complexity. While I suggest you practise evoking these feelings to get you started, I also suggest you experiment to find the emotions that work for you in your given context.

To start, practise embodying different feelings in your preparations, to get you in the mood, and experiment with varying the intensity level of each emotion. Being grateful can certainly help our neurology sync up, for example, but if the feeling of gratitude is too strong, it becomes a distraction in and of itself. Equally, the timing of when we activate certain emotions is key. Listening

Shape Your State

to the soundtrack of the movie *Rocky* may get us fired up, but if we listen to this music too far in advance, it might get us too fired up, too early, and leak valuable energy. In the days leading up to an event, we want to save our energy and stay calm and relaxed, with small pockets of high intensity as we practise being in flow. Within an hour of the event, we want our arousal and focus to increase towards the event gradually. We don't want to peak too early.

Ultimately, you want to be able to elicit a range of emotions to suit different contexts. There will be times when you need to generate feelings to help you relax and conserve energy, and there will be times when you need to be fired up, focused, present and alert. Keep experimenting until you have a few feelings, and preferred intensity levels of these feelings, that you believe will help shape your state at different stages of your preparations.

Sustain your attention

Learning to flicker your attention to an optimal position relevant to the task at hand is an important aspect of attentional control to master. But just as important, if not more so, is the ability to sustain our attention and concentrate for extended periods of time. With the many modern-day distractions – such as mobile scrolling, and the increased forms of neurodiversity and attentional 'disorders', such as attention deficit hyperactivity disorder (ADHD), common even in six-year-olds – your attention is

How to Find Flow

probably more distracted than you realise. For example, try focusing your attention on the flame of a candle, or on a single object, for longer than five minutes – see how in control of your attention you are.

Treating undistracted blocks of time as treasurable moments and engaging in deeply concentrated tasks is important attentional training for anyone, no matter their life goals, but it is especially important for flow. Billie Jean King, the tennis player, was known for staring at a tennis ball for twenty minutes prior to going on court, and for good reason. It helped her practise focusing externally, while managing rising internal distractions. Additionally, the ball became so important to her focal awareness that when she walked on court, the tennis ball was all she focused on; it seemed to be the size of a football. All the great athletes and leaders I have met have shown an ability for attentional control, whether they have developed it consciously or not. After scoring eighty-one points in an NBA game, basketballer Kobe Bryant explains: 'When you get in that zone ... everything is just one noise. You don't think about your surroundings like what's going on with the crowd or your team, you're kinda locked in.'[107]

Practise being present

It is clear that negative thoughts are unhelpful and make up a large portion of the internal noise that distracts our attention. But it is also important to recognise that positive thinking can be just as unhelpful. The advice to 'just think

Shape Your State

positively' is bandied about as a standard solution to mental distraction and doubt, but while it may help to counter the negative chatter in our consciousness, it is still a mechanism of our Thinking Brain. Positive and negative thinking are two sides of the same coin, and while positive thinking may be more helpful than projecting negative outcomes, contrasting the 'good' against the 'bad', the 'right' against the 'wrong', comes with a price; they both derail our attention from being present.

Ordinarily, we are so entrenched in our thoughts that we fail to recognise them as thoughts. For the most part, we identify so quickly with our thoughts that we get lost reacting to them; we become so attached to them that we fail to recognise our psychological environment.

It is helpful, therefore, to always remember that no matter how strong a particular thought, or thread of thoughts, may be, it does not represent who you are, and there is no need to react to it. Acknowledging that a thought is simply a transitory signal that appears in our consciousness, not always worthy of our engagement, helps to gain back control of our attention. It is in this non-judgemental diffusion from our own thoughts and self-dialogue that we become empowered to navigate through the noise rather than be reactive to it. As yogi Sara Page explains:

> 'We, as humans, have this intellect, this mind that is busy, that likes to delve into its memories and to

How to Find Flow

predict the future. Creating an array of thoughts in any one moment. All this complexity disconnects us from the moment and the task at hand. If we didn't have any of that, then we'd naturally be in a greater harmony. When we can see that most of our distractions are just imaginings of the mind, wishing to be entertained, then we're able to become present far more easily, and move into those deeper states, such as flow. It's so simple: when we still the mind, become present, we allow our true nature to flow. It helps to find ways to awaken the mind, not get on the bus and journey with our thoughts.'

There is no point disliking our thoughts, just as there is no point becoming angry with a pre-programmed computer. They are what they are, but that doesn't mean we need to take them seriously or bend our attention towards them. Deciphering whether every thought is helpful or unhelpful would be unbearably tedious and painful, if not impossible, and it would certainly be distracting when it comes to being in flow. In flow, our psyche is fused with the act, not the whim of any rising thought.

I have talked about the distraction of our thoughts, but the same can be said about our emotions, sensations, perspectives, volition or anything else that consumes your consciousness. If we give any one aspect of our attention too much attachment, we run the risk of jumping down that rabbit hole, reacting to it and then

Shape Your State

becoming enslaved to it. It is important, therefore, to become well practised in your ability to awaken your attention back to the present moment so that you can free yourself from your attachments to the contents of your consciousness and, at the same time, free up your attentional bandwidth for flow.

Aptly named, given the gift it provides, the 'present' is the perfect platform to become absorbed into the act and enter flow. Becoming comfortable with being present is a skill – something the ego and Thinking Brain will try hard to inhibit. If you do not practise the attentional skill of holding a state of presence, then even if you find flow frequently, you may not have the attentional control to sustain a flow experience for any length of time.

Are you ready to train your attentional flexibility? Let's put this into practice:
- When you are ready, stare at a wall in front of you. Alternatively, you can stare at an object, candle or a tree if it helps.
- Keep your eyes fixed on one small spot. As you hold a state of presence, every time you notice something appear in your consciousness, metaphorically put it on an imagined shelf a couple of feet in front of you.
- Given our natural state of embodied cognition, I suggest physically moving your arms to pick the rising distraction out of your head with your hand and then place it on the shelf.

How to Find Flow

- Practise awakening your mind from your distractions and become comfortable in the detached space. Experiment with prolonging your capacity for presence for as long as you can, not by trying to eradicate thought (this is impossible), but by becoming highly competent in detaching your attention from the rising contents of your consciousness. This attentional control is an integral skill for increasing the duration and intensity of flow experiences.

Protect your attention

The ability to say no and protect your space for concentration and connection is a necessary flow skill. Our psychic energy and attentional bandwidth are finite, after all. The quality of each moment is shaped by our attention, what we select to attend to and the intensity of this attention – also known as our psychological selection. While this moment-to-moment psychological selection is continuously being distracted by society, culture, colleagues and our devices, it is ours to give away. We may choose to readily give it away, as we scroll through social media, but if we are to frequently find flow we must protect our attentional bandwidth so that our psychological selection can fully concentrate on the task at hand. Whether it is saying no to immediately replying to incoming emails so that we can focus on a task or limiting a gathering to a few people to improve

Shape Your State

the quality of connection and clarity of communication, we need to create boundaries around our attention if flow is to flourish.

Control the controllables

When in the red, much of our mental bandwidth is consumed by things we cannot control. Whether it is how someone else will perceive how we look, how an opponent will perform or the behaviour of our kids as we enter the supermarket, our Thinking Brain loves to revel in these narratives. Why? Because when we cannot control something in its entirety, our response is to get triggered and think more – keeping the Thinking Brain rooted in the captain's chair. If you are unsure about what I mean, I suggest you reflect back to a time when you felt stressed. Go ahead, do this now. Was your attention on something that you didn't have 100 per cent control over?

At times, we may have a level of influence over something or someone, but, for the most part, we are limited to our equipment, our actions, our body, our words, our thoughts and our feelings. The saying 'control the controllables' helps us to focus our attention on what we have absolute control over. In doing so, we instantly become empowered. The friction and stress of trying to control something we do not have a dominion over disappears. We get back the full breadth of our attentional bandwidth and, once again, can steady ourselves for flow.

How to Find Flow

PROFESSIONALISING YOUR PREPARATIONS

Taking the time to set yourself up for success and shape your state works, full stop. In this chapter so far, I have hopefully explained that, in order to shape your state towards flow, you need to hold the reins to your attention. If not, you leave your consciousness open and subject to distraction. Attuning your attention by evoking emotions, detaching from rising thoughts, sustaining presence and proactively protecting it from the bombardment of noise out there are important skills to integrate into your preparations. Practically, however, it can be overwhelming to remember all of this, which is why I suggest building these lessons into rituals. Professionalising your preparation in this manner will help you embody these skills as habits, making it feel easy and natural to shape your state towards flow.

Preparing yourself, as an elite athlete would, for your daily challenges, may seem over the top, even weird. It may even feel laughable to think about ritualising your preparations before answering an email, having a meeting, picking your kids up from school or playing sport for your local club. But whether you are aware of it or not, you are probably already preparing your state before an event, but perhaps just not in the most optimal manner. Whether it is going to your favourite coffee shop before work, rubbing your hands before typing, listening to music as you pick your kids up or taking a deep breath

Shape Your State

before talking, these little rituals help to manage your mental and emotional states and empower focus before taking on a task. You may only notice these preparations being important to you when something derails your routine and you lose your composure, but these micro behaviours happen all the time. In fact, it is impossible for the brain not to prepare. Given the brain's predictive processing and need for homeostasis, the psyche is continually working to balance the scales. So choosing to not optimise your preparations, or not even entertaining the idea of ritualising your mental preparations, is, more accurately, taking a position to purposefully surrender your mental game – an act of experiential negligence. If there is no structure to your preparations and you 'wing it', simply expecting your psyche to deliver, you will miss the opportunity to systematically shape your state towards flow. Your performances will be at the behest of a thousand and one distractions, fluctuating like a roller coaster. In short, you will be setting yourself up for stress not success, friction not flow.

Once READY and using these skills to stay STEADY, you may find yourself naturally slipping into flow. However, in testing events, even with gold-standard preparations, when the time comes and we find ourselves dancing with the moment, the psyche may just need a little extra help to let it happen rather than make it happen. The next part will give you the skills to do just that.

How to Find Flow

> **LET'S RECAP**
>
> In this chapter, we have covered a range of flow skills to help set yourself up for success:
> - attuning your attention internally and externally, wide and narrow; improving your attentional flexibility
> - evoking helpful emotions to stay calm and conserve your energy, and to amplify your arousal leading into the event
> - practising sustaining presence
> - detaching from rising thoughts to clear the contents of your consciousness
> - protecting your psyche from external distractions
> - professionalising your preparations for any performance
>
> It is now over to you. Find a way to enjoy practising these skills and staying STEADY.

YOUR CHALLENGE

You do not need to be a professional athlete to value your day-to-day performance or experiential quality, nor do you need to be an elite performer to professionalise your preparations. Equally, professionalising your preparations only for important events is selling yourself short.

Shape Your State

I challenge you, therefore, to create your own ritual to help you stay STEADY throughout the day.

Write down how you will integrate a flow skill, or two, into your preparations to help you shape your state for an activity that is important to you. For example, you can choose to attune your attention, external and narrow, by focusing on a tiny mark when shooting free-throws; you may evoke the feeling of curiosity before going into a conversation by taking a deep breath and seeing the other person as a sum of their life experiences; you may practise putting rising thoughts on a shelf as you drive to work.

1) _____
2) _____
3) _____

When you feel you have these skills dialled in, change the list and embed some more skills from your toolbox into helpful habits. See what it does for your satisfaction and performance.

Part 3
FLOW

ALLOWED IN THE TEDx ARENA A FEW DAYS BEFORE I would face my biggest fear, I walked around the stage. It seemed bigger than I had anticipated. The empty velvet-lined seats gave me goosebumps. I imagined where I would stand, how I would hold myself and how I would use the presenter screen that was conveniently hidden in the floor at the front of the stage.

I had spent many nights thinking about my speech, rehearsing line after line and thinking how certain phrases would land with the crowd. As always, I had my accompanying digital presentation ready, loaded with impactful images to add meaning to my words and draw the crowd's attention away from myself, and, on the other speaker's screen, my speaker notes that I used to prompt my memory. Up until now, my Flow Mindset had been a lifesaver. Every time the thought of the event popped into my mind, I would prioritise flow and get READY. I'd embody my flow blueprint and imagine myself speaking with intent, moving my arms hypnotically and delivering the speech in flow. I was truly excited about the challenge. I was READY!

Flow

The day finally arrived, and I had the perfect start. I went for a swim in the ocean, had a tasty breakfast and enjoyed my morning coffee while going over my notes. Arriving at the venue, which was a prestigious university theatre, I could see the crowd lining up with their tickets, waiting to be funnelled into the entrance doors. Realising that the time was soon approaching, my heart fluttered. The impending reality of needing to be my best during one of my biggest weaknesses suddenly dawned on me. But, unlike many prior speaking engagements, I stayed STEADY. I reminded myself of my blueprint, invited the challenge and enjoyed the bump of arousal. I knew that this spike of arousal would help create the intensity I was going to need to get into the zone. I proceeded to head backstage.

I walked into the auditorium, to the speaker's area, and disposed of my belongings. When I greeted the other speakers and organisers, I could almost smell the stench of stress and fear that was wafting through the air. Well versed in staying STEADY and prioritising my preparations to ward off external distractions, I said my greetings and headed for a stroll outside. I was quickly stopped in my tracks by the speaker liaison, who asked me whether I minded going first. Feeling privileged, and maintaining my flow approach, I embraced the challenge and told the organiser that I'd loved to commence proceedings after a quick breath of fresh air.

Taking in the beautiful plants and trees of the university

How to Find Flow

grounds, I stayed focused on my STAFs. I imagined walking out confidently to meet the audience, delivering my first line with composure and clicking into flow as I became absorbed in my opening story. I felt physically pumped and mentally calm and composed. As the start drew near, I headed back inside.

The backstage was now pitch black. Three sound techs dressed in black appeared out of nowhere and proceeded to put a mouth mic on my head, test the sound and put me into position behind the curtain. Feeling a little flustered, I subtly swayed my body from side to side, finding a sense of rhythm and coherence. I directed my attention away from the chaos and distracting noise that was happening around me and went through my STAFs once again. Filling my consciousness with excitement and gratitude for the opportunity, I felt strong and STEADY! In fact, I was astounded by how composed I was feeling. I was even able to help another speaker calm their nerves and adjust their microphone.

The opening theme tune belted out of the speakers, and the audience came to a sudden, dutiful hush. As I peeked through a slit in the heavy curtains, I saw the announcer walking into the bright lights that hovered over the famous carpeted red circle. The applause from over 300 people silenced and, for a few seconds, you could have heard a pin drop. I listened to the presenter introduce the event, highlighting all the speakers to come, and then the stage crew gave me a one-minute countdown. It was time.

Flow

The next minute seemed to go on forever. All I wanted to do was to walk on stage, but with the host finishing off her speech, the crowd clapping in anticipation and the intro music and video staged to play before my entry, a mere sixty seconds felt like ten minutes. To keep my presence and protect my attention from any unwelcome invasion, I ran my finger around the slideshow clicker, using my sense of touch to occupy my consciousness. Finally, I got the nod. I pulled back the curtain and walked towards the red circle on the middle of the stage.

Nearly blinded by the lights, I stood still, waiting for the music and clapping to stop. I scanned the room to acknowledge the crowd and, in the corner of my eye, I noticed the presenter screen on the floor displaying the image the audience should have been looking at behind me. Thinking it might be a technical mistake, I glanced behind to see the same image on the wall. SHIT! I thought. Contrary to what I was told, the technicians had set up the screens to mirror one another. My presenter notes had gone. The prompting phrases that got me through virtually every keynote that I had ever done were not going to be available. Like a bolt of lightning, doubt hijacked my consciousness. The blinding lights suddenly felt very uncomfortable, and my mind went fuzzy and blank. All I could remember was my opening line. The room was now deafeningly quiet. Hundreds of expectant eyes watched on as I froze like a deer in the headlights.

You will find out at the end of Chapter 9 what

How to Find Flow

happened in my TEDx Talk, but, importantly, this experience was one of many that helped confirm the last stages of my cartography to flow.

So far, you have done a great job staying with me, learning to self-lead (READY) and self-regulate (STEADY) towards flow. Before building your personalised ritual for flow, we will now go over the last part of a Flow Mindset: how to give our experience a helping nudge into a state of absorption and effort-less action so that we can self-actualise and FLOW. In the following chapters, we will unpack how to allow ourselves to become absorbed and be effortless in our action. You will learn not necessarily to find flow but to *allow* flow. After all, flow is a natural state of harmony that we need to allow. This is the real icing on the cake – it has helped me personally and professionally, and continues to help athletes, executives and people across the world find their flow, as I'm sure it will for you.

Chapter 8

BE ABSORBED

IN PART 1, WE LEARNT THAT FLOW INVOLVES AN absorption into the act, characterised by concentrated action and a merging of action and awareness; we no longer think about ourselves, just the act, and we can often distort our normal sense of time. This absorption occurs primarily because the Thinking Brain is not holding the reins to our attention. Without the slow, conscious and reflective thinking part of our brain holding our experience, we are allowed to experience each moment as it unfolds and become absorbed into the task. Unnecessary aspects of our cognition that would slow us down get peeled back, allowing the Being Brain to grapple with the situation to much greater effect. This chapter will now dive into the practicalities of creating this absorption, most notably how to bridge the Thinking Brain and the Being Brain so that they can work in partnership.

MOVING BEYOND THE THINKING BRAIN

Common concerns I hear about becoming absorbed are, 'Don't we rely on our Thinking Brain to make decisions?' and 'Aren't we likely to make more mistakes when completely absorbed?' These are both great questions, though it is helpful to understand that decisions do not happen in our Thinking Brain alone. Hundreds of thousands of decisions are made during a performance – far too many to be made by our advanced frontal cortex (PFC) alone. Catching a ball, for example, involves thousands of micro decisions that are affected by the new information gained every microsecond by the stimulus from our body and the environment. The restrictiveness of our clothing, flexibility of our shoes, interference from the sunlight, softness of the ground beneath us, position of our shoulders, clarity of our vision and trust in our ability to dive towards the ball all go into the micro decisions we make in each moment. As scientist Duarte Araújo has dedicated years of research to point out, 'our perception, action, and environment are intricately linked to define the intelligence we use to make decisions'.[108] We don't just have embodied cognition, we also have ecological cognition: countless ever-evolving interactions with the environment that feed into our micro decisions.

The processing of this information is far too complex and rapid for the PFC to curate and process on its own. Rather, it is a result of our Being Brain, sensory receptors,

Be Absorbed

cognisant bodies and embodied intelligence working as one to receive and navigate each micro decision and permit the free-flowing information that we take for granted. If our Thinking Brain was to try to govern this process, it would drastically choke our ability; information processing would be limited, slow and overwhelmed at best. It is precisely the downregulation (i.e. deactivation) of the Thinking Brain and the absorption that amplifies our ability to make rapid decisions.

No matter how technical or analytical the task may be, the Being Brain is captaining our cognition and operating the ship when we are in flow. Consequently, activating the Being Brain on demand has been at the forefront of performance science for some time. For example, Dr Charles Limb, a neuroscientist at the University of California, found that, when using functional magnetic resonance imaging (fMRI) to examine the brainwave activity of jazz musicians and freestyle rappers, the neural activity of the medial and lateral PFC (often associated with Thinking Brain activity) significantly reduced when these performers were in the zone.[109] Accordingly, the US Air Force has experimented with transcranial direct-current stimulation (tDCS) to try to shut down the Thinking Brain when soldiers are learning and performing. By producing higher-than-normal electrical impulses to specific parts of the PFC, the Thinking Brain becomes overstimulated and effectively shuts down, inhibiting conscious and critical thought, and improving learning

How to Find Flow

speeds and performance.[110] Andy McKinley, a biomedical engineer at the Air Force Research Laboratory at Wright-Patterson Air Force Base in Ohio, explains:

> 'The military has been looking at how to improve vigilance for the past fifty or sixty years. If you imagine learning to ride a bike or a manual vehicle, your process is very conscious at first, because you're thinking about all the steps. But, as you do it more often, it becomes more and more unconscious. We wanted to see if we could accelerate that transition with tDCS.'[111]

Indeed, they did, cutting in half the training time it took for novice marksmen to become experts. 'We've never seen that with anything else,' explains McKinley. In an alternative study in Australia, tDCS was applied to thirty-three people as they tried to solve the notoriously tricky 'nine-dot' logic problem. Not one participant was able to crack it without stimulation, yet 40 per cent among those augmented with tDCS solved it.[112] It is also why studies examining the use of alcohol to inhibit our cognitive functions find that those who are moderately inebriated score better on insight-based creative tasks. Equally, studies that involve a secondary task specifically to distract the participant's Thinking Brain from the primary task consistently display improved problem-solving ability and enhanced skill execution. I'm sure you

Be Absorbed

can probably relate to this when, away from the desk, in a shower, playing sport or on a walk, your best ideas or insights seem to find you. As Albert Einstein once suggested: 'The intellect has little to do on the road to discovery. There comes a leap in consciousness, call it intuition or what you will, the solution comes to you, and you don't know how or why.'[113] Although, with modern neuroscientific research, we do know why, and how.

BRIDGING THE BRAINS

Edward Slingerland, Distinguished University Scholar at the University of British Columbia, outlines articulately in his book *Trying Not to Try* that our Being Brain (hot cognition) is inherently emotional, and our Thinking Brain (cold cognition) is the epitome of non-emotional cognition. Further, Slingerland highlights that it is the misalignment of these two brains that often leads us to feel that we need to do one thing yet think we should do another[114] – like debating at the café counter whether we should go for the pastry or not.

Like it or not, the two brains need each other. An untrained Being Brain, like that in a child, may result in biased, impulsive and low-quality decision-making, such as supporting someone in a debate because we are attracted to them rather than the validity of their argument; or withdrawing our life savings because gambling at the casino one night was fun. A life ruled

How to Find Flow

by an untrained Being Brain would likely take us back to tribal warfare. In turn, an untrained Thinking Brain will never take a risk and will ruminate until the cows come home. A life lived through the Thinking Brain will ultimately result in a highly rational, detached, sheltered, judgemental, boring, distracted and unfulfilled life.

Even in situations that require logic and consideration, utilising the Thinking Brain's assets alone may not be best suited; for example, many a dictator has presented logical justifications for their actions, yet their perspectives may not have been true or their actions right. Equally, a calculated decision or perfect plan doesn't necessarily lead to a better subjective experience; for example, in a study assessing the subjective experience of eating fruit jam, participants who had to explain the rationale to rating their favourite jam rated lower scores to the jam's quality than those who were asked to give an immediate answer.[115] The results indicated that those who were prompted to use their Thinking Brain to manage their experience and choices had an overall lower quality of experience. Similarly, in another study, participants who had to explain their reasons for choosing a poster to take home with them were found to regret their decision months later, while those who simply picked one instinctively, using their Being Brain, seemed more satisfied with their choice.[116]

I'm not saying that we should discard the Thinking Brain – neither brain is better than the other; rather, it

Be Absorbed

is when they try to work in isolation or conflict with each other that problems arise. The ability to turn the battle of the brains into a collaborative dance is a characteristic not only of allowing flow, but also of successful people in general. For example, Barbara Sahakian, a Professor at the Department of Psychiatry at the University of Cambridge, found that entrepreneurs and managers were equally compatible when using their Thinking Brain to make decisions throughout a number of tasks, but when it came to tasks that required rapid decision-making, entrepreneurs were far more adept in using their Being Brain.[117] In short, entrepreneurs had better-trained Being Brains and were better able to switch between brains – mostly likely because their Being Brain was better trusted by their Thinking Brain; there was a better relationship between the two parts of their cognition.

When trust and synergy prevail between the two brains, we get the best of both worlds, using each brain for what it is designed to do. In most cases, this looks like utilising our Thinking Brain to direct our attention and keep us on track, while the Being Brain is trusted to actualise the intended performance. Like the rider and the horse, when both brains are working in unison towards one aim, a beautiful synergy can occur that allows the horse to perform at its best. In this harmonious marriage, we allow focus to become absorption, and logical values to become lived virtues. Yet if the rider tries to over-control the horse, then the battle for power takes over and the special relationship doesn't stand a chance to bloom.

Power up your presence

To create this collaborative dance, we first need to find ways for the Thinking and Being Brains to be in unison. Typically, both brains are not dancing together because they are busy running after different agendas, so ordering them to suddenly cohere rarely works. To initiate this cohesion, it is critical that we take a moment to slow the brains down to interconnect, synchronise and then speed back up. Like encouraging two kids to play together, we need first to sit them down and explain why it will be to their benefit, helping them connect and align goals, and then let them run off to play.

When helping people bridge their brains, there is often a resistance to slowing down – people describe not having the time or luxury to do so. For example, when coaching an executive, Angela, who was trying to enjoy a high-performing and demanding lifestyle, her rhetoric continuously disallowed any notion of slowing down: 'I don't have time! I barely have time for this meeting,' she told me. I examined her schedule, and she was partially right. Every waking hour of every day was accounted for with meetings or appointments; she even had to schedule in time for her partner, otherwise he never got a look in. Her mind had created a strong justification for her hectic life: she had an important job and couldn't afford to let

Be Absorbed

herself or others down; she had to stay fit; she already didn't have enough hours in the day to get all her work done, she believed. She certainly had not come to me to hear the advice of slowing down! What she wanted to know was how she could speed up to supersonic. So, contrary to what she was expecting, I had to confront her with the quality of her presence. Accordingly, I pointed out every time her mind wandered in our sessions, and questioned the quality of her engagement in each of her tasks. On reflection, she could see how the depth of her presence was very shallow. She was quickly distracted, often thinking about the next task rather than focusing on the present one. She was so fuelled by her fears and achieving arbitrary goals that made her look productive, that she was locked in a hamster wheel chasing her own tail. To intervene, I suggested that sometimes we need to slow down to speed up. To help her understand, we practised a few tasks with different approaches: firstly, in a state of flux, which was her usual experience; and then in a state of absolute presence. To get there, she first had to take ten seconds to connect her entire psyche to her breath. This gave her less time to do the task, but, to her surprise, she completed it faster. Once she realised that she could get more done by paying more attention to each task throughout the day, she realised that she had more time than she thought. By slowing down and powering up her presence, she also became aware of her bias to micromanage, and realised that she probably

How to Find Flow

didn't need to have so many meetings in the diary. Slowly but surely, she realised that, counterintuitively, slowing down saved her time – for it was in the slowing down that she could synchronise discorded aspects of her psyche, reduce the stress and cortisol in her system that was otherwise powering her hamster wheel mentality, and minimise the background psychic conflict that was otherwise competing for energy. As a result, she could then speed back up in unison – more present, more effective and more productive.

Sharpen your senses

A tried and tested method to initiate this slowing down and synchronisation of your psyche is to sharpen your sensory perception and, by doing so, create an instant state of presence. By directing our Thinking Brain to focus on a Being Brain act, such as a sensory experience, we firstly build a bridge between the two brains and, secondly, mobilise the Being Brain by activating a sensory experience. Once synchronisation has taken place and both brains are trusting of each other and behind the same agenda, we can amp back up to smash the challenge.

Connecting to our senses is an innate skill that can be done by anyone, anywhere, even in the heat of competition or the intimacy of a conversation. In sitting in this space, it is common for any underlying conflict to eventually emerge. If so, this is great news, as the psyche

Be Absorbed

is providing you with an opportunity to shed a conflict that may be blocking you from entering flow. You now have the space to process and resolve accordingly.

Before we get started practising this skill, it is important to note that paying attention to something is different from thinking about it. Thinking about our breath, for example, is very different from filling our attention with the sensory experience of breathing. When we do pay close attention to a particular sense, it is almost impossible to have concurrent thoughts; they compete to fill our consciousness. Depending on where we place our attention, we can enhance specific senses to widen our periphery vision, hear more acutely, smell more intently, feel more intensely, embellish the taste, sense the temperature, feel a degree of pain or become more aware of our balance point or proprioceptive movements. While thoughts may come and go during an amplified sensory experience, our Thinking Brain is not dominant, as we need the capacities and resources of our Being Brain to connect with these alternative senses deeply. Since the Being Brain has a greater parallel processing capacity, when we put ourselves in a sensory-heightened state we receive more feedback and information from each moment, and thus have a richer experience. When we are present and alert to our senses, the world feels more real and we feel more alive.

Try it. Put the book down and practise heightening either your sense of *sight, hearing, smell, touch, taste,*

How to Find Flow

temperature, *pain*, *balance* or *proprioception*. I always recommend rubbing two fingertips together to see if you can feel the individual ridges and valleys of one fingerprint. Alternatively, breathe through your nose and see if you can feel whether the air going in your nose is hotter or colder than the air going out. As you move from thinking about the sense to experiencing it, witness how your psyche quickly moves from a Thinking Brain dominance to a Being Brain state of presence. And with it, feel how you may feel more connected to the world around you.

Utilising your sensory perception to boost your Being Brain during a task can be very effective. It is important, however, to focus your attention on a particular sense that facilitates the act. Focusing on your sense of pain while cooking will be distracting, but focusing on the smell of spices or feeling the texture of the vegetables as you cut them will bring you into the present moment with a heightened sensory experience that will add value to the task. As tango dancer Lucy Hare explains:

> 'Letting my thoughts go and instead bringing my attention to my senses took lots of practice, but it became easier the more I did it. The impact of remaining in my Thinking Brain was immediately tangible in my dancing. It would lead to stiff and awkward movements, and I would lose the synchronicity with my partner. I found connecting

Be Absorbed

with the "balanceo" [balance point] immediately sent my attention from my head down to my body, feet and the floor. It woke my feet up and gave them centre stage to flow.'

Be the breath

One of the most powerful sensory tools we have to synchronise our entire body is our breath. When we breathe, we move more than our lungs and our respiratory system. Our breath is intricately linked with our heartbeat, blood flow and oxygen levels, which feed life into every part of our body. The breath is often referred to as our 'centre' in yogic or Buddhist practices: 'Breath is the bridge which connects life to consciousness, which unites your body to your thoughts,' explains Thích Nhất Hanh, a Vietnamese Buddhist monk and peace activist.[118] Focusing our attention on the breath not only helps us to slow down and sync up, but it also allows us to modulate our nervous system, increase or decrease our arousal to an optimal level, and bypass distraction and conflict. It is a juncture point between our physiology and psychology, a gateway to affect our heartbeat, nervous system, feelings and energetic vibrations all at once. It is why women in labour focus on their breath when giving birth; Navy SEALs use a technique known as box breathing to stay calm in intense situations; freedivers use their breath to help concentrate blood flow towards vital organs in their body before descending to

How to Find Flow

great depths; rock climbers power-breathe before a difficult move; and yogis keep their breath continuous and stable during their poses. Tom Carroll explains:

> 'I think connecting with the breath is probably the biggest thing for me. I start by being aware of my breath and doing several breaths very, very consciously. The breath then takes me deeper and further into my body, as that's where I need to be. Quite often, my scattered and very short attention span takes me out of my body, so I use my breath to come back into my body. This helps to centre my mind, avoid the mental noise, and be ready for anything.'

To put this into practice, there are literally hundreds of breathing exercises and methods that you can use. Pranayama is a form of yogic breathing that aims to increase the life force between mind and body; the Wim Hof method of repeating exaggerated inhalations aims to oxygenate the system to train our autonomic system to deal with pressure; abdominal or belly breathing techniques increase relaxation, lower our heart rate and improve recovery; box breathing techniques cycle the breath in an in/hold/out/hold sequence for an equal number of seconds to build our CO_2 tolerance and deal with stress; kapalabhati involves long breaths in and short powerful breaths out from the belly, which

Be Absorbed

helps to awaken the mind and body as if drinking an espresso; breathing while holding your tongue to the roof of your mouth activates the vagus nerve, the farthest-reaching nerve in the body, resulting in the activation of our parasympathetic nervous system (responsible for calming our neurology) and a cooling down sensation; or nose breathing can be used to stimulate the production of the neurochemical nitric oxide and flush away excess cortisol and norepinephrine (i.e. adrenaline).

There is no right or wrong way to breathe, rather different practices that create different reactions. If you are under-aroused, you may want to engage in some kapalabhati breathing. If you are over-cooked, you may want to do some belly breaths. Regardless of the technique you use, you can use your breath to fully focus both your mental and physical attention towards a common goal and synchronise your two brains. A technique that I have used to great effect, and labelled as 'flow breathing' to help people remember, is to breathe out during pivotal actions. Breathing out just as you act, speak or think loosens the psyche. It heightens the parasympathetic nervous system and allows our muscles to move with greater fluidity. And it concentrates the mind on the process of the act, protecting the mind from being distracted. Try it for yourself. Whether you are throwing a dart, hitting a tennis serve, delivering the opening line of a speech or responding to a child throwing a tantrum, breathe out as you do it.

How to Find Flow

Flick between frequencies

While being present to our senses creates a bridge between the two brains, your Thinking Brain may still remain in charge if you don't surpass this conscious experience; to find flow, we need to move beyond consciously controlling a state of presence and instead become completely absorbed in the act.

Scientifically, this consciously controlled experience, through which we have become so accustomed to experiencing life, can be measured through brainwave frequencies. As outlined earlier, the brain is composed of billions of neurons all outputting electrical signals that communicate with one another. The sum of this electrical potential is emitted in patterns, which 'cycle' at varying rates. Thanks to electroencephalogram (EEG) machines we can interpret these movements as brainwaves and measure them in cycles per second, or 'hertz', as cognitive neuroscientists would say. Over time, studies have correlated specific brainwave frequencies to different human experiences and states of consciousness:

- During deep sleep, our brains produce the slowest cycle, called *delta* frequency (<4 Hz).
- In slightly more awake states, such as deep meditation, trance states or subconscious processing, *theta* frequencies (4–8Hz) cycle at a marginally faster rate.

Be Absorbed

- After theta, *alpha* waves (9–13Hz) become apparent; these are associated with being very relaxed and calm, and are often correlated with high performance and creative endeavours.[119]
- Then, when our Thinking Brain takes hold of our experience, an even higher frequency *beta* wave (14–30 Hz) occurs, for the most part accounting for our day-to-day conscious activities.
- Infrequently, scientists observe extremely high *gamma* waves (>30 Hz) representing the brain 'binding' or combining disparate thoughts from different parts of the brain into a single idea, and/or experiencing higher states of perception and consciousness.
- Lastly, and even more infrequent, are *hyper gamma* (~100Hz), *lambda* (~200Hz) and *epsilon* waves (<0.5 Hz) that occur at extreme polar ends of the spectrum and are associated with extraordinary states of consciousness, such as deep levels of insight, out-of-body experiences and spiritual insights. Gamma, lambda and epsilon waves typically occur after an initial period of delta or theta activity.

How to Find Flow

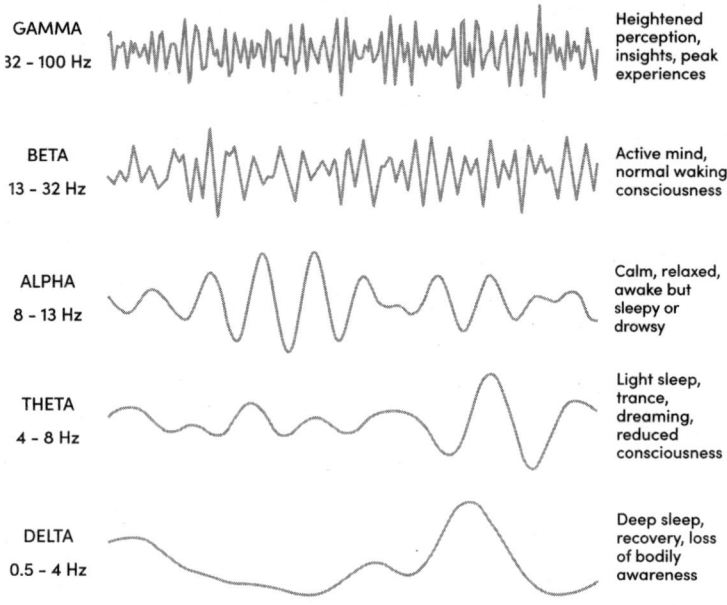

Standard brainwave frequencies

The cycling of our brainwaves can vary greatly, as outlined in this chart, even within one activity. But, for most of our waking day, we remain locked into *high-beta* wave cycles as our Thinking Brain dominates our waking consciousness. While research in this niche area is only just beginning, flow is an experience that appears to break the brainwave norms of how we typically deal with daily challenges.[120] In flow, the brain uses a variety of frequencies, interchanging between them at precisely the right time. This ability to flick between frequencies and go from high-beta to high-alpha and then to low-beta or even theta, for example, differentiates flow from

Be Absorbed

other ordinary activity states that consistently display high-beta waves. Nowadays, with wearable tech getting more accurate and immediate in its bio-feedback, you can learn what it feels like to be in these differing brainwave frequencies. Familiarising yourself with what it feels like to be in a low-beta and high-alpha state, and mastering the ability to flick between frequencies, is another flow skill to put in your toolbox and use when wanting to slip into flow.

Trigger a trance
Perhaps my most tried-and-tested flow skill to flick between frequencies and step into the Being Brain is a ritualised process using our sensory awareness that self-induces a mild state of trance. I am not referring to the time-consuming trance-inducing activities such as sweat lodges, raving and gaming, or the narcotics that temporarily flood our synaptic connections to mimic trance states. Instead, I am suggesting a surprisingly simple and quick self-induced technique that can readily dislodge the Thinking Brain. All you need to do to induce this mild trance state is to place your attention on your peripheral vision and simultaneously stack an additional sense.

Our peripheral vision probably does more to prime us for flow than anything else, and has the added benefit of being conducive to most tasks, especially physical activities. Why? Because our peripheral vision is deeply connected to our motor cortex, which is why we can

How to Find Flow

catch a falling glass without consciously looking at it. Experiencing the moment through your peripheral visual field is an art form that many an athlete has mastered, unknowingly. It is how martial artists can quickly react to a kick while looking at the opponent's shoulders, how a tennis player knows where their opponent is on the other side of the court when focused intently on the oncoming ball or how you can engage in a conversation with someone while also being aware of what is around you. Try it for yourself. Put the book down and let's create a mild trance state together:

- Place your conscious attention on a small square inch in front of you, or focus on a single letter on this page. Once you have fixed your gaze, keep your eyes here for the whole exercise – on the same square inch or letter.
- After ten seconds, widen your peripheral vision so that you can see to either side of the square – at the same time as keeping focused on the small square. Keep increasing your peripheral awareness to take in all your surroundings at the same time – above and below, to the left and to the right. Holding this peripheral fix for sustained periods is a skill that takes practice to build stamina.
- Once your peripheral field is maxed out, this may be enough to induce a trance state. However, most may need to simultaneously introduce

Be Absorbed

another sense into awareness. For example, while sustaining your peripheral vision, you may want to simultaneously feel the individual lines on your fingerprint when rubbing two fingertips together, or feel the chair against your body, to introduce touch.
- At some stage, if your attention is fully engaged in both your peripheral vision and one other sense, you will become absorbed into a trance state.
- You might also notice that it is near impossible to hold this deep sensory experience and think at the same time.
- As you halt this activity, you may suddenly feel somewhat disorientated as you come back to your usual mode of high-beta waking consciousness. This is normal – do not be alarmed.

When triggering a trance state just before an activity in which you want to find flow, make sure the secondary sense is helpful to the activity you intend to move on to afterwards. For example, before I return a tennis serve, I will always induce a state of trance. When getting ready, I focus my attention on a blade of grass or speck of concrete in front of me and widen my periphery so that I can see the court and the server. Then I feel my weight shift on to my toes, as I know this secondary sensual act will also help me to react faster. I look up at the ball in the server's hand and I continue to amplify the sensory

How to Find Flow

experience until I reach a deepened trance state – where thought is non-existent.

Once practised, this flow skill can be achieved in seconds and helps you to bridge your brains before you write, speak, interact, play or work. Professional rock climber Hazel Findlay, who is widely considered to be one of the best climbers in the world, shares that:

'Several winters ago I found myself near the top of El Capitan, a 1,000m overhanging face of sheer granite. My goal was to free climb the classic Salathé wall [by free climbing she means only using ropes or equipment as a protection aid, and not for help ascending the wall]. Our food and water were running low and, with a storm rolling in, the pressure was on. I found myself distracted by the desire to succeed, and other narratives: "What if I fail?", "I feel tired", "It's so exposed up here" ... Before I started the crux section, I connected to my senses until I was absolutely focused, present and connected to my body. I remember looking out at the amazing view, sensing the air beneath my feet, and I reminded myself of how lucky I was to be somewhere so beautiful. Then I stared at a little section of rock, focusing on the beautiful patterns in the granite crystals. I felt the chalk in my fingertips and noticed my belly push against my harness as I breathed in. Within seconds, I had completely

Be Absorbed

changed my mindset. Knowing I was back in the moment, I set off. I was able to tap into flow and complete the climb.'

This chapter has outlined several flow skills that you can use to help you trust your Being Brain and become absorbed into the task. In the next chapter, we get to the really interesting bit of experiencing flow and feeling a sense of effortlessness.

> **LET'S RECAP**
>
> In this chapter, we have discussed the following flow skills to allow absorption:
> - asking the Thinking Brain to trust the Being Brain
> - powering up your presence by heightening your senses
> - using your breath to bridge your brains
> - practising 'flow breathing'
> - flicking between brainwave frequencies
> - triggering a mild trance
>
> No doubt your Thinking Brain will be working hard by now to derail you from practising these tasks. These practices will loosen the Thinking Brain's hold on your psyche, which it will not like. Once practised, these techniques only take several seconds to

How to Find Flow

> deploy. Don't let the Thinking Brain tell you that you don't have the time. It will likely try to justify why these tasks are a waste of time, ineffective or why you even need to train your mind at all. Don't be alarmed, just laugh at the cunningness of your monkey mind and use these flow skills to slow down, bridge your brains and sync back up.

YOUR CHALLENGE

My challenge to you is to practise entering a state of trance before executing an activity. Set up a challenge for yourself wherever you are reading or listening to this book: hold a yoga pose, juggle, throw tea bags into a cup, do a handstand, write a poem, sing a song ... it doesn't matter what the task is. Before executing the task, take a moment to slow down and follow the script we've outlined to trigger a trance. Once in a trance, then engage with the activity. Practise slowing down, triggering a trance and then deeply engaging with the activity. See if you can use it to allow yourself to flow. Now go for it. Put the book down. I'll wait.

Chapter 9

BE EFFORTLESS

IN THE PREVIOUS CHAPTER, WE HIGHLIGHTED THE importance of becoming absorbed into the moment to enter flow. However, stepping into flow is so much more than going from a state of conscious presence to just being absorbed within the act – after all, we can be immersed while listening to someone read and yet be far from experiencing a high degree of control. Being in flow is also about feeling a high sense of control within the situation in which this control feels more effortless than usual. There is no inner critic or doubt; instead, our actions flow as if hardwired to our intuition. Even in effortful acts, our subjective experience of the act feels more effortless, smoother or more fluid than normal. It is precisely this effort-lessness to the act that releases the shackles and allows us to move out of an ordinary experience and into an extraordinary experience, self-actualising our most connected and capable best.

How to Find Flow

In this chapter, I will guide you through some of the practices I use with my clients every day to lean into this effortlessness. We will look at how our innate trust levels mediate this effortlessness, how to let go of over-controlling our actions and how to develop our intuitive voice to enable intuitive action. So strap in, as this is the best part of the book!

EXAMINING EFFORT-LESSNESS

While flow may feel effort-less, when we take a peek under the hood, there is actually a huge amount of activity occurring. More accurately, it is not that no effort is being expended; rather, it is the supreme level of efficiency and synchronised engineering of the mind and body that makes us feel like the words of an email landed on the page as if destined to be written in that manner, or the joke that came out of our mouth just flowed without us even thinking about it. While this high level of synchronicity may feel surreal, it helps my clients to realise that this high degree of effort-less control is not just a subjective phenomenon, but has measurable physiological reactions. Specifically, what allows this effort-lessness to occur is a greater coherence between our neurology and brain regions, and a reduced amount of perceived effort attributed to the task. To understand how we can create this coherence, let's take a look at these processes in detail.

Be Effortless

In flow, actions happen with greater fluidity because there is minimal neurological conflict between our brain and our body, causing messages to travel faster around the body – that 'cortico-muscular coherence' we met in Chapter 3. Using electromyography (EMG) machines to measure the electrical activity in muscles and electroencephalography (EEG) machines to measure the electrical activity in the brain, scientists can look at the extent of rhythmic signalling between the brain and body. The smoothness of movement that seems to be at the root of the flow sensation occurs when the movement is performed continuously without any neurological interruption, suggests Guy Cheron, a neuroscientist from the Université Libre de Bruxelles in Belgium.[121] When there is less interruption, less effort is attributed to overcome this friction and the act feels more effort-less. It doesn't stop there either. Within the brain, key neural structures responsible for attentional and cognitive control (such as the dorsolateral and ventrolateral PFC and left anterior inferior frontal gyrus) seem to sync up. Practically, this synchronicity results in a deeper sense of cognitive control, at the same time that our abilities that engineer goal-directed activity are 'switched on'. This coordinated chorus is just the beginning.

Contrary to what we might feel when we put our hand to our chest, the heart does not beat in a regular metronomic rhythm; instead the intervals between each beat vary, indicating much about our internal states, such as

How to Find Flow

how our nervous system is operating. When the heart beats, it sends out electromagnetic fields (EMFs) that continuously emit energy – stronger than any other organ in our body. Imagine a vibrating tuning fork that sets off another tuning fork across the room; even though we cannot see it, it happens. Between each heartbeat, the level of energy vibration varies. The scientific name for these variations is heart rate variability (HRV). Perhaps you have seen the jagged lines on a hospital heart rate monitor in the movies, before the actor's heartbeat goes flat. If so, on these graphs, you can see the varying smoothness of how the undulating line rises and falls. Jagged lines are termed as an 'incoherent' heart rate and often represent our normal waking consciousness. In contrast, a smooth undulating wave-like line is termed a 'coherent' heart rate and signifies a greater internal balance and heart–brain synchronisation.[122] Note that we are discussing not high or low heart rate levels, but rather the coherence of frequencies between heartbeats. Specifically, the synchronisation and frequency entrainment between the heart rhythms, blood pressure, and respiration rhythms; brain rhythm and the cardiac cycles. Importantly, when the heart rate is coherent, our reaction times are faster,[123] and decision-making and satisfaction improve,[124] helping to explain the increased efficiency and fluidity during flow. This coherence also helps to explain how we can have an internal level of harmony during flow, even if our heart rate is going through the roof.

Be Effortless

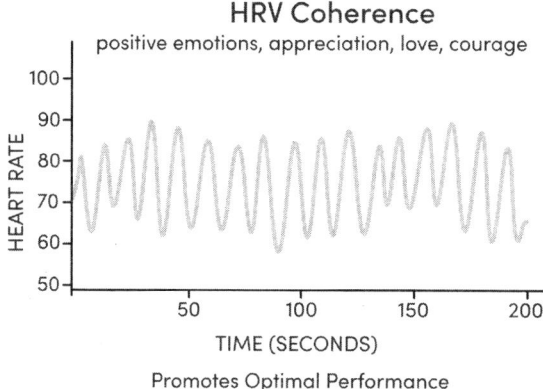

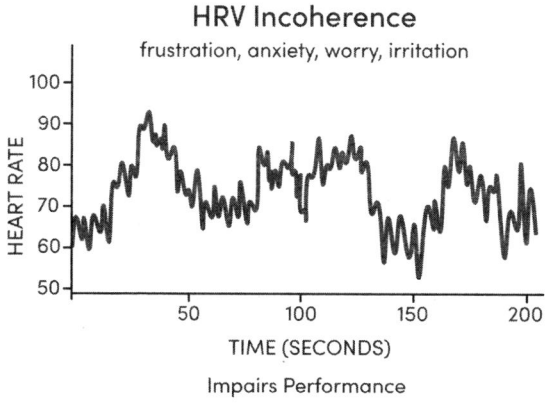

Heart rate coherence

Stick with me, there is more. In flow, our heart rate coherence increases and our respiratory depth falls in sync with the oxygen that is needed;[125] our left amygdala, a region responsible for triggering emotions, quietens down and our Thinking Brain hands over the steering wheel, allowing our decision-making processes to occur uninhibited by distracting emotions and thoughts;[126] our

How to Find Flow

somatosensory networks that allow us to sense internal and external stimuli physically sync up, allowing us to be more present to the situation and absorb more information;[127] and our left putamen, a part of the brain responsible for a complex feedback loop that prepares and aids the movement of our limbs, becomes hyperactive, increasing our ability to calculate outcome probabilities and respond effectively and efficiently.[128] In this rare biological synchronisation, our brain and body are allowed to act intuitively in a manner that best meets the momentary opportunity, as if dancing with the novelty of each moment.

As William James, who is considered the Father of American Psychology, suggests, 'The more of the details of our daily life we can hand over to the effortless custody of automatism, the more our higher powers of mind will be set free for their own proper work.'[129] All this internal synchronicity inherent within a flow experience often feels like the automation of muscle memory or automated patterns of behaviour simply repeating themselves without friction. But while this automation does occur in flow, enabling our behavioural blueprints and muscle memory, importantly, flow is not merely automated behaviour. As we've discussed, it is the *union* of the Thinking Brain and Being Brain that allows such focused attention and efficiency of action, not simply undirected habitual automation, which would be an act of the Being Brain alone. Aspects of flow may feel automatic, but

Be Effortless

practically it is far from it. In fact, rarely is any activity purely automatic or process pure; even driving a car down the same road for the thousandth time requires attributes of the Thinking Brain to direct where we want to go and adjust to unexpected events.

It is not just our biology that changes during this effortlessness in flow, but our perception too. The unusual effortlessness attributed to flow is often linked with a reduction in perceived conflict, known scientifically as the 'conflict-monitoring hypothesis'.[130] There is a specific area of the brain called the anterior cingulate cortex (the ACC), which has a specific function to detect and monitor any conflict when processing information – this conflict could be a threat to our competence or comfort, confusion in what we see or feel, or a mismatch between what we expect to happen and what is occurring. Once a conflict is detected, the ACC steps in to allocate more attentional load, or 'effort', to address the perceived conflict. While this ascription of effort enhances processing power, it also redirects consciousness inwards to order this apparent disorder. In other words, to counter a perceived conflict, the brain sends in reinforcements, but, in doing so, our attention and actions become more subjectively effortful. The greater the conflict, the greater the attentional loading to overcome the encounter, and the greater the felt effort. It is why simple tasks, such as doing the washing or getting out of bed, can *feel* like such an effort if it is perceived as a conflict, even though the act itself requires

How to Find Flow

little physical or attentional effort. Since an implicit level of trust is attributed to our actions in flow, any perceived sense of conflict subsides; the ACC becomes downregulated, fewer attentional reinforcements (aka nodes) are ascribed and less effort is felt within our effortful actions.

When we combine the reduction in felt effort, exceptional neurological efficiency, amplified sensory experience, increased Being Brain automaticity and reduced Thinking Brain distractions, we can start to understand how people feel like they are literally flowing in flow. We can also comprehend how this supreme level of collective synchronisation, unparalleled efficiency and reduced effort allows optimal functioning to occur and makes improved personal performance in flow a biologically inevitability. Not because we are on autopilot or have tapped into some supernatural energetic power, like many might believe, but because we are unladen by the ordinary glitchy and distracted processing of our psychophysiology and can therefore better meet with the moment.

Neuroscientific research will continue to grow and evolve to better help us understand what is happening neuropsychophysiologically in flow, but what is abundantly clear is that flow demands a coordinated orchestra of our cognitive systems, nervous systems and neurochemical activity to play together in perfect chorus. When acting in harmony, every system does what it has been designed to do, and the natural phenomenon of flow is allowed to occur.

Be Effortless

'Fascinating', I hear you say, 'but how do we practically create this coordinated chorus'. Let's get into it.

TOTAL TRUST

The extent to which we will allow such a biological harmony to occur depends very much on our own internal level of trust. Some are born with a natural tendency to trust their own physiology, like that of Mitchie Brusco, a skateboarding wonder kid who came second in the X-Games at only fifteen years of age. In a post-competition interview, he said, 'I just try to let my body do the work. My body knows how to do it better than my brain so I kind of just let it take over.'[131] By most standards, being world class at the age of fifteen is unheard of, let alone being second best in the world. Brusco manages to pull off some of the world's toughest skateboarding tricks, on a massive quarter pipe that would make most heads spin just looking at it, by simply *trusting* his body to act. Kids like Brusco have a refreshing ability to simplify matters without a developed Thinking Brain continuously critiquing and interfering. If we were all like Brusco, flow would undoubtedly show up far more frequently in our lives. But, for most of us, we need to relearn how to embody this high degree of self-trust and then work at maintaining it during crucial moments.

So how do we increase our level of self-trust? In the words of Ernest Hemmingway, 'The best way to know if you can trust yourself, is to trust yourself.'[132] Simple as

How to Find Flow

it sounds, in practice this is not always that easy. Over the years, however, I have found that, across individuals and activities, there are a number of aspects within our control that, together, make trusting ourselves far easier.

Try not to try

Sometimes, the situation is so intense, such as a life-threatening experience, that the event forces us to trust ourselves; we have no other option. But, for the most part, our biggest obstacle to trusting our innate ability is that we *try too hard*.

The deep level of trust happens naturally in flow, not because we are overriding our fear of failure or concerns, but because the underlying doubt or concern over losing control is absent. At its essence, one of the reasons flow experiences feel so unique is because we surrender the need to be in control.

As touched on earlier, there is a paradox to control that occurs in flow: the more we let go of the need to control, the more innate control we feel over our actions. This paradox can be difficult to trust and embody at first, but it is easily recognisable and in situ in our lives already. Take the act of falling asleep, for example. When we try to fall asleep, we are often far less successful than when we simply enjoy the weight of our head on the pillow. The same paradox of control is apparent when we try to relax, hit a powerful tennis serve, write poetry, go to the toilet, juggle, love or forgive. When we *try too hard* to do

Be Effortless

these acts, our performance and degree of control within them suffers. Therefore, one of the secrets to achieving a high degree of self-trust is not to *try* to trust yourself. By removing the forced sense of effort, typical of the Thinking Brain, we stop interfering and, by default, start trusting.

Soften your gaze

In trying not to try, and just do instead, it is helpful to become aware of how your body is feeling. Wherever there is distrust, there is tension and hesitation, not just in our mind but mirrored in our physiology. It can help to see the body existing in a sea of tension, as if every muscle fibre is held by an ocean of energetic tension. Where there is distrust, muscles tighten and constrict to try to stay more in control. When the tension becomes too taught, friction occurs and movement is limited. It is our responsibility to keep a sea of tension in our body that allows agility and intensity, but doesn't cause rigidity. As the Dalai Lama once said, 'When your mind is too intense ... you need to loosen it, like loosening the strings of a guitar.'[133] This is why 'flow breathing' works so well (see page 275) – whether you are about to write an email, present a report, serve a match point or apply the critical incision during surgery, if you notice tension in your mind or body and then intervene by breathing out as you act, your physiology will soften and be more agile and responsive.

This sea of tension can most noticeably be felt in our gaze. When trying too hard, there is a reciprocal

How to Find Flow

sternness and rigidity to our attention that can be felt around our eyes and forehead. In effort, our eyes narrow, causing the muscles around them to strain and our forehead to tighten. It is why we often rub our forehead, eyes or temples when stressed, to loosen this rigidity.

Try it for yourself. Actively over-try to read this sentence or force a physical push-up on the floor and notice how your face responds. Now that you are aware of this facial response, it is difficult to not feel it when trying too hard. You now have the power to intervene at will.

A tried and tested technique that you can instantly implement to soften this sea of tension is to soften your gaze. Since our attention is the gateway to our inner workings, softening your attention will also soften your approach. To allow the muscles around your eyes to relax, I suggest you look at what is in front of you using an imaginary third eye, existing in between your two eyes.

Try it. Put it to the test. Read this sentence but this time soften your gaze – direct your gaze through a point in between your eyebrows, and witness the subtle changes to the tension in your forehead and your experience as a whole.

I have used this skill successfully with surgeons entering critical moments of an operation, skiers getting ready to drop off a cliff and students and writers readying to put pen to paper. Now you too can use it when you need to loosen the strings of your mind and find a sense of effortlessness in your action.

Be Effortless

Importantly, this physical softening is not to be confused with surrendering intent or becoming too floppy – that may take us away from flow into passive relaxation. For flow, we need to remain intensely present and focused on the task. We want to keep the helpful arousal and felt intensity to activate our body, but, at the same time, we can use this eye gaze to soften any rigidity of our psyche.

Feel the rhythm

In flow, there is greater fluency or fluidity to our actions, as discussed earlier. The unrivalled coherence between mind and body, and the synchronisation of many of our functions, makes everything seemingly click – as if moving to the same groove. While we may not be able to entirely replicate this exact state of harmony instantly, we can certainly initiate the process. By swaying our hips to a rhythmic beat or gently dancing with fluidity, we can give the mind and body a nudge. As discussed earlier, focusing on our breath helps bridge the Thinking and Being Brains. It also sets an intention for both brains to be more cohesive, more fluid. Further, by physically moving our body, even for a cerebral task, the movement automatically activates and promotes the Being Brain.

For instance, when I present a talk or workshop online, displaying only the top half of my body on screen, I always start by swaying my hips. The physical sensation

How to Find Flow

of moving side to side rhythmically sets an embodied intention to find some rhythm and flow. It helps me get into my groove.

I have used this notion to help athletes sway their hips before dropping off cliffs, dance before facilitating a coaching session or find some rhythm before going on stage. Try it for yourself. Before engaging in your activity, spend a few moments developing fluency in your movement, then proceed.

If you want to step it up a level, there's something grounding and unifying about making a sound with your voice. Try it for yourself. Stop reading for a moment and hum or sing and hold a note. The vibrations of our own voice reverberate through our psyche, cohering our attention to one end. It feels great and helps to initiate an internal synchronisation process. I'm sure it is why religions use songs, monks chant and choirs feel so united. Try it. Intentionally use your voice as a preparatory tool to cohere your psyche.

Adopt the mantra 'Let go, let flow'

I remember watching Jazz, my then thirteen-month-old baby, exploring our new flat. She was knocking everything over, as only toddlers know how. I was lying on the floor intent on being at her height, so we could communicate as equals, admiring how big and interesting even the most mundane of objects are when you have the perspective of seeing the world 30cm above the ground.

Be Effortless

Jazz had recently discovered the joys of walking and was on the hunt for her next adventure. She wobbled over to the child-sized table and chair on the other side of the room, making it all the way without falling. I was proud of her. On her arrival, she grasped the back of the chair to hold herself steady. She looked up, as a climber would on the first day of ascending a mountain peak, and, to my surprise, she began to entertain a multitude of different angled ascents up onto the chair. None were working. Just when I thought she had been defeated, and her Being Brain had given up, Jazz launched a leg onto the chair and pushed her way up.

I laughed with a pride that many parents and coaches would relate to, and then it suddenly hit me. My daughter was now standing on the chair, out of breath, but apparently determined to scale the table.

I watched on, feeling out of control, as if my heart was in Jazz's body. My mind was urging me to pick her up, or at least offer my support, as most parents would have probably done by now. I needed to feel more in control. But there was also another part of me that didn't want to steal her thunder. In recognition that this need to act was based on my fears, my perceived limits and my need to control the situation and ensure that I wasn't being an irresponsible father, I decided to adopt her perspective instead. As I experienced this moment through Jazz's eyes, I morphed from a mental matrix of everything that could go wrong to a curious, playful, trusting and

How to Find Flow

determined mindset. I found myself absorbed in the next step of the summit.

Shifting between curiosity and concern, and back again, I let Jazz do her thing, but shuffled closer, ready to be a ninja dad if the need arose. Mindful not to transfer my more stifling map of the world onto hers, I watched with curiosity and caution as the chair wobbled beneath her already wobbly legs. Focused on the task, she briefly glanced down to check the foundations, and then turned her attention back to assessing the ascent. The chances of her scaling this table were slim, I thought.

I was unnerved from doubt and deliberation but, to my surprise, she launched herself up onto the table. Half rising from the chair and half hanging off the table ledge, her face scrunched up like a prune, her eyes widened and she nervously hesitated. I could see in her eyes the sudden shock of what she had just gotten herself into. But, unlike most of us adults, for her this panic lasted for only a second or two. She took a deep breath, and miraculously changed her state instantaneously. I watched as every ounce of her small and uncoordinated body found a very unconventional way to roll her body weight onto the table top. Sprawled out on the surface, recovering from the exerted effort, she paused for a moment. Then, with a heavy sigh, Jazz pushed herself up, standing like a boxer rising after a knock-out punch. Her legs shaking, she rose to triumphantly claim her summit. She waddled on the surface of the table, relishing her triumph with a pride

Be Effortless

and newfound confidence that was awe-inspiring. At the same time, I too let out a big sigh, knowing that I had been so close to stifling this magical moment of growth. Immediately curious about a piece of wrapping paper on the table, she manoeuvred over to play with it, and moved from her Mount Everest without a shred of ego.

In knowing that we cannot force our mind and body to self-actualise, rather we need to let go of the worry of needing to be in control; the same goes for how we treat or manage others. In life, I am constantly amazed at how leaders, coaches, managers and parents are continuously getting in the way of others' performances. Whether it is distracting their attention or triggering unhelpful emotions with throwaway comments, micromanaging someone else's task or using the stick and carrot to control someone's immediate actions to the loss of short- and medium-term performance standards, people in leadership positions readily feel the need to over-control the situation in order to produce results. Yet the consequences are monumental and often unseen in the moment, limiting the individual's volition, intrinsic motivation, confidence, potential and level of deep engagement. The net effect? A disempowering and demotivating leadership, even though the original intention may have been to help.

Take a moment now and reflect on how you have felt in your life when being over-controlled or micromanaged; perhaps reflect on how you may be doing this with others. There is obviously a time and place to be prescriptive

How to Find Flow

or give direct feedback when working with others, but can we do that and help them in their actions while also empowering them?

The words we use with ourselves and others are powerful. With just one word or phrase, we can easily trigger the Thinking Brain and activate a need to protect rather than prospect the moment – such as the sports coach shouting from the sidelines, giving technical or strategic feedback; while well-intended, it activates the player's Thinking Brain, causing them to overthink and become more effortful, often creating further mistakes. It can help, therefore, to proactively direct the thread of consciousness by adopting the saying 'Let Go, Let Flow'. By repeating this phrase, we instruct our Thinking Brain to let go of trying too hard, of over-controlling our actions or the situation and instead help the Thinking Brain to trust the Being Brain. This phrase is really supportive to helping us *let* it happen rather than *make* it happen, and can be ideal for when you find yourself nervous or holding on too tight.

INTUITIVE INTELLIGENCE

Once we stop trying too hard and instead learn to trust ourselves, the most unexpected thing happens: we allow ourselves to bind with our intuition and perform much better than we could ever consciously control. While a degree of phronesis, a type of wisdom or intelligence relevant to practical action in particular situations, exists

Be Effortless

in all of us, our Thinking Brain doesn't always allow us to go beyond the analytical and technical know-how when forming judgements and decisions – if it did, it would lose control. As a result, our intuitive voice is often suppressed or neglected, and becomes another voice lost in a boisterous crowd. To foster flow, therefore, it is our responsibility to change this status quo.

Research and practice tend to group our intelligence into three main intelligence centres: our head, heart and gut. Although this is intuitively old news, as we commonly say, 'My head is suggesting that I ...', 'My heart feels and believes that ...' and 'My gut instinct is telling me to ...', we are just starting to scientifically understand that each of these locations in the body represent an independent intelligence centre. The brain is still the kingpin of intelligence, boasting around 100 billion neurons that can sense, learn and remember. It is the master of thinking, perception and cognition. In the modern era, it is our most developed intelligence system, and schools almost exclusively foster its importance through their teaching styles, content delivery and assessments. The heart, however, has close to 40,000 neurons that can retain and initiate intelligence. It is the first organ to be created at birth, before the brain, and initiates some of our electrical signalling and neurochemical activity surrounding our emotions. For example, through measuring the heart's electromagnetic field, the heart is known to transfer energies between humans in close proximity without

How to Find Flow

passing signals through the brain.[134] Lastly, the gut has around 100 million neurons, and offers an intelligence that I like to think of as our inherited intelligence, passed down from prior generations. Most practically noticeable when recoiling from a flaming fire, it communicates by releasing chemicals into our bloodstream and sending electrical signals via the largest nerve in our body, the vagus nerve. The gut is primarily responsible for upholding our immune system. However, neurochemically, it also plays a pivotal role in managing our emotions. For example, close to 95 per cent of the body's serotonin, the neurochemical associated with happiness and well-being, is found in the gut.[135]

Practically, we often find ourselves rooted in one of these intelligence centres reacting to the stream of intelligence, most commonly our brain, in which our Thinking Brain habitually holds the reins, directing the majority of conscious activity. Fused and somewhat enslaved to one of these intelligence centres, rarely do people proactively de-branch themselves from this entrenchment and give all areas (head, heart and gut) an equal voice in decision-making. But when we do take a more egalitarian approach, and create an experiential space from each and all these intelligences, a curious thing happens. A fourth position emerges – a place that allows a sense of knowing rather than thinking, feeling or reacting. We no longer feel at the whim of our head, heart or gut, or their proceeding thoughts, emotions

Be Effortless

and instinctive reactions. Instead, a calm intuitive sense of knowing what to do next emerges. A natural wisdom or phronesis seems to take the reins and, if allowed to remain, this intuitive voice allows us to be and act with a level of certainty that almost feels predestined. There is no internal debate of right or wrong or better or worse; we simply click into a sense of knowing what needs to be said or done, and act with full commitment.

Rebecca Soni, six-time Olympic medallist, multi-World Record holder and World Swimmer of the Year in 2010 and 2011, recounts how building a relationship with her intuitive voice helped her find flow when she needed it most:

> 'It was my favourite event, the one I had been training for. In the earlier rounds, I was hoping to have gone faster, so the pressure was mounting for me to break the World Record. My goal was to break 2 minutes 20 seconds. I didn't necessarily feel physically at my best, as my mind kept reminding me: "Oh, you don't feel as good as you did the night before; you're sluggish; you're not feeling well; your pace isn't very fast." I just remember stepping up on the blocks and having this moment of "I don't think I can do this." I knew I could win, but I didn't think I could break 2:20. But then a second voice popped in and said, "It doesn't matter; you're going to do it." This voice was a familiar voice that

How to Find Flow

I had developed through training, and had helped me to stay grounded, calm and on point. It had helped me go beyond the usual distracting noise of my mind and the unhelpful thoughts that would often distract my attention when training for hours on end. So, standing on the blocks, I remember making a decision to listen to this intuitive voice and let go of the rest – in hindsight, that's when I entered flow. Once the race started, I just followed the game plan that I had practised in training, and everything started firing on all cylinders. Then pretty much when I came to the last five or ten strokes I probably snapped out of flow, and knew that I was doing pretty well, and by then I just sailed to the wall (breaking the World Record).'

While the science of intuition is still evolving and elementary at best, the latest thinking suggests that it originates from within our Being Brain operations and best represents an inherent personal wisdom, an intelligence derived from our cumulative experience on this planet.[136] Regardless of the neuroanatomy linked with intuition, what is obvious is that listening to and fostering the relationship we have with our intuition can revolutionise how we live, work, train and perform. It is a relationship, an experience that we need to foster.

Be Effortless

Develop your inner voice

Like any relationship, it takes intention and attention to build a strong relationship with our intuition so that we can promote it when it matters most. It can be confusing at first to know whether the voice we're listening to is our intuition or not. It can take time to resonate with the nuances of our intuition and develop the embodiment of this voice. A starting point that many have found helpful is to imagine your intuition as a third entity and take the time to get to know it, as you would chat with a friend. Practise differentiating its character and tone from the other intelligence centres. Ask yourself, 'What would my logic, feelings, instinct and intuition each say regarding this scenario?'

Common characteristics of our intuition include a sense of measured curiosity, calm and feeling grounded, whereas our knowledgeable head can often feel like a merry-go-round of urgent, incessant logic, our heart space can push and pull our attention with fleeting and often compulsive feelings, and our gut compels us to react with a sense of inherited instinct. Above all else, our intuition is most noticeable because it just feels 'right' or 'true'. Our intuition feels well placed for that particular moment in time, an expression of embodied wisdom, in harmony with all that you are.

Let's start developing your relationship with your intuition and finding that same inner voice Rebecca relied on to achieve her success.

How to Find Flow

Ready?

The task is to ask each intelligence centre the same question. Importantly, the meta-task, or deeper agenda behind this task, is to witness the different reactions you see, feel and hear inside you to get a feel for the character of each intelligence centre. The goal here is to understand how each intelligence shows up and is differentiated from the others.

I suggest you read the entire exercise that follows and then do it. Don't overthink your answers, just go with what immediately comes up; your answers will likely arise as flashes of images, thoughts or feelings. Your answer will usually come up within the first few seconds of asking the question. It is important not to linger for too long. If you do, the Thinking Brain will likely take the reins in disguise and end up answering the question. It also helps to close your eyes if you feel comfortable doing so while doing this exercise.

- First, place your hand over your forehead. Take a moment to embody your rational and logical thoughts. Then ask your Thinking Brain, 'What shall I eat for dinner tonight?'
- Second, place your hand over your heart space and take a moment to feel and connect with how you feel right now; identify with what you feel are your strong beliefs in life. Then ask your heart, 'What shall I eat for dinner tonight?'

Be Effortless

- Then place your hand two inches below your belly button and embody your inherited instinct; how you may react when you see fire, for example. Then ask your gut the same question: 'What shall I eat for dinner tonight?' This can often be a difficult place to connect with, so don't worry if nothing comes up.
- Next, keeping your eyes closed if you can, imagine taking a few steps back, leaving your body in front of you; you (Self A) should be looking at yourself (Self B), a few feet or metres in front. Imagine the pulsating information from each intelligence centre glowing in the body that is in front of you (Self B). Placing your attention on the space you feel in your current position (Self A), uprooted from the self in front of you (Self B), ask your intuition to come forth (in Self A). Allow that space of knowing to emerge: the place that best represents your personal wisdom; a space somewhat detached from the three intelligence centres, but that can be objectively inclusive of the information gained from each intelligence centre, as you would the information garnered from multiple consultants. Now ask this space the same question, and witness how the response feels: 'What shall I eat for dinner tonight?'

How to Find Flow

The answers from each area can be wildly different or the same, it just depends on how in sync your intelligence centres are. The more personal the questions, the more this exercise will resonate. I suggest trying this sequence with questions like: How do I feel about my job? How is my relationship with my partner? What should I do in my next spare evening? What do I want to achieve this year? What changes do I need to make in my life to allow flow to occur?

When we are young children, this intuitive intelligence comes very naturally to us. It helps to remember that finding and developing our intuitive voice is easier than we might think – we only need to reconnect with what we once knew very well: the voice that was present when jumping in the playground and practising cartwheels in the garden. We don't have to learn how to connect with our intuition, we already know how – we only need to re-promote it.

BEING MORE

Blurry-eyed, heart beating, I stood in the deafening dearth of noise on the TEDx stage, as if waiting for someone in the crowd to speak. I was thrown by the sudden realisation that I wouldn't have my visual pointers to depend on for the speech. 'How am I going to face my biggest fear, without the props that got me through every keynote and rehearsal to date?' I thought. Instead

Be Effortless

of being the calm and composed individual that I had embodied only moments previously, my Thinking Brain was now in overdrive.

While this moment would have only lasted seconds, my mind inverted and was doing a slow-motion critique of the situation. Mind racing, I thought, 'I can't remember the whole speech without my notes. This is a nightmare. I've got to speak. Why am I not speaking? I am a Flow Coach, an expert in matters of peak performance. Not performing fluently will diminish by credibility. I feel like I might stammer.'

On hearing this rhetoric, I immediately realised I was in the red of the Flow Model and strapped on my Flow Mindset. Feeling more empowered, I took a deep breath, and focused on my STAF, my opening line. While the rest of the speech evaded me, I decided it didn't matter. I was going to trust myself come hell or high water – I'd deal with the next line when I got there. Then, in making this decision, somewhat surprisingly, the little intuitive voice that I had been nurturing over the years in my work, relationships and sport spoke up. 'Let go, let flow,' it said. Almost instantly, my attention softened, my periphery took in the whole audience and my mouth spoke the first line of my speech. It had begun, and I was a passenger!

The next few moments seemed to unfold in and of themselves. While I couldn't grasp the whole speech, it didn't matter; I wasn't trying to remember it. The next words just came. I leant into the next lines, embodying the

How to Find Flow

focus and emotion of the story, and, in moving my arms to act out a tennis shot, I became absorbed into the story and into the speech. It suddenly felt light and flowy. The rest of the speech went by in a flash.

As the applause filled the auditorium, I suddenly came to, realising it was over. I felt somewhat awkward, as if I was an imposter coming in at the end of someone else's speech. I knew it had gone well, but my Thinking Brain couldn't recall what had just happened in detail. Slightly embarrassed, I left the stage before the applause had reached a crescendo.

The overriding sensation in my consciousness was one of pride and reward. The experience of facing my biggest fear, something that had plagued me for years, was now over. Instead of the usual relief I felt when finishing keynotes, this time I felt exuberant. Strangely, more satisfying than the success of the speech or the reaction of the audience was the feeling of knowing that I could trust myself and find my flow speaking publicly. Ever since, that overwhelming fear of speaking, that overbearing noise in my consciousness, which had plagued me all my life, became an insignificant whisper in the room.

Now it's your turn to find that intuitive action in your activity. The last two chapters have focused on being in flow for specific occasions, but there are many nuggets of wisdom I want to share with you about living a life filled

Be Effortless

with flow and integrating the philosophy of flow into your lifestyle – which is what the next chapter is all about.

> **LET'S RECAP**
>
> In this chapter, we have learnt that flow demands absolute trust of our innate capacities – without it, our actions become effort-full, not effort-less. To engineer this trust, we have discussed the following flow skills:
> - appreciating your incredible coordinated chorus when it occurs
> - trusting your innate capacities
> - not trying – just doing
> - softening your sight
> - feeling the rhythm or making a sound with your voice
> - letting go to let flow
> - developing your intuitive voice

YOUR CHALLENGE

Being more effort-less is real and attainable. I challenge you to play around with these ideas and hold them in your psyche as you attempt to drop into flow during an activity. Practise embodying them, experiencing the effects, and find what works best for you. With all learning, as we go from conscious competence to unconscious competence, the content will feel like a distraction. But stick with it so

How to Find Flow

that they become favoured habits of your psyche and allow flow to occur when you're not even trying.

To get a feel for these more nuanced skills of a Flow Mindset, pick a challenging activity that isn't your primary activity, such as speed chess, juggling, yoga, writing poetry, dancing and so on. It doesn't matter what activity – you can throw tea bags into cups, as long as it's challenging and you don't get distracted by making technical improvements as you learn.

Then, when at the crux of the challenge:

1. Allow yourself to move from a state of focus to **absorption**. For example, help bridge the two brains by stacking your senses or triggering a trance (see page 279).
2. Then, be **effortless** in your action. Trust yourself in each unfolding moment, surrender the need to control the outcome and move with fluency.
3. Lastly, follow your **intuition**. Allow it to guide the unfolding experience and your moment-to-moment decisions.

I suggest practising these points, one by one, as three separate skills to help build your sensitivity to each of these important aspects of flow. When you have found some success in each step, stack them on top of each other as one preparation. Once you are gaining some success, map this practice across and integrate these skills into your main job, sport or hobby.

Chapter 10
BEING FLOW

SO FAR IN PART 3, WE HAVE COVERED SPECIFIC SKILLS and focal points to get into flow for a particular event. This chapter covers important life attributes to consider. We will look at how the notion of play, self, time and your energetics can fit into your lifestyle to allow the Flow Mindset to take centre stage.

LIVING WITH FLOW

To truly embody a Flow Mindset, it is important that it becomes a lifestyle approach and is not just reserved for special occasions. Even when coaching elite performers looking to summit incredible feats, one of the first trainings I employ is to find flow in the everyday mundane tasks that otherwise go by unattended. If we can build habits around finding flow in our cooking, cleaning, hobbies and conversations, then flow will be far more habitual and attainable in moments when we need it most.

How to Find Flow

Flow scholars would argue that this questing for flow occurs already at deeper layers of our unconscious. After all, flow is not purely a momentary embodied state, but also a north star to much of our generative development. To be specific, organisms, such as humans, survive and evolve if they find ways to forestall entropy and become more capable and complex entities. As such, the brain has a radar and attraction for complex and flow-inducing situations that guide our moment-to-moment psychological selection. These experiences help us to become more complex and evolved human beings. It is one of the reasons that we are all attracted to activities that bring out the best in us.

Despite our deeper predilection for flow, however, given today's barrage of distractions, we can't just simply expect our consciousness to lasso itself into cohesion and congruence without guidance – we need all the help we can get to bring it into focus. While you already have the Flow Mindset to put on each morning and its READY, STEADY, FLOW rituals to aid your preparation for specific events, let's now look at a number of themes that can invite and increase the frequency of flow across our lives.

Create your tribe

Ultimately, we all become a product of our environment. In addition to giving ourselves permission to find flow, it helps to be around other people who do the same – groups that celebrate flow attainment. You will find that

Being Flow

certain people and groups allow space for flow and respect it when it happens; they do not try to moderate its importance or squander the space it needs to exist. Equally, they do not diminish the opportunity to train, make mistakes and practise trusting your Being Brain. If we are to find flow regularly, we need to choose and involve ourselves in locations, contexts and tribes that allow flow to flourish. From the schools we attend to the soles we wear on our feet, we make hundreds of choices every day that take us closer to or further away from flow.

It is helpful to remember that we are complex human beings who need support, and if we don't actively optimise the resources available to us, then we actively constrain our flow potential.

Live consciously

Investing in a flow coach is an obvious helpful resource to flow, but just raising your conscious awareness to the choices you already make can have massive consequences. We make hundreds of choices every day, from how we treat the planet to how we treat our neighbours, all of which leave a trail in our consciousness. If these choices are not aligned with your values, you will create conflict and be distracted as your mind tries to justify your actions. It is much more efficient to take the time to be conscious about your life choices than to live with the psychological consequences. Equally, we make choices every day that take us towards or away

How to Find Flow

from flow. For example, I found that taking a moment to breathe before stepping into the shower each morning radically changed my mindset, and choosing to put on sports clothes each morning encouraged movement and micro moments of flow in the mornings. So fully empower the choices you already make each day.

Prioritise your passion

While the pursuit to find and live with Aristotle's 'daimon' may initially seem hedonic or selfish, it is in this search for personal alignment that we are better able to click into a deeper rhythm of life, attracting luck, joy and the ability to give as we journey on. When we gain perspective about our limited time on the planet and relative stature in the universe, doing anything other than what we feel designed to do seems somewhat senseless. As philosopher and theologian Howard Thurman once said, 'Don't ask what the world needs. Ask what makes you come alive, and go do it. Because what the world needs is people who have come alive.'[137] By doing what makes us come alive and questing to self-actualise our ability, we lead by example and subconsciously give permission for others to do the same. In short, prioritise your passions, give them attention and give them space. In a world in which people are redefining careers and creating new professions each day, ensure that you, too, are on a path that captivates your attention.

For me, aligning my actualisation with the actualisation

Being Flow

of others was crystallised in the form of Flow Coaching, a job that is endlessly liberating and abundantly enriching. When we let go of personal success, hedonic pleasures, and extrinsic gains as the primary driving force behind our attention and actions, there is a natural liberation from all the fear, friction and expectation that so often makes life so dissatisfying. While the calling of Flow Coaching may not be for you, once you unpack the layers of 'shoulds', 'musts' and 'have tos' that may otherwise direct your attention and hold you back, perhaps you too can find a more eudaemonic pursuit – a life pursuit that allows you to pursue happiness by creating meaning and purpose, and that puts the betterment of humanity first and foremost. I have no doubt that, while a career shift won't free you from your ego, conflicts, distractions or selfish desires, once you discover a bearing that is harmonious with who you want to be, coming alive, being passionate about life and finding joy in all of life will be more forthcoming.

Assess whether you're in friction or flow

The duality of life echoes through everything around us. Be it religions, philosophies of life, political values, education, supporting a certain sports team or even deciding what to eat for dinner, many of our choices and justifications for what we think and do are done through a notion of duality: good or bad, light or dark, negentropy or entropy, right or wrong, strengths or weaknesses, advantages or drawbacks, love or hate, white or black,

How to Find Flow

and so on. We readily condense how we view our actions and our mind's intentions through a dual approach to keep our justifications simple, and 'in order'. While life and the choices we make are perhaps not so dualistic, often residing in the grey and complexity, I have found it helpful at times to adopt the dual approach of *friction* or *flow*. Simplifying the intentions behind a decision or action to a choice of either *friction* or *flow* has helped me, and others, to instantly reflect and optimise what we are doing, saying or thinking. Whether it is getting ready to hit a tennis serve, chatting with your partner over dinner or writing an email, you can use the simplicity of *friction* or *flow* to help assess and shape your core intentions and decisions towards flow.

Give yourself permission to play

One of the unfortunate consequences of the ever-increasing grasp of the Thinking Brain is that our ability to immerse ourselves in 'play' fades, until our very senior age and its accompanying degenerative brain helps us out. As the responsibilities of life take over and our mind becomes more burdened with staying on top of the day-to-day demands, it is very easy to become accustomed to thinking more, being more serious and concerning ourselves with control. For example, have you ever stopped yourself from being playful, belittling the act, while your mind goes, 'I don't have time for this! I have more important things to do!'? I'm sure we all have.

Being Flow

Being 'playful' is the last state before 'flow' in the Flow Model for a reason. As Peter, CEO, explains:

'Some of my best moments at work, which I'm sure are flow experiences, have come when I'm not too serious, just playing with ideas with colleagues. One moment we are throwing in ridiculous ideas, the next moment we are deeply engaged on a new practice or procedure that will help the company. When we allow ourselves to be playful with our ideas, that's when we all start to come alive.'

Why is being playful so helpful to finding flow? Because being playful demands us to be intuitive and creative. In play, we dance with novelty, explore the edges of our ability, test our capacities, sometimes pulling us into a state of absorption or demanding an intuitive action. As the ancient Greek philosopher Plato stated, 'You learn more about a person in an hour of play than in a year of conversation.'[138]

Proactively being playful is a valuable flow skill as it primes our mind and body to be in flow. Thankfully, play comes naturally to us all. It is one of the first things we do as a child – we only need to re-evaluate the act of being playful as a valuable skill for adulthood. When we start thinking of work as play, for example, rather than 'another day at the office', we become more curious and more open; a lightness and buoyancy to how we

How to Find Flow

feel and approach the task enters the equation. Though easy to prioritise in theory, committing to being playful when a task or life gets challenging can be troublesome. Even sustaining a state of play when out of pressure can be difficult. Try it. It is only a matter of time before the Thinking Brain steps in with a very sensible, practical and reasonable request, persuading us that there are 'more important' things to do: 'I don't have time for this', and so on. Yet sustaining a state of play for any length of time is the same battle we face when finding flow.

So build in a sense of playfulness to how you see the world, generate feelings of playfulness, loosen the expectations and outcomes you're holding on to and see if you can have fun with what you're doing.

Transform time

In deeper states of flow, we are so completely absorbed in the present moment that many people talk about time either slowing down or speeding up. As Chris 'Douggs' McDougall describes:

> 'When I put myself in a situation like jumping off a cliff or something similar ... There's no past, no future, there's just the present ... I can just see more ... I see things in the distance, like the cameraman sitting on the mountain. As I fly past at about 200km/hr, I can smile at him super casually. A microsecond seems to last for seconds. In that space, I can marvel at

Being Flow

water drops of rain as if they are hovering in mid-air; I can be upside down having just jumped off the roof of the building, waving at people in different floors, feeling like I have all the time in the world.'

While the logic of distorting time is up for question, the feeling of time slowing down or speeding up happens to us all. In fact, the physiology of what occurs during this time is fascinating (though if you are not seeking scientific interest, feel free to skip the next two paragraphs as they get juicy!). Firstly, as explained earlier, the depleting 'onion-peeling' effect of our higher cognition stops us computing time in our momentary experience. As attentional resources become increasingly reallocated and dedicated to the demands of the moment, areas dedicated to monitoring time become downregulated. However, there is also a loading factor of the brain's processing resources that impacts this phenomenon. Identical twins Andrew and Alexander Fingelkurts, who are neuroscientists and Co-Heads of Research at the Brain and Mind Technologies Research Centre in Finland, postulate that, as we gather and interpret information in any given moment, the speed of our processing can change, affecting how we experience time.[139] For example, a single second can be broken down into zeptoseconds, a unit of time equal to 0.000 000 000 000 000 000 001 seconds. Within these smaller fractions of time, the brain works hard to put together the jigsaw

How to Find Flow

puzzle of our reality in order to make sense of what we see – like examining the million bits of information in front of us and then cross-referencing the results with the brain's database to determine whether we are looking at a lemon or a tennis ball. The brain handles all this pattern recognition and detective work through a highly sophisticated computational process that has many operational modules (OMs), or predefined categories. These chunk-sized bits of information, or OMs, are what we become aware of in our conscious experience. Like a kaleidoscope, these individual OMs come together to give us a subjective experience, or a reality of each moment. We depend on this type of processing to anticipate and act efficiently. Importantly, during our normal waking consciousness, our OMs operate at relatively consistent and standard rates of processing to process our reality. But when in flow, our ability to process information gets turbo-boosted, and these OMs are processed at a quicker rate. As a result, space is freed up in our processing capacity, and more OMs are then able to compute the same given time unit.

This overflow of OMs makes our perception of time change as we rapidly flick between more modules within the same unit of time. This extra operating capacity also helps to explain why, when we later reflect on our flow experiences, we can often remember an amazing amount of detail in the experience, such as the colour and texture of the water within a section of the wave we just

Being Flow

surfed, or the exact facial expression on our client's face when ending the meeting. In effect, more OMs have been processing the experience, helping us to absorb more information. Conversely, our brain can naturally alter the processing speed to reduce the number of OMs in order to attend and process the new information adequately; as a result, we can also experience time slowing down. In short, the analogue clock will keep ticking, but as our level of processing alters to meet the demands of the moment, our perspective of time becomes malleable.

On a more conceptual level, time is mostly irrelevant. The universe certainly doesn't incorporate a discernible concept of time. An ant doesn't ask another ant, 'What time is it?' Time always has been, and always will be, a concept devised by the Thinking Brain's innovation lab to feel more in control of reality. Despite the obvious benefits to the concept of time, such as helping us to order our day or meet up with a friend at the right time, it can also be argued that time is an ever-consuming aspect of life that has over-reached its intended purpose. Over the centuries, time has become an ever-increasing fuel for conscious thought, rather than a helpful set of reference points as it was intended. The past and future may seem very real in our minds as we project to a future time or recall a past event, but these are just thoughts, hallucinations, abstract concepts and nothing more. The past and future are no more than frames on a movie reel stimulating mental and emotional reactions, diverting us

How to Find Flow

from the present – and then quickly forgotten. Yet we seem to spend more time projecting to the future or regressing to the past than being in the present. The Dalai Lama aptly stated, 'What disappears from memory is how much of any moment is spent worrying about the future.'[140] All that ever truly exists is the 'now'.

The present moment is all we have, and all we will ever have. It is the only time over which we have the privilege to govern. Yet our obsession with time causes our mind to continuously disconnect from the present moment as we spend most of our waking day thinking about what will happen or what has just happened. Time is so influential in our lives that we even strap metal objects to our wrists to constantly remind ourselves of the time. Instead of listening to our bodies, time typically dictates when we sleep, eat and move. This obsession with time has become a prominent feature of cognition and soaks up an enormous amount of attention and psychic energy and is a constant neurological distraction. So much so that when we do surrender to the present moment and let go of any time monitoring, it can feel liberating. Not only is letting go of the need to monitor time cathartic, but the extra psychic energy, which was otherwise occupied with monitoring time, can go towards our performance output.

In practice, knowing that time can be an obstacle to flow, I suggest letting go of the need to continuously monitor time, when you can. Whether that's bringing

Being Flow

your thoughts back to the present or vanquishing the watch from your wrist or clocks in your house, you can take lifestyle steps towards protecting yourself from the excessive distractions of time.

Surrender the idea of 'self'

In flow, we feel connected to our pen, clothes, equipment or another person. A common thread of this increased connection is that the boundaries of the 'self', a concept that is intricately integrated into our psyche, dissolve. In the pursuit to feel more flow in our lives, many of my clients, and myself, have had great success by actively letting go of this concept of 'self' to invite a more consistent connection into our lives.

One of the reasons flow feels so liberating is that in flow, and especially in deeper states of flow, we no longer feel self-conscious. In flow, we are not concerned about how we are being perceived (i.e. 'What are other people thinking of me?'); we are too absorbed for our ego to need protecting. A neuroscientific explanation for this decoupling of our usual self-consciousness relates to a specific network in the brain becoming inhibited. It is commonly accepted that the default mode network (DMN), a network consisting of multiple anatomical areas in the brain, is responsible for monitoring much of our waking and conscious experience.[141] Also known as the 'self-awareness network' in certain sub-disciplines, this network includes the medial PFC, posterior cingulate

How to Find Flow

cortex and angular gyrus, all regions of the brain that help us think about our place in relationships and the world around us. Because the depleting 'onion-peeling' effect of our higher executive functions occurs as we become more and more absorbed, it is posited that the DMN also becomes stripped back, helping to explain how the loss of reflective self-consciousness and the loss of our self-related thoughts occur.

It is not just the self-reflective thoughts that disappear in deep states of flow, but also a sense of self that typically delineates us from others. In deep states of flow, it is common to experience a profound sense of connection to everything around us. Mountaineers report feeling the heartbeat of the mountain, musicians say the instrument becomes an extension of their hands, lovers feel at one with each other and accountants feel hardwired to the spreadsheet. The treasured moments of feeling deeply connected, while enthralling and deeply motivating, are often cast aside as nonsense by our rational mind as they are seemingly illogical and difficult to explain. Though when examining this barrier between 'me' and 'you' more closely, it becomes more tangible.

Firstly, as our DMN activity diminishes, so too does the projected self that we want others to like and judge us by.[142] Using the terms of the well-known psychologist George Herbert Mead, who separated the self into 'Me' and 'I', in flow it is the projected self-image of 'Me' that evaporates.[143] What is left is the agentic I, the present-

Being Flow

orientated self that drives our volition, goals and actions to direct intention, attention and intuition. Or, in Freudian psychological terms, while the 'ego' remains to help us meet our inner desires, the 'superego', our hallucinated self-image, disappears.[144] This part of our self disappears because there is no need for it in flow – it would simply add friction and be a distraction to engage our obsession with what others think about us. Whatever term or language you prefer to use, what is undeniable is that, when the DMN goes down, we lose the strong sense of a representational self, which typically consumes much of our thinking, and is scientifically known as 'hypo-egoism'.

Another explanation involves a dissolving of the boundaries that we typically insert in our psyche. In addition, Andrew Newberg and Eugene D'Aquili, neuroscientists from the University of Pennsylvania, suggest that, when we experience a 'oneness', a specific area of our brain shuts down. Studying the brain activity of Tibetan Buddhists and Franciscan nuns during their experiences of absolute connection, they observed that the area in our brain most responsible for navigating our body's location and drawing the borderline of self from other, known as the orientation association area (OAA), stopped receiving signals and was temporarily blinded. According to Newberg:

'Once this happens, we can no longer draw a line and say this is where the self ends and this is where the rest of the world begins, so the brain concludes,

How to Find Flow

it has to conclude, that at this moment you are one with everything.'[145]

As William James once stated, 'We are like islands in the sea, separate on the surface but connected in the deep.'[146] In summary, the de-layering of the cognitive onion and consequential inhibition of self-reflection, egoism and self-monitoring helps to explain in part why deep states of flow liberate us from our incessant self-consciousness, and why deep flow experiences are repeatedly described as an experience of 'self-transcendence' or an 'out-of-body' experience.

In my experience, practising surrendering this 'self' is not so much a performance hack but a lifestyle approach. Thinking that we can *instantly* decouple our attachment to our projected superego is probably a cunning act of the Thinking Brain trying to fool us into its grasp, a trap in which our spiritual ego takes the reins in an act of hyper-egoism rather than hypo-egoism. Why does this happen? Well, once this egoic 'Me' is established, its foremost goal becomes that of protecting itself and justifying its self-existence, and it will do anything it can to advance itself. It seeds its way into our daily life, continuously hijacking the contents of our consciousness as we generate thoughts, feelings and perspectives to confirm and self-justify our manifested notion of self. We warp our reality to support and strengthen the egoic projection we have built. Whether it is the thought of needing to win to prove

Being Flow

to others that we are worthwhile or debating what to wear in the morning as it might impact on what other people think about us, most of this subservient thinking and behaviour that supports the notion of our reflective self is automatic and often goes unnoticed. While this sense of 'Me', and the stream of consequential thoughts, can feel sensationally real and dictate much of our life as we post selfies on social media, what we are really reacting to is a culmination of musings from our Thinking Brain. Allowed too much time in the captain's chair, over time, our Thinking Brain creates a superego, a psychic matrix or maze that keeps us locked in, and the Thinking Brain firmly in the driver's seat.

Being aware that this projected and reflected self is ultimately an illusion of our ego, albeit something that we have become very attached to, we can come to understand that it does not need to define us, nor shape us. We can learn not to take this 'Me' too seriously. The mind will always try to conjure its existence and justify its importance; it is a condition of being human. But if we can see the illusion of self as precisely that, a helpful illusion (at times), its walls of sustenance don't have to hold substance. In this new paradigm, we don't have to identify with our thoughts; we don't even need to react to them, if we don't want to. Instead, we can smile at our own ingenuity of any rising thoughts, let them pass and then choose to attach to those that take us closer to flow.

This might feel like a big ask, finding our way through

How to Find Flow

an internal maze, but the closer we look at the construct of a projected self, the more its fragilities become quite obvious. For example, does our name or status define who we are? No – we can change our name or job and still be the same person. Do our achievements, clothes, haircuts, thoughts, perceptions or body shape define who we are? No – remove any, or all, of these features that we ordinarily grip tightly to and we still exist. Even brain-damaged patients who have lost their personal memories and history can still display a strong sense of self.[147] Our sense of self, therefore, is far deeper than the projections we display to the world. In understanding that the genesis of 'me' is nothing but an illusion, we can learn to surrender the need to self-author a projected image of who we want to be in the eyes of others. In doing so, we can intentionally blur the self-installed boundaries of 'You' and 'Me', and move the demarcation lines to welcome a greater connection in our lives – removing a major barrier that ordinarily locks us out of flow. We still keep the volitional and authentic sense of self, but, by dropping this ever-constant 'Me', our thoughts, feelings and actions don't have to be at the whim of an ever-changing and fragile projected self. Moreover, we liberate an enormous amount of energy that is otherwise powering all this activity.

Reading this book, surrounding ourselves with others who don't cling to their superego, reducing the mirrors in our house and paying less attention to what we look like

Being Flow

on social media are all examples of lifestyle choices that deprive this 'me' of the sustenance it needs to exist; we interrupt the flow of information that it relies on to install its dominance in our minds. When we do, we give ourselves a window to escape the hamster wheel mentality that our projected self otherwise locks us into in order to support its existence, we liberate our consciousness from much of its pre-programmed instructions and use the gearbox of our mind to shift into a more connected and richer experience. As the story goes ... a man said to Lord Buddha, 'I want happiness.' Lord Buddha replied. 'First remove "I" that's ego, then "want", that's your desire, now you are left with happiness.'[148]

Next time you engage in your work, ask yourself, 'What boundaries of self can I dissolve here?'; 'Can I allow the keyboard to feel like an extension of my fingertips?'; 'Can I remind myself of the human connection I share with my colleague before speaking with them?' Whatever equipment or variables you are working with, see if you can allow yourself to feel less separated, more connected, and witness how your experiential tapestry grows ever richer – bridging you ever closer to flow.

Embody your energetics

'If you want to find the secrets of the universe, think in terms of energy, frequency and vibration,' explained physicist and electrical inventor Nikola Tesla.[149] In flow, we seem to go beyond the restraints of technique,

How to Find Flow

pain, fatigue, time and self. Every cell and atom work cohesively towards one aim. In doing so, we seemingly gain access to an abundance of energy, channelling it perfectly, as if we are turning on a tap that we have kept hidden for special occasions. How the movement and transference of our energy is stored, harnessed, released and expended is somewhat difficult to comprehend, as we can't see it with our own eyes. However, what is undeniable is that energy runs through our bodies like electricity in the walls of our house or the love we feel for our family. We cannot see this energetic force with our eyes, yet it, too, is undeniable. What if you could tap into this energetic feeling outside of flow? What would it do for your life? Would it lay the foundations to help you springboard into flow more easily?

Interestingly, we are always emitting energy to varying levels, depending on what we are doing. For example, Dr Akira Seto and his team reported that martial arts experts have measured significantly higher pulsating magnetic fields from their palms when preparing for an energetic punch.[150] Seto's studies revealed that the emitted chi from the subjects' palms produced a magnetic field a thousand times stronger than a human's normal biomagnetic field, which also created significant changes in measures of infrasound, electromagnetism, static electricity, infrared radiation, gamma rays, particle and wave flows, organic ion flows and light. Energetic scientists would argue that energy channels are the most fundamental systems in

Being Flow

our body and give rise to, and regulate, all other innate systems – a logic that many civilisations have long adopted in their examination of the human body. For example, yogic science describes a network of 72,000 'Nadis' or energy channels throughout the body; and ancient Chinese practices outline twelve 'meridians' or energy highways that facilitate our energetic movement. Dr Oschman suggests that these energy pathways differ from the common scientific explanations of internal communication, such as diffusible gases, neurochemical exchanges or nervous system communication, and provide a much faster avenue for communication.[151] He highlights that communication within energy fields can travel at speeds near that of the speed of light – around 180,000 miles per second. He suggests communication can occur almost instantaneously using the body's connective tissue and continuum pathways. Whether it is the examination of magnetic fields, electrophotonic emissions, brainwave frequencies, bioelectromagnetics or other scientific areas of interest, the future study of energetics will hopefully shed light on much that we can feel but cannot yet explain rationally.

While we are still understanding how our energy systems work, it is clear that, at the most basic level, our body is made up of matter, or billions of vibrating atoms in the form of protons, neutrons and electrons. Your hand, for example, is made up of tissues, bone, veins, blood, ligaments and nails. Each of those components is made up of millions of cells. Each cell is made up of a cell wall, cell membrane, cytoplasm, nucleus, mitochondria, ribosome, endoplasmatic reticulum and other cell organelles. At the most basic level, each of these components is made up of millions of atoms, pulled together to create a specific form. Derek Leinweber, a quantum physicist who featured in Professor Wilczek's 2004 Physics Nobel Prize Lecture, suggests that these atoms are composed of mostly 'empty space'.[152] In the case of a hydrogen atom, 99.9999999999996 per cent 'empty space' and 0.0000000000004 per cent hydrogen. This 'empty space' is not actually vacant but instead made up of invisible vibrating energy, electrostatic fields. Meaning that 99.999... per cent of what we are is energy.

While the idea of being a stream of energy can be mind-blowing, it is an important notion to get our heads around if we want to use our energetic awareness to help increase flow. Ordinarily, we might see ourselves as physical beings that radiate energy; for some, this may be the first time thinking about ourselves in this manner. However, importantly, this is not accurate. Rather, we are undoubtedly, first and foremost, an energetic being holding matter. In essence, we are a cohesive energy stream containing billions of atoms that take a physical form to the naked eye. We may only see and feel our physical body, but at a minute level, we are all vibrating.

When we see ourselves primarily as an energetic being and perform from this perspective, we can begin

Being Flow

to free ourselves from many of the mental and physical distractions and limitations that often plague our actions. Homero Diaz, eight-time National Champion Enduro rider, describes how he prepares for a competition:

> 'Every single time, right before I start, I put the bike in neutral, and then I rub my hands together to create a little bit of energy. This is something I do when the pressure is on, to get out of my head. When I start thinking in terms of energy, I'm able to connect to what's real in life. When I feel the energy between my hands, I cannot be sad or nervous. I feel energised, in a good way. Then, after feeling the energy, I clap my hands really hard, and then rub them again. It only takes five seconds and then I'm ready to start. That's my secret!'

Like Homero, it is by tuning into this energetic awareness that many of my coachees have moved beyond doubt, fatigue and distraction to instantly *be* more. By simply helping clients to improve their sensitivity to energetics, I have helped executives better connect with colleagues, artists express themselves, athletes overcome pain and fatigue, and many people release trauma and emotional blockages. For example, working with a runner, Kelly, I used this energetic approach to help her rise above her own limitations and that of her critics. After I helped her to connect with her energetic body, when times got

How to Find Flow

tough, Kelly was able to go to a different place free from distraction and conflict. There are many times during her races when the mind and body are so fatigued that they just want to give up or slow to a halt. Yet it is at precisely these times that the champions of these sports have the resolve and ability to find another gear and keep advancing. Just as Kelly's body wanted to become heavy, strained and sore, we worked on imagining herself running as a free and liberated energetic being, leaving her physical body trailing a few steps behind. This new perspective immediately gave her a lift, making her body feel lighter, leaving any pain behind, out of consciousness. Months later, with a Flow Mindset installed and Kelly seeing herself as an energetic runner, she was able to win, on multiple occasions, her most sought-after races.

If you choose to see yourself as an energetic performer, you, too, can feel lighter, increase your vitality, embody a greater fluency, curate quantum coherence and create a suitable platform for flow. As Amanda Brennan, a screen performance acting coach, commented in a podcast we did together:

> 'Everything we do radiates some kind of energy; our posture, our bodily actions, our words, our feelings, all communicate a type of energy. Trying to change each component to match a performance can be highly complex, being a distraction in and of itself. Instead, when we look to embody a type of energy

Being Flow

that we want to exuberate, these more complicated components just fall in line.'[153]

Harnessing your natural flow of energy is not something that you need to think about, but rather something that you need to embody and feel. It requires a sensitivity that is foreign to our Thinking Brain, but central to our Being Brain. Connecting with your bodily energy, and developing this sense, is often easier than one might first assume. You only have to rub a balloon against your hair to see how a small electrical charge can make the balloon stick to the bottom of a hand or cause the strands of hair on your head to stand upright, without the balloon even touching it.

Want to feel the buzz of energy yourself? Now it's your turn to be the energetic performer. Read the following flow skill and then put down the book and give it your full attention.

You are going to feel some energy, and heat, in between your hands. During this exercise, place your entire awareness on the space between your hands. Whilst you might be tempted to think about what's happening in this exercise, I encourage you to feel and sense what is occurring.

Ready?

- Rub your hands together for thirty seconds, or until hot, and then hold them close *without touching*, about 3cm apart.

How to Find Flow

- Once your hands are closely separated, you may start to feel a slight fuzziness, something that feels like a low vibration just beyond the surface of your skin. When you tune in to this feeling, you might start to feel a slight repelling force between the hands, like two opposing magnets. It helps to move the hands ever so slightly apart and then closer together again (but not touching) to feel this repelling sensation. Tune in to this sensation. It can help to close your eyes in order to maximise your commitment to the task and give it your full sensory attention.
- If you can feel a slight repelling feeling, then you are connecting with the energy of your body. More importantly, did you notice that the more you attuned towards this energetic space, the more present your experience? It is almost impossible to be consumed by distracting thoughts or emotions and be tuned into an energetic experience at the same time.

Play with this task. You can practise moving your hands wider apart while keeping the magnetic feeling of energy between them. Make a ball of energy, fill it with confidence and then eat it or gift it to someone else. Once you get a feel for it, practise finding that magnetic feeling between your hands without rubbing your hands and first creating heat.

Being Flow

Now that you are aware of how you can use being an energetic performer to your advantage, go ahead and use it. Imagine how you would perform, move or be in flow if your energy was unrestricted. Integrate it into your preparations, bring it into your performances and share this flow skill with others.

> **LET'S RECAP**
>
> In this chapter, we have looked at several principles to invite flow into your life:
> - surrounding yourself with flow-minded people
> - being conscious about your life choices
> - prioritising your passions; enjoying inspired action, personally and professionally
> - self-assessing whether you're creating friction or flow
> - giving yourself permission to play and practising sustaining a state of play
> - letting go of the need to monitor time
> - surrendering the idea of your projected 'self'
> - embodying your energetics to move beyond your mental or physical constraints
>
> Don't just use these principles in your main activity – allow them to infiltrate into all areas of your life; allow these flow skills to become lifestyle skills.

How to Find Flow

YOUR CHALLENGE

I challenge you to not only utilise the lessons in this book to advance your satisfaction and performance in your primary activity, but to go further and optimise multiple aspects of your life. Let's start by assessing flow in the different areas of your life:

Rate (out of ten), how frequently you find flow in your:
Favourite hobby   _____
Family interactions   _____
Romantic relationship   _____
Fitness routines   _____
Musical participation   _____
Primary sport   _____
Work   _____
With children (your own or others)   _____
Other   _____
Other   _____
Other   _____

In examination of your life, which areas lack flow? Please feel free to add other areas to this list. Now choose three areas that could do with more attention. For each area, write down next to your score a principle from this chapter that you could integrate into this area. For example, in wanting to find more flow within a special relationship,

Being Flow

I might choose the skill of seeing ourselves as energetic beings to improve the connection.

Next, write down one action, for each of the three areas, that you are willing to commit to, and that will help you embody these principles. Using the example just given, my action before engaging in the conversation might be to feel some energy between my hands or visualise the other person as billions of vibrating atoms as opposed to seeing their looks and clothes. Be realistic; it is better not to shoot too high and feel like a failure.

1) _____
2) _____
3) _____

To keep yourself accountable and ensure these actions happen, externalise them. Write them down and stick them on your wall at home. Tell your partner or friends about the changes you want to make. Breathe life into your commitments.

Now go back and do the same for every area of your life, then make one committed action for each area.

Conclusion

OVER TO YOU

IN THIS BOOK, I HAVE PROPOSED THAT ADOPTING A Flow Mindset will give you a new way to meet the challenges in your life, provide you with a natural resilience to deal with life's stressors and help to buffer the stress of everyday life. Prioritising flow, above other agendas, will help improve the quality of your experiences and help bring a sense of meaningful engagement towards your actions. It is my experience that when we pivot towards flow, the satisfaction that we gain from our endeavours increases, personal performance improves and we are able to actualise our potential during important moments.

You now have a mantra, 'READY, STEADY, FLOW', to use in the moment when you are feeling friction or fear in your life. If you find yourself trying too hard, or being nervous, stressed or bored, you can use this mantra to take charge of your experience.

READY will remind you to think less to be more. It will

Over to You

help to rewire your mental approach to your challenges and achievements, away from outcomes and towards a true north of flow. It will remind you that you are driving your self-leadership and every task has the potential for a deeply engaging optimal experience.

STEADY will remind you that you have to manage your moment-to-moment consciousness to protect yourself from internal and external distractions and conflicts. It will help you to build psychophysiological blueprints to train your psyche to be in flow when the moment arrives, ensuring you invite the intensity of a challenge or the fascination of complexity. And it will encourage you to take charge of your preparations before events so that you can progressively shape your state towards flow.

FLOW will remind you that, no matter your preparation, you can't simply expect to fall into flow; you need to trust your Being Brain, give yourself permission to become absorbed and let go of the need to control the situation to find a sense of effortlessness within the moment. It will prompt you to build a relationship with your intuition and trust your innate capacities to deal with the moment as it unfolds.

While 'READY, STEADY, FLOW' is a tried-and-tested pre-performance ritual to get you firing and buzzing when you need it most, perhaps more importantly, the Flow Mindset is a lifestyle philosophy that will reward you richly the more you adopt it.

Now that you have the skills that I have spent decades

accruing and teaching to others, the success of these skills will depend on one last critical component: you. Just inhaling the overarching theme of the book – flow matters – will allow flow to seep into your thinking and awareness from time to time. Putting flow first when engaging in life's challenges will hopefully be transformative. But if you actively use your flow skills daily and adopt a Flow Mindset across your life, then the world is your oyster, my friend.

FLOW MATTERS

We live in a world in which the pace of change constantly requires a faster and smarter operator, one who can self-manage their own well-being, thrive in competitive environments and innovate for breakfast. The rise of technology is forcing many traditional jobs to be overtaken by AI; as such, graduates are now expected to evolve their own jobs, be more agile and adaptive than ever before, and be prepared for a future of over forty different jobs in twelve completely different career paths within their lifetime. The pressures to survive, let alone thrive, are immense.

Most of the time, our inner states are not prioritised, let alone optimised. We readily alienate our experience and put it to one side as we get on with more 'important' and productive things, treating the present as a means to an end and diminishing its quality. We keep busy,

Over to You

striving and naively hoping that, eventually, we will be rewarded for all our hard work, neglecting this accrual of sub-optimal, and often poor, daily experiences. But in doing so, we douse our inner flame and subconsciously give permission for others to do the same; we watch the quality of our life dwindle, day by day. This industrialised mindset of prioritising our external over our internal, productivity over presence, outcome over process is a problem. It diminishes the very locus of control required for us to optimise our inner experience towards the satisfaction and performances we seek, dampening our engagement, choking our connection and reducing the quality of life in the process.

The McKinsey Global Research Institute conducted a survey in which they asked leaders across industries what ingredient they thought was most often missing for them and for their colleagues, and they almost invariably replied: a strong sense of meaning.[154] Even though the 5,000+ executives interviewed in this study admitted that they were five times more productive in flow, they reported that both themselves and their employees were in flow well below 10 per cent of the time. 90 per cent of the executives asserted that the bottleneck to unleashing more flow lay not in intellectual or emotional solutions, but in the ability to add meaning – a sentiment that is echoed by the 83 per cent of employees who report 'meaning' to be a top priority at work. In other words, what society seems to need more than the 'change-makers' found in

How to Find Flow

Silicon Valley are 'meaning-makers'. This call for greater *meaning* goes beyond defining direction or attaching a virtuous goal to the workload – this is already a tactic applied in many organisations. Rather, the experience at work needs to be richer, more complex and of higher quality. Mixed with the unacceptable rate of mental health issues and an anxiety-driven population that is simply burnt out, disempowered and far too distracted to find their own flow, there has never been a more important time to crystallise the human skills of self-actualisation.

Albert Einstein once said that 'The world we have created is a process of our thinking. It cannot be changed without changing our thinking.'[155] Putting flow first and adopting a Flow Mindset offers a new way to approach all of life's challenges. Personally, it has the potential to fundamentally improve the way in which we live, learn, create, engage and perform. Professionally, putting flow first provides a solution to how we can increase creativity, efficiency and productivity, without negatively affecting motivation or participation. On an individual level, flow's alignment with an inner harmony offers an exciting opportunity to bridge the quest for well-being and performance, allowing both happiness *and* excellence. The Flow Mindset offers a simple, unified approach to our development, enabling us to enjoy both our personal and professional challenges.

Prioritising flow in our lives can be the difference not only between success and failure, but also between

Over to You

living a fully engaged life or not, a meaningful life or not. In prioritising the quality of personal experience, we fabricate a richer, more complete and complex self. In the process, we free ourselves from much of the dysfunction that ordinarily reaps disorder and dissatisfaction, chaos and conflict. We become more liberated to love, more capable to create and more committed to connect. Since our future prosperity depends on how attention is invested in the now, the Flow Mindset can take us closer to both our personal and professional prosperity and offers a beginning to Aristotle's age-old calling for us all to find and live with our true selves.

While the personal development of flow may seem like a selfish pursuit, putting flow first fundamentally helps us to better contribute to society. Developing internal harmony is not just self-regarding; it also spurs a resilient and harmonious collective future. Every time we invest attention in an idea, pick up a book, turn on the TV, purchase a product or choose one activity over another, the texture of our future changes, even if in microscopic ways. Across all individuals, the psychic energy culminating from these microscopic decisions, in no small manner, actively builds the quality of our life, and that of our culture and society. For humanity to evolve beyond our genetically coded desires for power and pleasure, investing our attention into improving the quality of our experience will help to challenge those next to us, to also *be* more and create cultures that are

How to Find Flow

structured to produce the same. As flow becomes a more conscious goal for many, it will be passed down from one generation to another, becoming part of the fabric of future generations.

Collectively, if we are brave enough to re-prioritise our focus towards flow above the outcomes of trophies, affirmation or profit, then we can empower positive cultural and systemic change. Putting flow first provides a solution to find sustainable personal prosperity without the need for the continued consumption that seems to placate this need, producing unnecessary carbon emissions and overusing the planet's limited resources in the process. Prosperity without growth – what a world this will be.

In schools, instead of using top-down education processes to force content into a diversity of minds (who may not best learn in this manner) – processes that kill the love of learning and shame those brains that are not developed enough to rote-learn information and recall on demand – having flow as a focus can put the quality of student learning at the centre of the classroom. By prioritising the learner's experience, we can develop delivery styles that help students to cultivate innate positive tendencies towards discovery, such as autonomously inspired experiential learning, as is often the way we best learn as adults in the field.

In business, we can move beyond the Thinking Brain's need for control and surveillance of short-term compliance, and instead focus on nurturing curiosity,

Over to You

engagement and self-regulation towards personal performance. By building autonomously motivated workforces that make intuitive decisions based on their first-hand experience, not that of a distant manager, businesses will be better able to serve their clients, and improve productivity in the process. They will be better placed to be value-driven not task-driven, empower employees rather than control them, foster innovation over automation, and offer an inviting place to work.

In leadership, with flow as a guiding star, we can let go of the need to control everything. Instead, promote authenticity, mastery over compliance, challenge over comfort and learning over blame. We can be inquisitive rather than adversarial, enactive over reactive and enjoy being a facilitator rather than an influencer.

Given today's rate of burnout, disengagement, anxiety and mental health-related issues, perhaps there has never been a more vital time to develop the personal skills for flow, and yet rarely have we been so in need of something, yet so idle about finding it. As more and more people reject spiritual beliefs and values, humans are actively looking for ways to add meaning and richness to their experiences and enhance the quality of consciousness.[156] Just look at the rise of coffee shops or the trillion-dollar drugs industry. Most of what we do, from searching out better coffee shops to enjoying a glass of wine while researching our next holiday, is to improve our experience of life. We often claim that we

How to Find Flow

are 'smarter' than ever before, yet, while most of us are already looking for a richer state of consciousness, we are looking in totally the wrong place. It is as if we enter the supermarket knowing that we want wholesome food, only to repeatedly get distracted by the well-packaged unhealthy products that promise short-term pleasure. We may know we have the potential to feel better and perform better, but we continually get in our own way, and, in doing so, deny ourselves the richness of self-actualisation.

YOU MATTER

Whether you like it or not, your time on this planet is very short, relatively speaking. It is not a rehearsal. The more you can appreciate the fragility of your own life, the true value of each day, the more you will treasure the time you have left. Correspondingly, the more you will appreciate that your experience of each moment matters – and, in turn, flow matters. After all, the collective sum of these moments will forge your life tapestry, and the collective quality of these moments will form the quality of your life.

The price you are paying for not managing your inner states and settling for sub-optimal experiences is unfathomable. You deserve more; you are worth more; you are responsible for what you are passing down the generational chain. While many of us tend to think of our

Over to You

potential as capped or fixed, as if we have a specific shoe size to fit into, the work surrounding neuroplasticity and brain growth states the opposite. Increased capacity and regular flow are available to us all. No buts. We may choose to get in our own way and talk ourselves out of opportunities, but the opportunity-cost and experiential-loss is enormous and frankly unacceptable in this day and age. The search for meaning in all that we do must start now, if it hasn't already.

The benchmark in which you measure a good life is entirely up to you. My hope is that this book will remind you to value your inner experience and journey beyond results. It will serve you to:

- value flow as a worthwhile lifestyle pursuit
- continuously develop your experiential intelligence; to hold the reins of your experience, attune your attention and curate the contents in your consciousness so that you can readily enjoy what this world has to offer – no matter the adversity thrown at you
- to think less and be more; encourage your Thinking Brain and Being Brain to work in unison, pulling each other towards complexity
- adopt a Flow Mindset to give you a new approach to live beyond the distractions and conflicts that mar your daily experiences
- to practise the READY, STEADY, FLOW preparatory skills of a Flow Mindset so that you have a proven

How to Find Flow

strategy to ritualise your preparations for the moments that matter

Becoming flow-fit

Walking in what I can only describe as my life flow, or what Hindus and Buddhists call their 'dharma' or life's purpose, I seem to have been rewarded tenfold. The greatest of these rewards has been recently returning to the tennis court after twenty-three years. After a breakthrough in science re-diagnosed my injury, from tennis and golfer's elbow to neurogenic thoracic outlet syndrome, which revealed a compression of my radial nerve at the first rib and brachial plexus, I engaged in some experimental treatments and, slowly but surely, my everyday pain decreased. With less restricted movement, my nerves started to heal, and my strength and capability grew. Stirred by this newfound freedom, I gradually made my way back onto the tennis court to play with my kids and, to my surprise, realised that my arms could handle more load. My ability to play for longer grew every month and, after twelve months, I was able to play for a full hour without too many repercussions. Not long after, I got invited to play for my local club, which I accepted with great excitement and trepidation.

Simply walking back onto the court in a competitive manner was overwhelming. I was paired up with a spritely twenty-years-younger budding tennis player. Sure enough, as the match started, I felt completely out of my

Over to You

depth. The accuracy and confidence that I once had as a teenager felt out of reach. Still unable to serve over-arm because of my injury, I was serving under-arm, giving my opponent an easy shot on every return. This only made matters worse as I watched my opponent hit many of my returns out of my reach. Nervous and flabbergasted by the occasion, I rapidly lost the first set 6–1. It soon became obvious that, despite my best efforts, I was not match fit either; huffing and puffing, trying to slow the game down, I quickly fatigued. My opponent was in total control.

At the change of ends, grabbing a banana out of my bag, I saw the Flow Model printed on a piece of paper in between my spare racquets. On seeing the blue and red arc, I suddenly realised that the occasion of finally being back on court after twenty-three years was so overwhelming that I had been ignoring my experiential intelligence. I had left my Flow Mindset at home and was now paying the price. I realised that I was barely enjoying being on court, when only a year ago I would have given my right arm to get this very chance. Playing a competitive match had felt so foreign that I had gone into reactive mode. My mind was focused on trying to control the score and my Thinking Brain was having fun beating myself up for not doing better. I was anchored in the red.

I stopped. Thankfully, I knew exactly what to do. I reset and embodied the flow approach. Before each new point, I set a STAF to consume my attention. Letting go of trying to control the outcome of the point, I focused on

How to Find Flow

finding my rhythm and allowing my intuition to find flow within each shot. And in a very short time, I was starting to surprise myself again. To the annoyance of my opponent, who threw his racquet over the fence into a field, I found my effortless returns and the result took care of itself; I won. Face in my towel, shedding an exhausted tear at the end of the match, I was crying with an unexpected joy and satisfaction. Not only had I just had my first match of competitive tennis in twenty-three years, but I finally felt free of the self-shackles that I never knew how to remove in my youth.

Although my body still limits my time and application on the court, I've been able to get back competing, win the Australian National Championships 40+ and enjoy playing the senior International Tennis Federation tour. Not long ago, I even got to represent my country at the senior World Cup – a privilege I never imagined could happen – and made the last sixteen of the senior Individual World Championships. Finding my flow in the ultimate crucible, in my favoured flow activity, was a dream I had long let go of. To be back, mixing with the very best again, was insanely rewarding. Joy, surprise and elation still fill my heart when I look back. Parts of me that had long felt fractured were now reunited.

Every time I play, I can feel that space of uncertainty and intensity, and relish the opportunity to practise putting on my Flow Mindset. Like every human, I still get triggered by many distractions and conflicts when challenged and

Over to You

in the pressure cooker. Though, now that I have a tried-and-tested framework to use, the stress of it all seems less significant, and somewhat enjoyable no matter the stakes. Just as self-actualisation is not an outcome, but a process of actualising self, the same can be said for flow. By embodying a 'flow-fit' attitude, as we would a 'get-fit' attitude for becoming physically fit, finding flow is never an outcome that I need to hit, rather a continual process or journey that I can enjoy. It is not a skill that I will eventually master, rather an art form that I can fine-tune and practise across business, sport, relationships and almost every aspect of my life. No matter how small or big the challenge or level of complexity I face, with flow as my true north, life unfolds as a series of wondrous moments. As Craig Hatkoff, co-founder with Robert De Niro of the Tribeca Film Festival, once told me, 'I have always tried to live by the "awe principle". That is: Can I find awe, wonder and enchantment in the most mundane things conceivable?'

A challenge I give to all those who I coach – and now you – is to adopt the same flow-fit attitude. We will not get strong or fast overnight; we need to train for it and enjoy the training, otherwise it will taper off. We are all human and will always be imperfect. If you can embrace the journey, however, and enjoy applying your flow skills at any given opportunity, then you will be flow-fit.

How to Find Flow

YOUR FLOW RITUAL

The aim of this last section is to give you a personalised ritual to help you apply your Flow Mindset. In the diagram that follows, I have included some of the important tools for you to choose from. This list has helped hundreds of others before you, so please use it; treasure it.

Over time, once a Flow Mindset is embedded, you may only need to implement one of the flow skills to get your flow going. For example, sometimes you might be slightly too conscious and other times you might be holding on too tight. If you have first done your practice, then you may start to intuitively realise which tool from your toolbox you need to wield in any given moment. Ultimately, all these lessons are a variety of flow skills for your toolbox; use them intuitively, as you see fit.

Having said that, using the Flow Ritual provided, or creating your own one, is essential to initially help install your Flow Mindset. You do not need to use every item in sequence – this may be a distraction. Rather, pick one that resonates with you at the time. I also encourage you to draw symbols, fill in the blanks, add pictures and customise it to make it your own.

Remember to keep it simple – don't let the Thinking Brain take control! Update it, refresh it; keep the Thinking Brain on its toes.

There is so much our attention has to attend to throughout the day that it is easy to forget about the

Over to You

lessons in this book in the moment. To stop that from happening, I suggest you create a one-pager that will remind you of the important lessons that resonate with you. You can start by using your flow ritual – that you will fill in shortly – and then add any important phrases or images. Print it and put in your kit bag, on the fridge or on your desk at work – somewhere you will see it before or during your activity. In addition, many people have chosen to wear a blue wristband that symbolises the blue arc of the Flow Model and the intended message of adopting a Flow Mindset – a constant reminder whenever our peripheral vision catches sight of it. Some even write, 'READY, STEADY, FLOW' on it, to give the mind an extra nudge. I wear a blue wristband, and I encourage you to do the same; it really does work.

Your life's experiential tapestry awaits. It is now up to you to put knowledge into practice for your future wisdom. If you want flow to be the engine of your evolution and propel yourself to the heights you inherently know you are capable of, then give it your attention; give it time. The journey to flow has been one of my greatest adventures, and your greatest adventure is waiting for you too.

How to Find Flow

FLOW MINDSET – 'READY, STEADY, FLOW'

Where is your experience?

'READY'	'STEADY'	'FLOW'
Release & Reset	Set Up for Success	Be Absorbed
☐ RELEASE any sticky emotion. Acknowledge it, accept it and let it go. ☐ RESET your psychophysiology. Chicken dance, shake up your mind and body.	☐ FLOW BLUEPRINT. See it, feel it and embody your projection in flow. ☐ INVITE the INTENSITY. Ignite your motivation. Optimise the level of challenge or complexity. 'Challenge me'.	☐ SYNC UP. Promote your Being Brain to unify your psyche. ☐ TRIGGER a TRANCE and power up your presence.

Over to You

'READY'	'STEADY'	'FLOW'
Ready Your Flow Mindset ☐ THINK LESS, BE MORE. ☐ Position flow as your primary intention. Be in the BLUE. ☐ 'LEARN, GROW, FLOW'. Be compassionate and collaborative in your journey for mastery.	☐ SHAPE your STATE. Protect and attune your attention towards presence and play.	Be Effort-less ☐ SOFTEN your gaze. ☐ Feel your RHYTHM. Sway your hips, move with fluidity. ☐ TRUST your intuition. ☐ 'LET GO, LET FLOW'. ☐ Be an ENERGETIC Performer.

To download the 1-Page Flow Ritual, comprehensive workbook, and all the illustrations featured in this book, visit www.cameronnorsworthy.com

REFERENCES

All interviews/quotes in this book have been referenced, otherwise they were interviews conducted directly with the author. The occasional client's name has been changed to protect confidentiality.

INTRODUCTION

1   https://www.gallup.com/workplace/349484/state-of-the-global-workplace.aspx#ite-659738

2   Doser, L. (2014). In Afterword, Leskowitz, E. D. (ed.). *Sports, Energy, and Consciousness: Awakening Human Potential Through Sport.* Createspace, p. 196.

3   https://www.sas.upenn.edu/psych/seligman/aparep98.htm

4   Csikszentmihalyi, M. (1991). *Flow: The psychology of optimal experience* (Vol. 41). HarperPerennial. p. 42.

5   Orlans, H. (2002). *T. E. Lawrence: Biography of a Broken Hero.* McFarland. p. 97.

CHAPTER 1: RECOGNISE FLOW

6   Campbell, Michael. 'Behind the Name: Meaning, Origin and History of the Name "Aristotle"'. *Behind the Name: The Etymology and History of First Names.* www.behindthename.com. Retrieved 6 April 2012.

References

7   Norton, D. L. (1976). *Personal Destinies.* **Princeton Univ. Press.**

8   Documentary, Kobe Bryant – Explains Being In the Zone 2009 NBA productions – CauserHost – https://www.youtube.com/watch?v=T9M8TvDfbjQ also see https://business.uoregon.edu/news/flow-experience-and-sports-products

9   Quoted in Shainberg, L. (1989). 'Finding the zone'. *New York Times Magazine*, 38, 34–6.

10   Norsworthy, C., Jackson, B., & Dimmock, J. A. (2021). 'Advancing our understanding of psychological flow: A scoping review of conceptualizations, measurements, and applications'. *Psychological bulletin*, 147(8), 806.

11   Norsworthy, C., Jackson, B., & Dimmock, J. A. (2021). 'Advancing our understanding of psychological flow: A scoping review of conceptualizations, measurements, and applications'. *Psychological bulletin*, 147(8), 806.

12   https://www.mckinsey.com/capabilities/people-and-organizational-performance/our-insights/increasing-the-meaning-quotient-of-work#/

13   https://www.nytimes.com/2013/11/03/magazine/jumper-cables-for-the-mind.html

14   Shernoff, D. J., & Anderson, B. (2014). 'Enacting flow and student engagement in the college classroom'. *The Wiley Blackwell Handbook of Positive Psychological Interventions.* Wiley Blackwell. pp 194–212.

15   Delle Fave, A., & Bassi, M. (2000). 'The quality of experience in adolescents' daily lives: Developmental perspectives'. *Genetic, Social, and General Psychology Monographs*, 126(3), 347; Bassi, M., Steca, P., Delle Fave, A., & Caprara, G. V. (2007). 'Academic self-efficacy beliefs and quality of experience in learning'. *Journal of Youth and Adolescence*, 36(3), 301–12; Bassi, M., Steca, P., Delle Fave, A., & Caprara, G. V. (2007). 'Academic self-efficacy beliefs and quality of experience in learning'. *Journal of Youth and Adolescence*, 36(3), 301–12.

16   Rathunde, K. (2023). 'Montessori education, optimal experience, and flow'. *The bloomsbury handbook of montessori education* (eds Murray, A., Ahlquist, E. M. T., McKenna, M., Debs, M.). Bloomsbury. pp 271–80; https://etcmontessorionline.com/blog/enhancing-flow-in-a-montessori-classroom/

17   Dietrich, A. (2015). 'Flow Experiences: From Mystery to Mechanism'. In *How Creativity Happens in the Brain.* Palgrave Macmillan UK. pp.163–83.

18 Sosik, J. J., Kahai, S. S., & Avolio, B. J. (1999). 'Leadership style, anonymity, and creativity in group decision support systems: The mediating role of optimal flow'. *The Journal of Creative Behavior*, 33(4), 227–56.

19 Zubair, A., & Kamal, A. (2015). 'Work-related flow, psychological capital, and creativity among employees of software houses'. *Psychological Studies*, 60(3), 321–31.

20 Baumann, N., & Scheffer, D. (2011). 'Seeking flow in the achievement domain: The achievement flow motive behind flow experience'. *Motivation and Emotion*, 35(3), 267–84.

21 Škerlavaj, M., Dysvik, A., Černe, M., & Carlsen, A. (2016). '25. Succeeding with capitalizing on creativity: an integrative framework'. *Capitalizing on Creativity at Work: Fostering the Implementation of Creative Ideas in Organizations*, 335.

22 Sartori, R. D., Marelli, M., Garavaglia, P., Castelli, L., Busin, S., & Delle Fave, A. (2014). 'The assessment of patients' quality of experience: Autonomy level and perceived challenges'. *Rehabilitation psychology*, 59(3), 267; Preziosa, A., Riva, G., & Delle Fave, A. (2008). 'L'esperienza soggettiva dell'obesità: implicazioni diagnostico-terapeutiche'. *Psicologia della salute*.

23 Ley, C., Krammer, J., Lippert, D., & Barrio, M. R. (2017). 'Exploring flow in sport and exercise therapy with war and torture survivors'. *Mental Health and Physical Activity*, 12, 83–93.

24 Crawford, R. T. (2016). *The Impact of Ocean Therapy on Veterans with Posttraumatic Stress Disorder* (Doctoral dissertation, Grand Canyon University).

25 https://www.cdc.gov/nchs/products/databriefs/db419.htm

26 https://www.cdc.gov/nchs/products/databriefs/db419.htm

27 https://www.aihw.gov.au/mental-health/topic-areas/mental-health-prescriptions

28 https://media.nhsbsa.nhs.uk/press-releases/5171d616-95ea-4282-959b-15f8bfed6a0f/nhs-releases-2023-24-mental-health-medicines-statistics-for-england

29 Brauer, R., Alfageh, B., Blais, J. E., Chan, E. W., Chui, C. S. L., Hayes, J. F., Man, K. K. C., Lau, W. C. Y., Yan, V. K. C., Beykloo, M. Y., Wang, Z., Wei, L., Wong, I. C. K. 'Psychotropic medicine consumption in 65 countries and regions, 2008–19: a longitudinal study'. *Lancet Psychiatry*. 2021 Dec. 8(12):1071–82. doi: 10.1016/S2215-0366(21)00292-3. PMID: 34801129; PMCID: PMC9766760.

References

30 www.nature.com/articles/s41562-021-01093-w

31 Keyes, C. (2025). *Languishing: How to feel alive again in a world that wears us down.* Random House.

32 https://www.nytimes.com/2021/04/19/well/mind/covid-mental-health-languishing.html

CHAPTER 2: GET OUT OF YOUR OWN WAY

33 Roosevelt, E. (1983). Foreword. *You learn by living.* Westminster John Knox Press; https://www.goodreads.com/quotes/36802-the-purpose-of-life-is-to-live-it-to-taste

34 Dr Anita Ward at a 22 July seminar held at the Cleveland Clinic Lou Ruvo Center for Brain Health, 888 W. Bonneville Ave. https://my.clevelandclinic.org/-/scassets/files/org/locations/nevada/multiple-sclerosis/2020-cclr-brain-guide-ms.pdf?la=en

35 Tolle, E. (2021). *The power of now: pedoman menuju pencerahan spiritual.* Bhuana Ilmu Populer.

36 https://www.who.int/news-room/fact-sheets/detail/anxiety-disorders

37 https://www.abs.gov.au/statistics/health/mental-health/national-study-mental-health-and-wellbeing/latest-release

38 Twenge, J. M. (2000). 'The age of anxiety? The birth cohort change in anxiety and neuroticism, 1952–1993'. *Journal of personality and social psychology*, 79(6), 1007.

39 http://www.bbc.com/sport/42871491

40 https://employmenthero.com/resources/wellness-at-work-report/

41 https://research.com/education/student-stress-statistics

42 https://iamfearlesssoul.com/joe-dispenza-you-are-the-creator-of-your-world/

43 Kabat-Zinn, J. (2003). 'Mindfulness-based interventions in context: past, present, and future'. *Clinical psychology Science and practice*, 10(2), 144–156.

44 Norsworthy, C., Jackson, B., & Dimmock, J. A. (2021). 'Advancing our understanding of psychological flow: A scoping review of conceptualizations, measurements, and applications'. *Psychological bulletin*, 147(8), 806.

45 Ulrich, M., Keller, J., Hoenig, K., Waller, C., & Grön, G. (2014). 'Neural correlates of experimentally induced flow experiences'. *Neuroimage*, 86, 194–202.

46 Slingerland, E. (2014). *Trying not to try: The ancient art of effortlessness and the surprising power of spontaneity.* Canongate Books.

47 *New York Times*, 1984 https://www.nytimes.com/1984/11/18/books/a-conversation-with-edna-obrien-the-body-contains-the-life-story.html

48 https://www.amnh.org/exhibitions/permanent/human-origins/understanding-our-past/dna-comparing-humans-and-chimps

49 https://www.abc.net.au/science/articles/2005/06/30/2839498.htm?site=science_dev&

50 Del Giorno, J. M., Hall, E. E., O'Leary, K. C., Bixby, W. R., & Miller, P. C. (2010). 'Cognitive function during acute exercise: a test of the transient hypofrontality theory'. *Journal of Sport and Exercise Psychology*, 32(3), 312–23.

51 Joy, S. P., & Furman, L. (2014, August). 'Progressive change in formal qualities of art produced over the course of frontotemporal dementia'. Paper presented at the annual meeting of the American Psychological Association, Washington, DC. https://www.researchgate.net/publication/264662859_Progressive_Change_in_Fomal_Qualities_of_Art_Produced_over_the_Course_of_Frontotemporal_Dementia. Accessed 15 Jan. 2015; Sawyer, K. (2011). 'The cognitive neuroscience of creativity: a critical review'. *Creativity research journal*, 23(2), 137–54.

52 Oppezzo, M., & Schwartz, D. L. (2014). 'Give your ideas some legs: The positive effect of walking on creative thinking'. *Journal of experimental psychology: learning, memory, and cognition*, 40(4), 1142.

53 Berkovich-Ohana, A., & Glicksohn, J. (2014). 'The consciousness state space (CSS)—a unifying model for consciousness and self'. *Frontiers in psychology*, 5.

54 Johansen, R. (2012). *Leaders make the future: Ten new leadership skills for an uncertain world.* Berrett-Koehler Publishers.

55 Seth, A. (2017). 'Your brain hallucinates your conscious reality'. [online] Ted.com. Available at: https://www.ted.com/talks/anil_seth_how_your_brain_hallucinates_your_conscious_reality?utm_source=newsletter_weekly_2017-07-22&utm_campaign=newsletter_weekly&utm_medium=email&utm_content=talk_of_the_week_button#t-1008774 [Accessed 11 Oct. 2017].

56 Tolle, E. (2004). *The power of now: A guide to spiritual enlightenment.* New World Library.

References

57   Lush, P., Dienes, Z., & Seth, A.K. (2023). 'Expectancies and the generation of perceptual experience: Predictive processing and phenomenological control'. In T. Cheng, R. Sato, & J. Hohwy (eds), *Expected Experiences: The Predictive Mind in an Uncertain World*. Routledge. pp. 47–75. https://doi.org/10.4324/9781003084082-4

58   Descartes, R., Williams, B. (1996). 'Meditations on First Philosophy'. In Cottingham, J. (ed.). *Descartes: Meditations on First Philosophy With Selections from the Objections and Replies*. Cambridge Texts in the History of Philosophy (Revised ed.). Cambridge University Press. pp. 1–11. doi:10.1017/cbo9780511805028.006. https://plato.stanford.edu/entries/embodied-cognition/

59   Wagstaff, C. R. (2014). 'Emotion regulation and sport performance'. *Journal of Sport and Exercise Psychology*, 36(4), 401–12.

60   Ulmer, K. (2017). *The Art Of Fear: Why Conquering Fear Won't Work and What to Do Instead*. HarperCollins.

CHAPTER 3: DEMYSTIFY FLOW

61   Csikszentmihalyi, M. (1988). 'The flow experience and its significance for human psychology'. *Optimal experience: Psychological studies of flow in consciousness*, 2, 15–35.

62   Csikszentmihalyi, M. (1995). 'The evolving self: A psychology for the third millennium'. *Journal of Leisure Research*, 27(3), 300.

63   Csikszentmihalyi, M. (2013). *Flow: The psychology of happiness*. Random House.

64   As outlined by Norsworthy et al. (2021). *Psychological Flow Scale*.

65   Weber, R., Huskey, R., & Craighead, B. (2016). 'Flow Experiences and Well-Being'. *The Routledge handbook of media use and well-being: International perspectives on theory and research on positive media effects*. Routledge; Ulrich, M., Keller, J., & Grön, G. (2016). 'Dorsal raphe nucleus down-regulates medial prefrontal cortex during experience of flow'. *Frontiers in behavioral neuroscience*, 10, 169; Bian, Y., Yang, C., Gao, F., Li, H., Zhou, S., Li, H., ... & Meng, X. (2016). 'A framework for physiological indicators of flow in VR games: construction and preliminary evaluation'. *Personal and Ubiquitous Computing*, 20(5), 821–32; Nah, F. F. H., Yelamanchili, T., & Siau, K. (July 2017). 'A review on neuropsychophysiological correlates of flow'. In *International Conference on HCI in Business, Government, and Organizations*. Springer, Cham. pp. 364–72.

How to Find Flow

66   Tang, Y. Y., & Bruya, B. (2017). 'Mechanisms of mind-body interaction and optimal performance'. *Frontiers in Psychology*, 8; Jacobs K. A. (2014). *Flow State in Dancers: Autonomic Regulation During Performance*. MS Thesis, California State University, Northridge; Keller J., Bless H., Blomann F., & Kleinbohl D. (2011). 'Physiological aspects of flow experiences: skills-demand-compatibility effects on heart rate variability and salivary control'. *J. Exp. Soc. Psychol.* 47, 849–52; Thomson, P., Jaque, S. V. (2011). 'Psychophysiological study: ambulatory measures of the ANS in performing artists'. *Int. Symp. Perform. Sci.* 1, 149–154; de Manzano, O., Theorell, T., Harmat, L., Ullén, F. (2010). 'The Psychophysiology of flow during piano playing'. *Emotion* 10, 301–11. 10.

67   De Manzano, Ö., Cervenka, S., Jucaite, A., Hellenäs, O., Farde, L., & Ullén, F. (2013). 'Individual differences in the proneness to have flow experiences are linked to dopamine D2-receptor availability in the dorsal striatum'. *Neuroimage*, 67, 1–6.

CHAPTER 4: PRIORITISE FLOW

68   Csikszentmihalyi, Mihaly (1990). *Flow: The Psychology of Optimal Experience*. Harper and Row.

69   Swann, C., Keegan, R. J., Piggott, D., & Crust, L. (2012). 'A systematic review of the experience, occurrence, and controllability of flow states in elite sport'. *Psychology of sport and exercise*, 13(6), 807–19.

70   Norsworthy, C., Dimmock, J. A., Nicholas, J., Krause, A., & Jackson, B. (2023). 'Psychological flow training: feasibility and preliminary efficacy of an educational intervention on flow'. *International Journal of Applied Positive Psychology*, 8(3), 531–54. Norsworthy, C., Thelwell, R., Weston, N., & Jackson, S. A. (2017). 'Flow training, flow states, and performance in élite athletes'. *Int. J. Sport Psychol.*, 49, 134–52.

71   Gladwell, M. (2008). *Outliers: the story of success*. Little, Brown and Company.

72   https://www.goodreads.com/quotes/904186-if-you-always-do-what-you-ve-always-done-you-ll-always

73   Slingerland, E. G. (2015). *Trying not to try: Ancient China, modern science, and the power of spontaneity*. Broadway Books.

References

74 Deci, E. L., & Ryan, R. M. (2012). 'Self-determination theory'. *Handbook of theories of social psychology*, 1(20), 416–36; Elliot, A. J., & Dweck, C. S. (2005). 'Competence and motivation'. *Handbook of competence and motivation*, 3–12; Lippke, S. (2020). 'Enactive mastery experience'. In *Encyclopedia of personality and individual differences*. Springer, Cham. pp. 1362–65; Dweck, C. S. (1988). 'Goals: An approach to motivation and achievement'. *Journal of personality and Social Psychology*, 54(1), 5–12; Dweck, C. (2016). 'What having a "growth mindset" actually means'. *Harvard business review*, 13(2), 2–5.

75 Selye, H. (1975). 'Stress and distress'. *Comprehensive therapy*, 1(8), 9–13.

76 Mbiydzenyuy, N. E., & Qulu, L. A. (2024). 'Stress, hypothalamic-pituitary-adrenal axis, hypothalamic-pituitary-gonadal axis, and aggression'. *Metab. Brain Dis.* 39, 1613–36. https://doi.org/10.1007/s11011-024-01393-w; Smith, S. M., Vale, W. W. (2006). 'The role of the hypothalamic-pituitary-adrenal axis in neuroendocrine responses to stress'. *Dialogues Clin. Neurosci.*, 8(4), 383–95. doi: 10.31887/DCNS.2006.8.4/ssmith. PMID: 17290797; PMCID: PMC3181830.

77 http://sportsenergygroup.com/

78 http://espn.go.com/golf/story/_/id/7568923/phil-mickelson-roars-tiger-woods-win-pebble-beach

79 Oman, D. (2024). 'What is a mantra? Guidance for practitioners, researchers, and editors'. *American Psychologist*.

80 Riemsma, R. P., Pattenden, J., Bridle, C., Sowden, A. J., Mather, L., Watt, I. S., & Walker, A. (2003). 'Systematic review of the effectiveness of stage based interventions to promote smoking cessation'. *BMJ*, 326(7400), 1175–7.

81 Soman, D., & Cheema, A. (2004). 'When goals are counterproductive: The effects of violation of a behavioral goal on subsequent performance'. *Journal of Consumer Research*, 31(1), 52–62.

82 Freund, A. M., & Hennecke, M. (2012). 'Changing eating behaviour vs. losing weight: The role of goal focus for weight loss in overweight women'. *Psychology & health*, 27(sup2), 25–42.

83 Ordóñez, L. D., Schweitzer, M. E., Galinsky, A. D., & Bazerman, M. H. (2009). 'Goals gone wild: The systematic side effects of overprescribing goal setting'. *The Academy of Management Perspectives*, 23(1), 6–16.

84 https://www.bbc.com/worklife/article/20171117-why-we-should-all-give-up-on-goals-already

85 Ordóñez, L. D., Schweitzer, M. E., Galinsky, A. D., & Bazerman, M. H. (2009). 'Goals gone wild: The systematic side effects of overprescribing goal setting'. *The Academy of Management Perspectives*, 23(1), 6–16.

CHAPTER 5: BUILD A BLUEPRINT

86 Hebb, D. O. (2005). *The organization of behavior: A neuropsychological theory*. Psychology Press.

87 Fields, R. D. (2005). 'Myelination: an overlooked mechanism of synaptic plasticity?'. *The Neuroscientist*, 11(6), 528–31.

88 Doidge, N. (2007). *The brain that changes itself: Stories of personal triumph from the frontiers of brain science*. Penguin.

89 Ranganathan, V. K., Siemionow, V., Liu, J. Z., Sahgal, V., Yue, G. H. (2004). 'From mental power to muscle power--gaining strength by using the mind'. *Neuropsychologia*, 42(7), 944–56. doi: 10.1016/j.neuropsychologia.2003.11.018. PMID: 14998709.

90 https://www.abc.net.au/news/2025-03-24/cliff-young-potato-farmer-who-ran-from-sydney-to-melbourne/105023078

91 https://alicenter.org/meet-ali/in-his-own-words/

92 https://www.theguardian.com/football/2012/may/17/wayne-rooney-visualisation-preparation

CHAPTER 6: INVITE THE INTENSITY

93 Norsworthy, C., Jackson, B., & Dimmock, J. A. (2021). 'Advancing our understanding of psychological flow: A scoping review of conceptualizations, measurements, and applications'. *Psychological bulletin*, 147(8), 806.

94 Oschman, J. L. (2006). *Energy medicine in therapeutics and human performance*. Butterworth-Heineman.

95 Coyle, D. (2010). *The talent code: Greatness isn't born, it's grown*. Random House.

96 Gallo, C., & Mangan, S. (2011). *The innovation secrets of Steve Jobs*. Bolinda Audio.

97 https://observervoice.com/john-galsworthy-quotes-47806/

98 https://www.cnbc.com/2021/12/16/google-20-percent-rule-shows-exactly-how-much-time-you-should-spend-learning-new-skills.html

References

99   Auld, D. P. (2014). *Flow and learning in computer-mediated learning environments: A meta-analytic review* (Doctoral dissertation, Fordham University).

100   Shernoff, D. J., Csikszentmihalyi, M., Schneider, B., & Shernoff, E. S. (2014). 'Student engagement in high school classrooms from the perspective of flow theory' (p. 3). In *Applications of flow in human development and education*. Springer, Dordrecht. pp. 475–94.

101   Deci, E. L., & Ryan, R. M. (2012). 'Self-determination theory'. *Handbook of theories of social psychology*, 1(20), 416–36.

102   Csikszentmihalyi, M., & Csikzentmihaly, M. (1990). *Flow: The psychology of optimal experience*. Harper & Row. Vol. 1990, p. 1.

103   https://www.goodreads.com/author/quotes/18540.T_S_Eliot#:~:text=Humankind%20cannot%20bear%20very%20much%20reality.&text=If%20you%20aren't%20in,know%20how%20tall%20you%20are%3F&text=I%20will%20show%20you%20fear%20in%20a%20handful%20of%20dust.&text=To%20prepare%20a%20face%20to%20meet%20the%20faces%20that%20you%20meet.

104   https://www.forbes.com/quotes/11194/

105   Migliaccio, G. M. (2023). *The Science of Deep Sleep, Towards success: Unleashing energies in sports and life thanks to quality sleep.* Sport Science Lab srl.

CHAPTER 7: SHAPE YOUR STATE

106   https://pmc.ncbi.nlm.nih.gov/articles/PMC3477383/

107   https://www.youtube.com/watch?v=T9M8TvDfbjQ

CHAPTER 8: BE ABSORBED

108   Araújo, D., Hristovski, R., Seifert, L., Carvalho, J., & Davids, K. (2019). 'Ecological cognition: expert decision-making behaviour in sport'. *International Review of Sport and Exercise Psychology*, 12(1), 1–25.

109   López-González, M., & Limb, C. J. (2012, January). *Musical creativity and the brain.* In *Cerebrum: the dana forum on brain science* (Vol. 2012). Dana Foundation.

110 McKinley, R. A., McIntire, L., Nelson, J., Nelson, J., & Goodyear, C. (2017). 'The effects of transcranial direct current stimulation (tDCS) on training during a complex procedural task'. In *Advances in Neuroergonomics and Cognitive Engineering*. Springer International Publishing. pp. 173–83.

111 https://www.bbc.com/future/article/20140603-brain-zapping-the-future-of-war

112 Kounios, J., & Beeman, M. (2014). 'The cognitive neuroscience of insight'. *Annual review of psychology*, 65.

113 https://www.forbes.com/quotes/173/

114 Slingerland, E. G. (2015). *Trying not to try: Ancient China, modern science, and the power of spontaneity*. Broadway Books.

115 Wilson, T. D., & Schooler, J. W. (1991). 'Thinking too much: introspection can reduce the quality of preferences and decisions'. *Journal of personality and social psychology*, 60(2), 181.

116 Slingerland, E. G. (2015). *Trying not to try: Ancient China, modern science, and the power of spontaneity*. Broadway Books.

117 Sahakian, B. (2008). 'The innovative brain'. *Nature*, 456(7219), 168.

118 https://www.goodreads.com/work/quotes/105847-the-miracle-of-mindfulness-a-manual-on-meditation

119 Lopata, J. A., Nowicki, E. A., & Joanisse, M. F. (2017). 'Creativity as a distinct trainable mental state: An EEG study of musical improvisation'. *Neuropsychologia*, 99, 246–58; Lustenberger, C., Boyle, M. R., Foulser, A. A., Mellin, J. M., & Fröhlich, F. (2015). 'Functional role of frontal alpha oscillations in creativity'. *Cortex*, 67, 74–82.

120 Katahira, K., Yamazaki, Y., Yamaoka, C., Ozaki, H., Nakagawa, S., & Nagata, N. (2018). 'EEG correlates of the flow state: A combination of increased frontal theta and moderate frontocentral alpha rhythm in the mental arithmetic task'. *Frontiers in psychology*, 9, 300.

CHAPTER 9: BE EFFORTLESS

121 Cheron, G. (2016). 'How to Measure the Psychological "Flow"? A Neuroscience Perspective'. *Frontiers in psychology*, 7.

122 https://www.heartmath.org/

123 Leskowitz, R. (2014). 'The 2013 World Series: A Trojan Horse for Consciousness Studies'. *Explore: The Journal of Science and Healing*, 10(2), 125–7.

References

124 https://www.heartmath.org/; Edwards, D. J., Edwards, S. D., Buscombe, R. M., Beale, J. T., & Wilson, M. (2015). 'Effect of HeartMath workshop on physiological coherence, sense of coherence, zone, mood and resilience perceptions: Health'. *African Journal for Physical Health Education, Recreation and Dance*, 21(3.1), 891–901.

125 Tang, Y. Y., & Bruya, B. (2017). 'Mechanisms of mind-body interaction and optimal performance'. *Frontiers in Psychology*, 8.

126 Nah, F. F. H., Yelamanchili, T., & Siau, K. (2017, July). 'A review on neuropsychophysiological correlates of flow'. In *International Conference on HCI in Business, Government, and Organizations*. Springer, Cham. pp. 364–72

127 Klasen, M., Weber, R., Kircher, T. T., Mathiak, K. A., & Mathiak, K. (2012). 'Neural contributions to flow experience during video game playing'. *Social cognitive and affective neuroscience*, 7(4), 485–95.

128 Weber, R., Huskey, R., & Craighead, B. (2016). 'Flow Experiences and Well-Being'. In *The Routledge handbook of media use and well-being: International perspectives on theory and research on positive media effects*. Routledge; Ulrich, M., Keller, J., & Grön, G. (2016). 'Dorsal raphe nucleus down-regulates medial prefrontal cortex during experience of flow'. *Frontiers in behavioral neuroscience*, 10, 169; Bian, Y., Yang, C., Gao, F., Li, H., Zhou, S., Li, H., ... & Meng, X. (2016). 'A framework for physiological indicators of flow in VR games: construction and preliminary evaluation'. *Personal and Ubiquitous Computing*, 20(5), 821–32; Nah, F. F. H., Yelamanchili, T., & Siau, K. (2017, July). 'A review on neuropsychophysiological correlates of flow'. In *International Conference on HCI in Business, Government, and Organizations*. Springer, Cham. pp. 364–72.

129 https://www.forbes.com/quotes/10027/

130 Harris, D. J., Vine, S. J., & Wilson, M. R. (2017). 'Neurocognitive mechanisms of the flow state'. *Progress in brain research*, 234, 221–43.

131 https://www.youtube.com/watch?v=2ZFATM2BszA

132 https://www.brainyquote.com/quotes/ernest_hemingway_383691

133 https://tibetanbuddhistencyclopedia.com/en/index.php?title=How_to_See_Yourself_As_You_Really_Are

134 https://www.heartmath.org/research/science-of-the-heart/energetic-communication/

How to Find Flow

135 https://www.apa.org/monitor/2012/09/gut-feeling#:~:text=Gut%20 bacteria%20also%20produce%20hundreds,both%20mood%20and%20GI%20 activity.

136 Patterson, R. E., & Eggleston, R. G. (2017). 'Intuitive cognition'. *Journal of Cognitive Engineering and Decision Making*, 11(1), 5–22; Luoma, J., & Martela, F. (2021). 'A dual-processing view of three cognitive strategies in strategic decision making: Intuition, analytic reasoning, and reframing'. *Long-Range Planning*, 54(3), 102065.

CHAPTER 10: BEING FLOW

137 https://quoteinvestigator.com/2021/07/09/come-alive/

138 https://quoteinvestigator.com/2015/07/30/hour-play/

139 Fingelkurts, A. A., & Fingelkurts, A. A. (2014). 'Present moment, past, and future: mental kaleidoscope'. *Frontiers in psychology*, 5.

140 https://www.goodreads.com/quotes/885801-the-dalai-lama-when-asked-what-surprised-him-most-about

141 Sadlo, G. (2016). 'Towards a neurobiological understanding of reduced self-awareness during flow: An occupational science perspective'. In *Flow Experience*. Springer, Cham. pp. 375–88.

142 Nakamura, J., & Roberts, S. (2016). *The hypo-egoic component of flow. In The Oxford handbook of hypo-egoic phenomena.* Oxford University Press.

143 Mead, G. H. (2015). *Mind, self & society.* University of Chicago Press. p. 133.

144 Freud, S. (1995). 'Psychoanalytic theory'. *A Review of Personality Theories*, 10.

145 Eames, K. J. (2016). *Cognitive Psychology of Religion.* Waveland Press. p. 25.

146 László, E. (2022). 'The Quest for a Quantum Leap in Human Affairs'. *Vidwat*, 15(1), 2–4; https://www.goodreads.com/quotes/837455-we-are-like-islands-in-the-sea-separate-on-the

147 Schmidt, J., & Ownsworth, T. (2022). 'Special issue editorial: The self after brain injury'. *Neuropsychological Rehabilitation*, 32(8), 1669–75. https://doi.org/10.1080/09602011.2022.2120504

148 Egan, J. (2015). *3000 Astounding Quotes.* Lulu.com.

149 https://www.youtube.com/watch?v=rieJef500nU

References

150   Seto, A., Kusaka, C., Nakazato, S., Huang, W. R., Sato, T., Hisamitsu, T., & Takeshige, C. (1991). 'Detection of extraordinary large bio-magnetic field strength from human hand during external Qi emission'. *Acupuncture & electro-therapeutics research*, 17(2), 75–94.

151   Oschman, J. L. (2006). *Energy medicine in therapeutics and human performance*. Butterworth-Heineman.

152   http://www.physics.adelaide.edu.au/theory/staff/leinweber/

153   flowcentre.org

Or Brennan, A. (2016). *The Energetic Performer: An Integrated Approach to Acting for Stage and Screen*. Singing Dragon.

CONCLUSION: OVER TO YOU

154   https://www.mckinsey.com/business-functions/organization/our-insights/increasing-the-meaning-quotient-of-work

155   https://www.goodreads.com/quotes/1799-the-world-as-we-have-created-it-is-a-process

156   http://www.pewforum.org/2010/02/17/religion-among-the-millennials/ and http://www.abs.gov.au/ausstats/abs@.nsf/Lookup/4102.0Main+Features30Nov+2013

157   Peifer, C., & Tan, J. (2021). The psychophysiology of flow experience. In Advances in flow research (pp. 191-230). Cham: Springer International Publishing.

ACKNOWLEDGEMENTS

THIS BOOK HAS BEEN IN THE MAKING FOR MANY YEARS. To the authors noted herein, and many who didn't make the edit, you have helped pique my curiosity and cultivate my passion; I am eternally grateful. Without your meaningful work, there would be no book. We all stand on the shoulders of giants, and this book is undoubtedly a tribute to you all. None more so than Mihaly Csikszentmihalyi, a great thinker of our time, whose work continues to inspire me daily.

I have had the privilege of working with many of the professionals featured in this book (some names have been changed to protect anonymity), as well as with those who were not quoted. It has been an honour and a continuing highlight of my life to work with you. Your achievements and commitment to your greater selves are inspiring. Thank you for your trust and for letting me into your lives.

Acknowledgements

A special thank you to John Hendry, Sue Jackson and many other flow enthusiasts who have helped shape my ideas with great insights and injected enthusiasm into our efforts to make flow education accessible to all. To those who guided, inspired and championed my love for sport throughout my younger years, including my first tennis coach, Roger Froud, tennis partner, James Manyoni, and my dear friend, John Robinson, your energy and belief in me still flame my inspiration today.

To my family, for their endeavour to facilitate a tennis career that never found fruition, and for the immense support they have offered me throughout the rollercoaster of life. To Dad, Mum, Gordon and Jo, who have helped edit the earlier troublesome versions of this book, and my wife, Hannah, who has never stopped supporting me and my work surrounding flow, I am eternally grateful and very lucky to have you in my life. Thank you.

Lastly, to my children, Jazz and Levi, who inspired me to write this book. Hopefully, the words herein give you as much hope, clarity and direction that they have given me. Let it flow.

Dr Cameron Norsworthy is a coach, keynote and TEDx speaker, author, and founder and CEO of The Flow Centre. He has studied and worked as a 'Flow Coach' with hundreds of clients for over 20 years, including world champions, leaders, entrepreneurs and high-profile military personnel. He has a PhD on flow science and was awarded the Outstanding Academic Achievement prize for his work in flow and performance. A former junior British tennis player, Dr Norsworthy has experienced first-hand the importance of refocusing and finding flow after personal and professional setbacks. Originally from England, he coaches clients, plays tennis on the senior world tour and delivers keynotes all over the world. When he's not travelling, Dr Norsworthy lives in Australia with his family.